THE MAKING
OF A SOUTHERNER

THE MAKING OF A SOUTHERNER

Katharine Du Pre Lumpkin

Foreword by Darlene Clark Hine

BROWN THRASHER BOOKS

THE UNIVERSITY OF GEORGIA PRESS

ATHENS AND LONDON

Published in 1991 as a Brown Thrasher Book
by the University of Georgia Press, Athens, Georgia 30602
© 1946 by Alfred A. Knopf, Inc., 1974 by Katharine Du Pre Lumpkin
Afterword by Katharine Du Pre Lumpkin © 1981
by the University of Georgia Press
Foreword by Darlene Clark Hine © 1991
by the University of Georgia Press
Printed in the United States of America

95 94 93 92 91   P   5 4 3 2 1

Library of Congress Cataloging in Publication Data
Lumpkin, Katharine Du Pre, 1897–
    The making of a Southerner / Katharine Du Pre Lumpkin ; foreword by Darlene
Clark Hine.
        p.   cm.
    "Brown thrasher books."
    Includes bibliographical references.
    ISBN 0-8203-1385-8 (pbk.: alk. paper)
    1. Lumpkin, Katharine Du Pre, 1897– . 2. Afro-Americans—Southern
States—History. 3. Afro-Americans—Civil rights—Southern States.
4. Southern States—Social life and customs. 5. Southern States—
Biography. I. Title.
F215.L86   1991
305.896′073075—dc20
[B]   91-26583
                                                                                                              CIP

British Library Cataloging in Publication Data available

The Making of a Southerner was originally published as a Borzoi Book in 1947 by
Alfred A. Knopf, New York.

CONTENTS

FOREWORD

by Darlene Clark Hine

KATHARINE DU PRE LUMPKIN's carefully constructed, wincingly honest autobiography explores and dissects the "southern" essence of her identity. Who she was and became remained inseparable from the social and economic history of the South. Thus, this autobiography reflects both the state of social science scholarship in the 1940s and the details of Lumpkin's intellectual journey. In other words, Lumpkin constructs her life in such a way that it becomes more than a familiar coming of age tale of an upper-class child of the Old South caught in the transition to the New South. Rather, much like *The Emancipation of Angelina Grimké* (Chapel Hill: University of North Carolina Press, 1974), the autobiography chronicles an intellectual transformation and conversion to the cause of racial equality and social justice.

Though a century separated the lives of the two women, the parallels between the career of the aristocratic white southern feminist and antislavery crusader and Lumpkin's own twentieth-century odyssey are striking. Given the nature of her intellectual and emotional heritage, the circumstances of her early upbringing, and the depth of the southern commitment to racial hierarchy and gender stratification, Lumpkin's rejection of the ideology of white supremacy and her questioning of the status of women was downright radical. This autobiography is a unique and compelling document prepared by a southern white feminist scholar of a generation that boasted few such persons.

Katharine Du Pre Lumpkin was born in Macon, Georgia, on December 22, 1897. She received her bachelor of arts degree from Brenau College in Gainesville, Georgia, her master's degree at Columbia University, and, in 1928, her doctorate in economics at the

Foreword

University of Wisconsin. She taught economics and sociology at several women's colleges, including Mount Holyoke and Smith. In addition to *The Making of a Southerner* (1947) and *The Emancipation of Angelina Grimké*, Lumpkin published *Child Workers in America* (New York: International Publishers, 1937) and *The South in Progress* (New York: International Publishers, 1940), both with Dorothy W. Douglas.

In the six chapters (she calls them books) that comprise *The Making of a Southerner*, Lumpkin records her intellectual struggle to come to grips with the contradictions and tensions inherent in being not only a white southerner but a member of the privileged but disinherited class of former slaveholders. In the first half of the volume (books 1, 2, and 3) Lumpkin describes what it meant to be southern, white, female, and privileged in the opening decades of the twentieth century. In the final three books she recalls the process of her transformation into a liberal democrat, fully aware of the economic inequities, racial proscriptions, and sexual restrictions suffered by those southerners who were poor white, black, or female. To be sure, Lumpkin's voice is atypical, but that is why her book is so arresting. Lumpkin painstakingly unravels the old tapestry of myths, distortions, and stereotypes that had blinded her to the existence of white poverty and black oppression. Epiphanies abound. After years of study and soul-searching she exhibits a fully awakened racial consciousness: "What struck me now was the circumstantial convenience of a belief in inferiority to the existence of a slave institution and the perpetuation of its aftermath" (p. 228).

In book 1, ironically entitled "Of Bondage to Slavery," Lumpkin provides a classically idyllic description of the institution of slavery as it allegedly existed on her great-grandfather Billy's moderate-sized Georgia plantation. To be sure, the description is more reminiscent of Ulrich B. Phillips's *American Negro Slavery* than of the modern revisionist portraits painted by Eugene Genovese, John Blassingame, and Herbert Gutman. A good master, as her family lore would have it, was "a just and kindly man, as well as one who was firm, maintaining in his charges a never wavering obedience" (p. 30). In addition to the Lumpkin forefathers we are introduced to Aunt Sarah, "Runaway" Dennis, and to the hardworking slave foreman Uncle Jerry, who "was six feet, eight inches in his stocking feet,

Foreword

they said, and weighed three hundred and twenty pounds." Lumpkin leaves no aspect of slavery unremarked, including child labor, work routines, cotton cultivation, the care of aged slaves, diet, illnesses, marriage, and slave discipline, purchase, and sale.

Lumpkin's portrait of slavery reflects the master's point of view, and from this perspective slavery was as much a burden to the master as it was to the slave. Great-grandfather Billy had his patience tried repeatedly by "Runaway" Dennis, "a quarrelsome slave, nagging and rousing the ire of his fellows until he would overstep the bounds with some transgression, and, fearful of punishment, would take to the swamps" (p. 13). Troublesome property was an exception on the Lumpkin plantation; still, ruling over so many slaves known "for their warm devotion and willing obedience," often proved taxing for even the best planter.

Occasionally a Lumpkin master, caught in the irony of human ownership and management, mused about who owned whom. But as the great-granddaughter of the "peculiar institution" points out, slavery and plantation management had their good moments. "There was a pleasurable side to ruling over a plantation. Indeed, my father seemed to remember this side with especial vividness. The men hunted and fished as a favorite pastime. They went up to town, to Athens or Augusta, to market their cotton and purchase supplies. They might travel even greater distances to attend conventions of church or political party, or go up to the legislature. More than anything else, they and their kinsmen and friends visited among each other" (p. 39).

This southern world of kindly masters, obedient slaves, and visiting kin met its apocalypse in the Civil War. In the war's aftermath the Lumpkin clan tried to make sense of a new order that left them bereft of "faithful slaves" and too dependent upon "'unreliable free Negro labor'" (p. 60). And when the Black Codes the landowners demanded to control their former slaves were nullified by Congress, Lumpkin acknowledges that "southern men who but two or three years before had owned their labor [slaves] now felt themselves at their wits' end" (p. 67). "Planters were frantic, cotton was at a high price; they were eager to grasp at this advantage, so they hit upon crop-sharing as a means of inducing freedmen to work for them" (p. 69).

Foreword

"Georgia's very first postwar legislature of 1866 (the same one that enacted the Black Code) passed legislation—and it remained in force—to protect the landlord who advanced supplies to his tenants. It permitted him to have a lien on his laborer's share of the crop to cover the advances he had made" (p. 72). The freedmen favored the crop-sharing plans because such schemes allowed them to determine their own work rhythms, gave them the opportunity to live with their families, and enabled them to hope for their own plots. Although the failures of the sharecropping system became apparent in later years, some historians would agree that given the lack of alternatives, it was initially not that inequitable an arrangement.

In the end, though the South may have lost the war, the shackles white landholding elites fastened on the freedmen proved almost as debilitating to black dreams of economic freedom as had centuries of slavery. Planters drove out merchants and controlled two-thirds of the furnishing stores, and as a result croppers remained perpetually in debt. Try as they might, whites found it impossible to restore the old order completely. Lumpkin's father and grandfather grew increasingly disgusted with the political assertions of blacks and their northern white "carpetbagger" and southern white "scalawag" allies. Repeating family legend, Lumpkin records that soon the "roads began to know the thudding horses' hoofs of strange, white-clad figures" (p. 78).

At this juncture it is imperative to underscore the strategy Lumpkin employs in her autobiography. She uses the first half of the book to recapture an intellectual world that she had already rejected by the time she wrote this autobiography. Her treatment of slavery, reconstruction, and redemption is the version of reality that conditioned her childhood. She is essentially presenting the story of her father, William Lumpkin. She interjects, "I only know the story as participants who were fearful antagonists afterward told it. I know what they said happened to them, and, from first-hand accounts heard in my childhood, what one side felt and did about it" (p. 85). Lumpkin recalls, "In my childhood, Father only told us of Negroes' 'insolence' and 'uppitiness.'" Her father's painful memories made an indelible impression. She observed, "Yet it seems that he felt he must tell the story, lest we have no concrete images such as haunted him.

Foreword

'Lest we forget,' he would say to us. 'On the streets of Union Point, a darkey,' so he put it, 'pushed me off the sidewalk and spit on me. . . . And we were helpless: . . .' He also said: 'My mother, walking down the street, was jostled by a negress, who then sassed her, nor would the woman give an inch of sidewalk to let my mother pass'" (p. 86).

Lumpkin sets the stage for the description of the birth of the Ku Klux Klan with these words: "This much is certain. To my people, as to me in my childhood, who was reared in their history of those fateful months, no 'two sides' to what happened was conceivable. To them there was but one side, made up of true Southerners engaged, they verily believed, in a struggle for existence, for this is what 'white supremacy' was to them" (p. 87). In the closing decade of the nineteenth century, perhaps because of frustration, William Lumpkin elected to leave Georgia and move the family to Columbia, South Carolina. Lumpkin writes poignantly of the pain of relocation: "The Lumpkins came to the Palmetto State as strangers. To be a Georgian in South Carolina was not to feel immediately at home. We were torn loose not alone from our past and from all its material symbols of superiority and comfort; we were set down among the clans of Carolina for whom name was paramount, and to whom our Georgia name in South Carolina genealogy was unknown" (p. 101).

Two essential southern institutions helped to ease their acclimatization: religion and a sense of "family." "Undoubtedly it helped that we were Episcopalians," Lumpkin remarks, "and immediately established our connection with socially elite Trinity Church" (p. 102). And even though unknown in South Carolina, the Lumpkins were identifiably "good family" people. "The meaning of 'family' was warp and woof of our heritage of ideas, and with it, of appropriate actions" (p. 103). To be of "good family" meant that no matter one's material fortune, you could still hold up your head.

As a child in South Carolina Lumpkin became intimately acquainted with the Lost Cause, as men of her father's generation endeavored to keep the spirit, if not the reality, of the Old South alive. Katharine Du Pre Lumpkin admitted candidly that she was a "daughter of an eloquent father, reared in a home where the Confederacy is revered as a cause, holy and imperishable." The great Confederate reunion of 1903 was held in Columbia, and such rituals, reunions,

Foreword

parades, and ceremonies glorifying old Confederate soldiers, and the building of monuments to the Lost Cause, became an all-consuming passion. Of these gatherings, Lumpkin maintains, "While yet the old men lived, on whom centered all the fanfare, it was a lusty movement and fervently zealous. I chanced to know it at the peak of its influence" (p. 113).

These years of conditioning in the atmosphere of an ostensibly inviolate way of southern life affected young Lumpkin and her brothers and sisters, though not as deeply perhaps as her parents would have wished. Still she recalled, "It was inconceivable, however, that any change could be allowed that altered the very present fact of the relation of superior white to inferior Negro. This we came to understand remained for us as it had been for our fathers, the very cornerstone of the South" (pp. 127–28). Yet it was inevitable that cracks would appear in the intellectual edifice so elaborately constructed to subordinate blacks and maintain white hegemony. For young Katharine Lumpkin it began, perhaps, with a chance sighting of her father's brutal reprimand of the family's cook for commiting the dreaded offense of "impudence." The incident produced the first tremors of doubt and misgivings: "Our little black cook, a woman small in stature though full grown, was receiving a severe thrashing. I could see her writhing under the blows of a descending stick wielded by the white master of the house. I could see her face distorted with fear and agony and his with stern rage" (p. 132). Note that Lumpkin refers to her father as "the white master," reflecting her perhaps unconscious distancing. Nevertheless, having witnessed this scene, Lumpkin became blindingly aware that she was white. "I began to be self-conscious about the many signs and symbols of my race position that had been battering against my consciousness since virtual infancy" (p. 133).

Lumpkin was too perceptive and too intelligent to remain imprisoned by fabrications designed to buttress the institutions of white supremacy and the fantasies of the old order. The latter half of the autobiography is radically different from the first part. It is largely a tale of personal reconstruction, of her remaking herself into a southerner free from old biases and lies. Lumpkin finds her own voice. She rejects the stories of her father and demonstrates the fruits of years of research and scholarship. In *The South in Progress*, Lumpkin explains, "I am mindful of how greatly we need to study our his-

Foreword

tory. Southern problems cannot be understood fully except in the light of an extensive examination of our historical background . . ." (p. 13). The problems explored in the last part include the desperate lives of croppers and farm laborers, workers in mill villages and cities, black peonage, the subjugation of women, the oppressive nature of southern religion, and the hypocrisy of northerners concerning the treatment of blacks.

Many critical events facilitated the remaking of Lumpkin. The first major event was William Lumpkin's removal of his family to a farm in Richland County, South Carolina. It was there in the Sand Hills that Katharine Lumpkin came to know white southerners with "pasty faces, scrawny necks, angular ill-nourished frames, straw-like hair" (p. 151). Shortly after the move, William Lumpkin died, and for a while the rest of the Lumpkin family tried to make a living off the farm by hiring black croppers. Lumpkin even tried her hand at picking cotton, "far removed from our house where they [Negroes] could not see me" (p. 157). In so doing she developed a deeper appreciation and antipathy for the "bending-and-picking, bending-and-picking," "back-breaking weariness" (p. 157).

It was the world of the "lower class" whites, though, that held her enthralled. She comments on every aspect of their desperate lives, from the religious revivals to the inadequate schooling, the "immoral" liaisons, the violence, and the alcoholism. She was equally observant of the lives of southern white women. Readily apparent, for example, was her fascination with "Miss Sarah" who was considered a sinner because she "lived with a farmer with no marriage words said over them, keeping his house for him for many a year" (p. 165). But Miss Sarah apparently "walked proudly as if she had nothing to be ashamed of, and this nonplussed people" (pp. 165–66). Lumpkin's observations about the lives of white southern women anticipates the historical works of Anne Firor Scott, Jean Friedman, Jacqueline Dowd Hall, and Elizabeth Fox-Genovese. Meanwhile, Lumpkin declares, "In the Sand Hills for the first time in my experience I had been set down to live day after day in close companionship with deep poverty suffered by whites, a poverty to which I had not hitherto been impreceptibly hardened. . . . I saw more than I otherwise would have" (p. 182).

The years Lumpkin spent as an undergraduate at Brenau College, 1912–15, left as indelible an impression as had her Sand Hills so-

Foreword

journ. Lumpkin's student involvement with the interracial commissions and the summer conferences sponsored by the YWCA and YMCA challenged her to overcome many racial taboos and southern sacred cows. One of the more poignant instances involved the first time she was asked to address a black woman lecturer to her YWCA group as "Miss." This episode, recounted in detail, reveals how difficult it was for her to let go of old customs. "The only time we had ever said 'Miss' or 'Mrs.' or 'Mr.' was in telling a 'darkey joke,' or in black-faced minstrels—'Now, *Mister* Johnson . . .' and the crowd would roar with mirth. It had always been a source of slight amusement to us, the way Negroes seemed to insist upon addressing one another as 'Mr.' and 'Mrs.' Why do such a thing, I used to wonder? To imitate white people, I supposed, in their desire to make themselves as much like us as they could" (p. 190). But one day "it struck" her "with stunning force" that though she may have been "wrestling with inferiority of race" and how "deadly serious the white South" took "its signs and separations," race "was nonexistent, only a fiction, a myth, which white minds had created for reasons of their own" (p. 215).

By the 1920s Lumpkin's search for a deeper understanding of the South and its people unveiled the "rigors of Southern destitution" of the white "lower classes." She concluded, after stints of working in the mills and factories where she observed more poverty and hopelessness, that "the mass of whites in a purely economic sense also had their 'place,' in which they too seemed meant to stay" (p. 222). The autobiography ends with a resounding condemnation of assumptions that working-class whites and blacks were kept separate because of "innate" and "inevitable" differences. Her critique of the economic forces that consigned the majority of its people to poverty led her to declare that "wage-earning whites and Negroes were, functionally speaking, not so unlike after all" (p. 222).

For the 1980 reissue of her autobiography, Lumpkin added an afterword in which she briefly surveys all the changes that occurred in the South in the wake of the 1954 *Brown v. Board of Education* United States Supreme Court decision and the modern civil rights movement. She applauds the dismantling of racial segregation and insists on documenting the ultimate futility of the massive resistance of southern Congressmen to the inevitable. Lumpkin astutely re-

Foreword

minds us that blacks were the vanguard of the change and that the transformations in race relations in the South grew out of their defiance. To underscore this point she declares, "The protest movement furnished incontrovertible evidence to any and all who had failed to comprehend, that black people were asserting that the time was now for an end to their burden of discrimination and segregation" (p. 250).

Why should anyone read the autobiography of an upper-class southern white woman? The reasons are numerous. First, Katharine Du Pre Lumpkin's book is an effective examination of what it takes to make a white southerner. Together with Benjamin Mays's *Born to Rebel*, Richard Wright's *Black Boy*, Anne Moody's *Coming of Age in Mississippi*, and Pauli Murray's *Proud Shoes*, which describe what goes into the making of black southerners, *The Making of a Southerner* reveals the layered depth of different perceptions and experiences shaped by gender, race, and social status.

Second, Lumpkin's autobiography opens a window onto the past attitudes and values that prevented elite whites from seeing the harsh realities and often demeaning lives led by blacks, poor whites, and many women. Lumpkin was exceptional in many ways, but most especially in her ability to see beyond form and structure to essence. Like the autobiographical writings of such other atypical white southern women as Lillian Smith and Virginia Durr, Lumpkin's volume is one of illuminating power. She penetrates the contradictions, myths, and ironies so deeply embedded in southern culture—in its religion, its economy, its race relations, and its gender conventions. Hers is the poignant testimony of a woman steeped in traditions peculiar to her class and region, who through education and will removed the cataracts of racism, curing herself of the blindness that hid pervasive and unrelenting white poverty and the grinding exploitation of agricultural, factory, and mill workers.

BOOK ONE
Of Bondage to Slavery

1.

GREAT-GRANDFATHER WILLIAM LUMPKIN had a sum total of twenty-one children. His first wife gave him five and died. His second, my great-grandmother, Susannah Edwards, had sixteen and survived her husband. It was upon her death that the estate was divided.

I can imagine how the court must have scratched its head over the problem. Adoniram Judson Lumpkin, my grandfather, "Uncle Jut" he was called, was principal executor, though he was child number nine, with two or three boys ahead of him. It was said he was a man to whom many in the county looked to handle just such affairs.

Having sufficient land was not so much a problem. It is true Great-grandfather's twelve hundred or more acres—he was always buying and selling, so it would be hard to say just how many he had at any one time—would have allowed very little land per heir, yet fully half of the fifteen living children were old enough to be well established on their own properties. My grandfather, for instance, was in his thirties when William Senior died. In any event, land had been going begging in Georgia for a good many years, where by legislative lottery acts between 1803 and 1831 some twenty-two million acres were distributed.

Valuable slaves, however, were hard to come by. Everywhere the price of prime field hands was rising. In middle Georgia they were selling at over a thousand dollars per head. That was on the open market. The valuations placed on Great-grandfather's slaves at the time of distribution ran lower. Only a small proportion of any old estate were "prime field hands," especially where the slaves had been in the family a long while. A question that must have arisen often was how to place values on temperamental differences, after the matter of size and weight and health and age had been taken into account. Surely "Runaway Dennis," powerful physical specimen though he was, and a mighty field hand, could not begin to rate with strong, dependable, docile Moses. As a matter of fact, Great-grandfather's Moses was valued at $825, while Runaway Dennis was set at three hundred less.

Nothing was too much for man's ingenuity apparently. Once they had set arbitrary dollar values on each slave, the problem was solved as follows. "Georgia, Oglethorpe County, 1852"— Great-grandmother Lumpkin had just died—"By virtue of an order from the Honorable Superior Court . . . authorizing and requiring us to make distribution of the negroes of the William Lumpkin Dec'd among the distributees of said estate. . . . We ascertained there were fifteen distributees. . . ." To match the number of heirs, the slaves, some thirty-seven of them now remaining, were grouped and divided into fifteen lots. For example, lot no. 1, consisted of Jerry and wife, old Aunt Winny, not field hands at all, and certainly no longer "prime," who together were valued at $400; also Caroline at $400, and Celia at $400; total value $1,100; whereas, lot no. 2, comprised of Clabourn and wife, $900, and Hazeltine, $300, totaled $1,200. To even up each child's share, those whose lots were worth more paid something back to the estate; those whose lots were worth less, received a few dollars; hence each child's inherited slave property came—in dollars—to precisely $1,136.66.

The decision as to who should get which lot was settled by the simple method of drawing numbers. Says the court order, ". . . The shares were numbered commencing at one and running to fifteen. . . . The names of the distributees were written on a piece of paper and placed in a hat." Similarly, the lot numbers were also written on pieces of paper and placed in another hat. "The hats were well shaken," declares the court. "A name was then drawn from the hat containing the names. Then a number drawn from the hat containing the numbers. . . ." A. J. Lumpkin, my grandfather, drew lot no. 11, consisting of Frederick valued at $500, and Sally and child at $750—it would seem by the valuations, a lucky draw. This totaling $1,250, he had to pay back to the estate $113.34.

It was an exceedingly pleasant country the several Lumpkin brothers saw, who first came to middle Georgia from Virginia in the late eighteenth century. Georgia's legislature had induced emigration from the older colonies by granting virtually free lands —one shilling per acre for the first hundred, and sixpence for the remainder up to a thousand acres. Men could have it for this so long as they took the oath of allegiance to the state and settled their families on their new holdings within a twelvemonth. It was rich, rolling country with dense virgin forest of hardwood and pine, acres of fine loam land waiting to be made ready for plowing, well-watered lowlands, abundant drainage. Rivers and creeks, brooks and rocky formations, gave beauty and variety, not to say a highly utilitarian aspect. Nothing could be easier in pioneer days than to find a large tract filling every agricultural need—land for cultivation, pasture, woods, and water for stock ready at hand. Nor was it a drawback, but the contrary, that in those early years the forests abounded in deer and bear, and men could ride to the fox hunt, a sport my father began enjoying with his elders at the early age of seven. Fine bass and perch, as well as plenty of eels and catfish for the less particular, stocked the streams.

Rivers served a more indispensable purpose, which men looking the territory over for settlement could not fail to anticipate. They saw in them fine arteries of transportation to the broad, navigable Savannah, in its upper waters only a few miles from the Oglethorpe line. Thence the Savannah would carry them to Augusta, already a town of some importance, and destined to become more so, as cotton market and distributing center for all the fertile agricultural country on both the Carolina and Georgia sides.

When once Eli Whitney, working, so local tradition records it, on his aunt's plantation near Augusta, had brought the sweeping revolution in cotton by invention of his ginning machine, then indeed did the Broad and Little Rivers, flowing close by Oglethorpe's two boundaries and into the Savannah, come into their own. Down Broad and down Little River went the laden flatboats carrying their burden of heavy cotton bales. Post roads were used

5

also. Some plantations laboriously hauled their produce in wagons drawn by four or even six horses. In any event, the planters themselves used the post roads, traveling by horseback, stopping at wayside inns and enjoying the good company of their fellows bent on similar business.

Just a year before Georgia gave Eli Whitney his patent and thus launched the era of great prosperity for the cotton planter, Joseph Lumpkin moved from Virginia to Oglethorpe County, there to join his brothers George and Robert, who had preceded him by ten years. With Joseph was his eleven-year-old son, William, my great-grandfather-to-be. In due time the children of these men, and their children's children, were scattered over the three adjacent counties of Wilkes, Clarke, and Oglethorpe.

Oglethorpe County where they settled was Black Belt country, yet very different from many other regions so named. It had no likeness to Georgia's coastal plain, very fertile in its choicest sections, where some of the immense plantations lay. If flat, monotonous fields, interspersed with dank swamps and flowing gray moss were appealing—as they were for many—it was for reasons which middle Georgia did not offer. In like manner, middle Georgia had no relation to the vast lands of southern Alabama, Mississippi, and the Delta, where again were plantations of huge size. These, in the most typical sense, were "Black Belt," once slavery had overrun them, increasing the black population to far more than the white, at the same time increasing cotton production well-nigh proportionately. Lands so inviting to expansion, so easy of cultivation, so profitable in yield, as in this deepest South section, might, and undoubtedly did, compensate for their unlovely monotony, their frequent unhealthfulness. Or it may be that to those acclimated to them, the deep bayous and flat fields came to be immensely attractive.

In Oglethorpe, however, settlers like my great-grandfather's parents found rich uplands ideal for growing short staple cotton as its bottomlands were for corn, more of course than in later years after the land had been worn out by wasteful tillage. So prosperous became plantation farming, and so profitable the labor of slaves (there were but three free colored persons in all the county on the eve of the Civil War), that by my grandfather's time the number of Negroes had been increased to twice that of all white people in the county.

As would any plantation whose location could be freely chosen with an eye to every natural advantage, the William Lumpkin place lay hard by running streams. The fork formed by an arm of Little River on the one side (North Prong, it was called) and Syls Fork Creek on the other, furnished agricultural land on the river bottoms and richly rolling acres on higher ground. It also provided plenty of water for stock on the place and wide, lush meadows. In the forests were good trees of hardwood when lumber was needed for building, along with plenty of small stuff to burn. The great Savannah River was but twenty-odd miles distant, while almost at hand was Little River which flowed into it, giving a ready-made water highway for flatboats to Augusta and the sea.

It was my grandfather's privilege, among his father's fifteen living children, to purchase from the estate the home tract of land with the family homestead. He had already been making his home there with his widowed mother since his father died, while continuing to supervise his own properties. Here in the old home, William Senior's since his first marriage in the early eighteen-hundreds, my father, an only child, was born and spent his first years until war came and altered everything.

The plantation "big house" (still standing, though parts of it are gone) was situated on a rise of ground above the road leading to the county seat of Lexington. Lexington was twelve miles distant; on the way to it at Stephens was Antioch Baptist Church. Once there must have been a picket fence immediately surrounding the dwelling; Father so often talked of excitedly swinging on the gate at Christmas time to watch for his uncles and aunts and their families to drive up from the roadway through the avenue of great trees as they came for the annual gathering at the old home. (That is Father's story. But how could even a few of William Senior's many offspring, plus their wives and children, ever be housed in the old home for the holiday? How indeed they were ever housed as children remains in my mind a mystery. And what a cavalcade it must have made on Sundays, as the patriarch William and his train, women and smallest children in carriages, men and boys each on his own horse, started out, as befitted the family of an oft-time deacon, regularly as clock-work, to attend preaching at Antioch Baptist Church. How many pews must be reserved for the William Lumpkin family?)

The old home was not a mansion of stately pillars, immaculate whiteness, ostentatious lines. Until I learned better I thought none were "big houses" save those of this exceptional description. Ours had been strictly utilitarian, yet with those fine square lines which in New England are called colonial farmhouses. Solidly built, with great chimneys at either end and square rooms running alongside a hall upstairs and down—"wide enough to drive a four-horse team through," so Father would speak of it. Cool breezes could sweep through this hallway, front to rear, in the heat of Georgia summertime. A narrow stairs went steeply to the "attic," which in so large a household was an integral part of the house. From the first-floor hall went a broader staircase downward, for the house was built on ground that fell away in the rear, and the large dining-room was on a level lower than the first floor. Looking out from the dining-room porch or from the windows in the rooms above, one's eye could sweep westward across wooded hills and pasture slopes, or, coming nearer, follow the stream flowing through the barnyard below, down under the hill, a stream whose water never failed, however prolonged the drought, because of the good springs ever feeding it.

As usual in such homes, the kitchen in Grandfather's place was in a separate building, some thirty feet removed from the house, connected with it by a firm walk fashioned of oak trees split and set solidly in the ground, flat side up. Aunt Sarah ruled in the kitchen, from whence, to and fro on the split-log walk, went the slave "boys"—men house-servants—who waited on table. In my father's day, when only the family were at home, it would take only two men waiting on table, Fed (not Fred) and a helper; "but with guests it would likely take four," even Pit having to do duty, though usually he was relegated to the post of kitchen helper, for invariably he grew excited and dropped something.

In the kitchen Aunt Sarah had no stove. Her cooking was done in a huge open fireplace with ovens, spiders, skillets, pots, and implements of copper or wrought iron. On certain very special occasions she would untuck her vast folds of calico skirt which had been turned up over her petticoats and held in at the waist to keep from impeding her movements, don a stiffly starched white apron, and, accompanied by a small slave boy carrying a great bowl of batter, she would enter the dining-room to make waffles over the huge open fireplace, to be served directly to the table. It was said she did this only for those whom she delighted to honor.

As plantations went in that section, Grandfather's was a large one. It was among the six or seven in Oglethorpe of a thousand acres or more. In some parts of the state, especially the low country, there would be huge estates with many thousands of acres and several hundred slaves. Not so in middle Georgia. The bigger places there had forty, fifty, some a hundred slaves.

Hence, while Grandfather and his father before him, might be "big" planters in the county, or in the surrounding counties of Georgia, they would not have been so regarded among big planters from the deepest South or the low country. Actually they were much more true to type of Southern planter than the large-scale owners.

Neither men nor women on Grandfather's kind of working plantation had much time to cultivate leisure-class occupations or ways, in the sense true of large-scale landlords. More often than not the latter were absentee owners, for at least a part of the year, keeping up town houses in the more sophisticated surroundings of city life. They traveled more, built more elegant dwellings, lived more richly altogether. It is of these planters that I, as a child, used to read in romantic Southern stories, filling my mind with their exotic luxuriousness. I certainly heard father tell of life as it was on his own plantation. It may seem strange to have missed the difference. Somehow the two pictures became blurred and blended until later years.

Masters on Oglethorpe plantations might not work with their hands—what master did who had a goodly number of slaves to train and direct at the wide variety of tasks? Yet they would be poor managers if they did not know how to do the work to which they set their slaves: they must closely supervise all the soil preparation, and planting and cultivating and harvesting; they must decide what must be planted and when, and how well crops had stood up under a drought, and how good was the cotton stand,

and whether it required reseeding; they must be certain of repairs on houses and barns and slave quarters and the upkeep of farming implements; their slave-artisans must be skilled, but the master must know how well they were exercising their crafts at the carpenter's bench or the blacksmith's forge. Above all, the masters must see to it that the plantation paid, for by it they made their living, which, while comfortable, was in no wise luxurious, as the great plantations were. Simple and abundant would more truly describe it. To let affairs on the plantation get out of hand for a moment would mean losses and debts and hardship for wife and children.

In middle Georgia men lived on their land and were not wont to go seeking out cities except as politics or church affairs or other business sent them on brief excursions. Lexington, the county seat of Oglethorpe, twelve miles distant from Grandfather's place, had but a few hundred souls twenty years after the war, although one account of the eighteen-eighties has it that the town "was noted for its refined and cultured society. Here some of the most distinguished men of Georgia have resided—William H. Crawford, Thomas W. Cobb, Stephen Upson, George R. Gilmer, and the Lumpkins."

It would seem that "the Lumpkins" were usually spoken of in the plural. So numerous was the clan that it always remained a tangle in our minds, to which branches belonged the names of those who in Georgia archives particularly distinguished themselves. Among the Lumpkin men were physicians, preachers (Baptist), even teachers now and then: one teacher among us, it is said, instituted the law school in Athens, giving it his name, which later became attached to the University. Of all occupations, however, Lumpkin men were, first, planters, and with it, frequently, lawyers who went in for politics. (During the war of course, young and old were all soldiers.) From this tradition of the law, feeding on the careers of the first Chief Justice of Georgia, Joseph Henry Lumpkin, and another Justice by the same name, his grandson, and still another named Samuel; and the Governor and United States Senator, Wilson Lumpkin, for whose daughter, so the tale ran, the city of Atlanta was named; and many, many Lumpkins who held this or that lesser political office—from this tradition,

10

fostered by these men and their activity, derived almost a cult of family role, which in its completeness embraced the conception of planter lawyer-in-politics gentleman.

It did not follow that middle Georgia planters in general were educated men, though Lumpkins seem frequently to have gone to college, medical school, or law school, a very few even attending universities in the North. Somehow a strong professional tradition had seeped into the Lumpkin clan, however closely bound up it was with farming.

Oglethorpe County did very little to encourage education. It had fewer schools than its neighbors. Less than a score of teachers and schools could be found in all the county in Grandfather's day, with hardly more dollars of public money put into them than there were pupils. Such schools were for those who could pay next to nothing. For the well-to-do, several "academies" were scattered about, supported by the wealthy for their own children to the amount of several thousand dollars a year. Some children had tutors at home. A few might be sent to stay with relatives in Washington in Wilkes County, or in Athens, where distinguished old academies could be found. In the 1830's or '40's the Baptist Convention had put some fine, dignified buildings in neighboring Wilkes County, to house newly established Mercer University. Here went many middle Georgia sons, of planter and professional standing, for their higher learning. Great-grandfather believed in Mercer and for years was one of its most faithful trustees. It was not my father's fortune to go there. At fifteen he entered the university of war.

If anything, it was of religion that people seemingly could get no surfeit. In the County of Oglethorpe, whose white population was less than five thousand in Grandfather's day, there were ten Baptist churches accommodating nearly seven thousand persons, if they could ever have been filled. Besides this, the Methodists had as many churches, though smaller, and the Presbyterians a few. To find Episcopalians one had to go to the cities or the low country.

Religion was in no way incidental to these middle Georgia antebellum planters. As they were solid, ambitious men, conscious of responsibilities of rulership, so were they pious and God-fearing,

11

at least the better of them, with an acutely developed sense of duty. This latter heritage we children had ample reason to be acquainted with in later years.

It was a simple faith with little adornment: these men believed in church, in going to church, in training their charges, be they children or slaves, in religious duties; they believed, without undue commotion about it, in heaven and hell and prayer, in the Bible and salvation, and of course in immersion. Antioch Baptist Church, six miles from the old home, was an active element in the lives of Grandfather and Great-grandfather. For Father too, it was very present during his childhood while he lived near it and, I suspect, remained very present in all his years.

This honest devoutness of men like my forebears—and it would be unreasonable to suppose that they, who I know were possessed of it, stood alone among their fellow planters in this regard—added a peculiar ingredient to their make-up. They were a very special blend: slaveholder, Southern Baptist, and Southern gentleman rolled into one.

2.

ONE THING can be said of the distribution among his heirs of the slaves "Grandfather Billy" (my great-grandfather) passed on: families were kept together. "Jerry and wife," "Clabourn and wife," "Frederick and Sally and child," "Easter and child"—so went the listing. The feeling their master had for his charges makes me believe he would have been very reluctant to permit his own slave-families to be broken up.

But just as there came birth and death and accident, all beyond man's willing or control, so were there circumstances, painful though they might be to my great-grandparents, under which it was legitimate and necessary for slave man and wife and child to be torn apart. It was not a prescribed set of circumstances, not something laid down in a code, but circumstances which according to the judgment of the master required the sale of a slave.

Of Bondage to Slavery

If for generations one's forebears had been slaveholders, how natural the slave order would seem, and how permanent. It was so for my people, bred in the very bone of their heritage. Before they could migrate to Georgia from Virginia in the late 1700's they must sell their lands, and sell or take with them their movable property. Eloquent of this is a trivial deed of sale by Joseph Lumpkin of Pittsylvania County—("Know all men by these presents")—who "bargained, sold, and by these presents delivered unto Pittman Lumpkin," in the selfsame category as "four negroes, Let, Delphy, Lucy and Fanny," "also one sorrell horse, one bay mare and one black mare. Also one feather bed and furniture for the consideration sum of one hundred and ninety pounds current money of Virginia . . ." whereupon he did "warrant said slaves, horses, and feather bed from the claim and claims of any person or persons whatsoever. . . ."

We never heard much talk of buying and selling under slavery. It was not of such things that we thought. Doubtless Great-grandfather Billy often threatened to sell "Runaway" Dennis, a quarrelsome slave, nagging and rousing the ire of his fellows until he would overstep the bounds with some transgression, and, fearful of punishment, would take to the swamps. Surely, it would try a master's patience, in particular that of a gracious, kindly man; and it would puzzle him too, for from Uncle Jerry, the foreman, on down, my grandparents' slaves were known for their warm devotion and willing obedience.

Occasionally on Great-grandfather's place a slave would be purchased. On these old plantations of moderate size where the owners had lived for a long time, keeping the same slaves, they would cling to the individual Negroes, even when their chattels grew so feeble as almost to be useless. So if field work was to be coped with, they of necessity must replenish their stock of slaves from time to time.

The way to go about their purchases would offer no difficulties. Slavery had been a settled institution so long as to make it almost as simple as the purchase of real estate. Indeed, when the institution first took root on this continent, once it was established that human beings could be regarded under the law as property, it surely required very little ingenuity on the part of legal authorities

13

to adapt existing property conceptions to the new category. "The slave being a personal chattel," they put it, "is at all times liable to be sold absolutely, or mortgaged, or leased, at the will of the master . . ." This was language already familiar in the business community for describing property transactions of any kind. "He may also be sold by process of law for the satisfaction of the debts of a living, or the debts and bequests of a deceased master. . . ." And this further angle: "A slave is one who is in the power of a master . . . to sell him, dispose of his person, his industry and his labor. He can do nothing, possess nothing, nor acquire anything, but what must belong to his master."

Complying with legal formalities presented no problems for the would-be slaveholder. It was simplicity itself. A Northerner settling in Lexington, Georgia, provided he had the money, could go to the county courthouse, find out what he had to do to own a Negro, secure the necessary papers, and complete his transaction in a very short space of time. His difficulty would be his inexperience. A stranger to slavery would not have the faintest notion of whether he was getting his money's worth, or what qualities to look for, and how to judge them when the man or woman stood before him, or where to go to get a good buy.

Not so men like my grandparents, steeped in an experience handed down from generations of slaveholders. Let Great-grandfather Billy once decide upon his need, whether of man or woman, of field hand, or of slave-craftsman to supplement his carpenter-blacksmith who was getting old, and his several next steps were obvious before him.

Any planter in such a case would cast his eye down the advertising columns of the county weekly newspaper, or the *Athens Banner*, or the *Augusta Chronicle*, for "Negroes for Sale." "A negro woman, 24 years of age, and her two children . . . eight and . . . three . . . will be sold low . . . or exchanged for groceries." He wanted a single man or woman; preferred not to separate families; did not need a seamstress with his expert Sally still young. Again, ". . . Subscriber has just arrived from Virginia . . . one hundred twenty likely young negroes of both sexes and every description . . . most reasonable terms . . . ploughboys, several likely and well-qualified houseservants of both sexes, several women with

14

children, small girls suitable for nurses . . . several small boys without their mothers. . . ." This was a trader advertising from distant Charleston. Under settlement of estates or debts he would find items: ". . . In La Grange, Troup County [this in Georgia; he was reading the *Southern Whig*], one negro girl, by the name of Charity, aged about ten or twelve years, as the property of Littleton L. Burke, to satisfy a mortgage fi. fa. from Troup Inferior Court, in favor of Daniel S. Robertson vs. said Burke."

Young as I was when Father died—nor would it probably have occurred to me to do it—I never asked if they made purchases of slaves at markets. By the time of my childhood, slavery was commonly regarded as well-ended, although by altogether wrong means. We were wont to say: "We should gradually have got rid of slavery if it had not been forcibly taken away." The slave market, I know, was relegated in our thoughts to a twilight zone, vague and but faintly recollected, and it was rare for us to turn to this vague shadow in remembering the old days.

On the other hand, one can find slave markets still preserved and still marked in Southern cities. I once chanced on the one in old Charleston. At dusk of a spring evening not many years ago I saw its sign down a side street toward the harbor, indistinct in the dim light shining through the heavy open door. What once had seen the buying and selling of slaves now welcomed the visitor to a tidy, almost gay souvenir shop selling candy and postcards and knicknacks. The second floor had presumably housed the market. Now it is a "museum of slavery." It was closed that afternoon, so I could only gaze up the short flight of roughhewn stairs and ask curiously of the caretaker what one would find in the museum. She replied, I thought a little sharply, that it had "only pleasant reminders. We don't go in for slave horrors. . . ."

It is unlikely that so small a county seat as Lexington in Oglethorpe had a regular slave market. Washington, in adjoining Wilkes County, had a well-known resident trader, a Jamaican by birth, who served as local middleman. The near-by city of Augusta, trading center as it was for a rich and wide plantation country in Carolina and Georgia, was probably the nearest regular market. No doubt Great-grandfather Billy preferred to make his infrequent purchases by some more reliable means than a market, but he would be well acquainted with them. What planter was not?

They were not attractive places. In large cities, where several might be found, run by different traders, they were often grouped in proximity. Thus, when an auction was on, the trader would hang out his little red flag to indicate activity, or even go to the door of his place and sing out along the narrow, unsightly street. Whether one or several, the markets' interiors were similarly fitted. Not much was needed for the transactions taking place. Bare rooms were usual, with a table or desk of sorts for the paper end of the business, a few chairs or benches on which the clients could rest between sales, and a "block," so called, in the center, in the nature of a small platform a few steps higher than the floor, so that when men stood about to get a view of the offering, they could see over one another's heads. Off at the side might be a screen or a room adjoining; this was needed for better examination of men and boys, who could be taken there to strip to have their muscles tested, their skin looked over for disease or sores, their general appearance assessed as could not be done when they were clothed. On the open floor the offerings would be required by the prospective purchaser to open their mouths for careful inspection of their teeth; and also they must open and close their fists to show their strength of grip for the tasks awaiting them in the fields. This examination of hands and fingers, they tell us, was always a matter of particular concern to the buyer, as a trait of first-rate importance.

Sales may sometimes have been coarse and brutal, even to the eyes of a contemporary accustomed to the scene. I am ready to believe that more often they were calm, business-like occasions, unclouded by any human consideration one way or the other. After all, it was primarily a matter of dollars and cents to all parties concerned as to who should get the best bargain.

We are told of a dark woman, with two children beside her and a baby at her breast, who mounted the block while the auctioneer sang out: "Well, gentlemen . . . here is a capital woman and her three children, all in good health—what do you say for them?" Neither our thoughts today, nor even the English visitor's who witnessed the scene, could quite reproduce the tenor of the buyer's mind, who was absorbed in a transaction to which he was entirely accustomed, and for whom it was nothing more than a means of carrying on legitimate business. "Well, now, gentlemen, here is a right prime lot. Look at this man; strong, healthy, able-bodied; could not be a better hand for field-work. He can drive a wagon, or anything." Persuasively: "A strong-boned man, fit for any kind of heavy work. Just take a look at him. . . ." They retired behind the screen, presently returning. And peremptorily, "Pray, gentlemen, be quick . . . I must sell him."

Great-grandfather Billy may have taken the long journey on horseback over the post road to the Augusta slave market when he needed a new slave. It is more probable that he could find what he needed by inquiries among relatives or friends in Oglethorpe and adjoining counties. He might even get a Negro from another member of the numerous Lumpkin clan. Three of George Lumpkin's sons had plantations within a fifteen-mile radius of William Senior's. Over the line in Clarke County lived Samuel P. and Joseph Henry and other Lumpkins. Besides these, there were the numerous grown sons and daughters living on their own places.

Certainly my grandparents would have preferred to supply their needs from relatives or acquaintances. For one thing, it was a much safer investment; one could know precisely what he was getting. Beyond that, to them it would be a more seemly procedure to purchase from kinsmen or friends. It would be but natural for kindly men, men of generous impulse and high ideals in all their relationships, other things being equal, to choose if they could the more seemly path.

It was the more true because by their day, slavery in its uglier aspects was openly the subject of sharp controversy. Bitterly and with indignation, Southern newspapers printed accounts of the rising tide of abolitionist sentiment, the better to fling back answers to the harsh epithets of castigation. A Southerner need not be shaken in his acceptance of slavery to be made extremely sensitive by criticism. Men like my grandparents, devout Christians as they were and deeply imbued with the Baptist theology of personal sin and salvation, would more than ever look to their personal conduct to have it beyond reproach, as they saw it, in relation to their slaves. They would search the Scriptures, as their preachers

17

did for them, to cite divine sanction for this institution which they could in no wise do without. With it all, they would follow meticulously, according to their lights, humane ways of acquiring and ordering the lives of their charges.

They would make the best of the bitter that must go with the sweet. No sensible man could do less. In this so imperfect world, many times would come when they must concur in less than perfect conduct.

We know of one occasion when William Lumpkin, Senior, with his fellows, was confronted with just such a dilemma. For some twenty-eight out of a period of thirty-four years he was chosen by his congregation at Antioch Baptist Church as delegate to the Georgia Baptist Convention. He faithfully attended, and faithfully shared in the deliberations; nor could it be said of these religious gatherings that they were remote from daily life. In the eighteen-thirties a query arose among Georgia Baptists, "Whether, in case of involuntary separation [i.e. sale] of such a character as to preclude all future intercourse, the [slave] parties may be allowed to marry again?" Such a highly practical problem could arise only if it had been of concern in devout men's minds, pushed forward, it may be, by the backwash of raging anti-slavery criticism. Being a problem of immediate moment to the multiplication of one's slaves, it was surely discussed around the fireside of every Baptist slaveowner. William Senior was in a position where he must share in finding the answer to that query.

It must have come very close home to him. Unlike some planters, who regarded as an inconvenience the slaves' personal relationships, interfering as they might with their maximum profitability, my grandparents encouraged marriage and family life. As any master would, Great-grandfather Billy no doubt preferred to have his slaves choose their mates on his own plantation, but he permitted them to marry property of his neighbors. Once they had made their choice, with the blessing of his permission, it was his custom so to clothe the occasion about with ceremony as to make it outstandingly a time to be remembered.

To my grandparents' slaves, Christmas was of all times a favorite for weddings. It was an exciting time in any event, and with so many of the master's relations there for the holiday, little gifts from the white family would be multiplied. The bride would have a wedding gown, the castoff garment of the mistress or her daughter; the groom, similarly, would look about to find a suit. The wedding would be held in the evening by the light of torches, in the back yard, beneath the dining-room veranda. In the afternoon Aunt Winnie, wife of Uncle Jerry, who in all things having to do with the women and children of the slave quarters was her mistress's deputy, would come, bringing with her the shy bride to stand before her mistress for inspection and a little extra furbishing.

Wedding time arrived with the fall of darkness. Lighting the pine torches was the signal for the master and mistress and family and guests to gather on the dining-room veranda; the signal, also, for the procession of men and women and children and babes in arms to begin from the slave quarters. Even a few slaves from neighboring plantations would be present for the festivities, whose first duty on arrival would already have been fulfilled when they went before Great-grandfather Billy to bob their heads or do their curtsy and present to him their passes from their own masters. At the end of the motley procession, torches ablaze in the hands of young men, came the bride and groom and Uncle Jerry.

On many places the master performed slave marriage ceremonies. On my grandparents', Uncle Jerry, plantation preacher as well as foreman, officiated, as he did at funerals and baptisms. In the wavering light of many torches, out under Georgia's mild December night sky, would boom forth the mighty voice of Uncle Jerry, uniting the young slave couple in holy matrimony, in the name of their Lord and Savior, Jesus Christ.

Jerry's blessing pronounced, the wedding proper was over. However, something still remained before the bride and groom could return to their fellows at the quarters, to join in song and dance until dawn. They must accompany Uncle Jerry into the big house to the dining-room, there to stand before their master. Seated in his accustomed place at the head of the dining-table, Great-grandfather would talk to the boy and girl, sensibly and solemnly, telling them of the serious step they had taken, and discoursing quietly on the duties of husband and wife. In this manner, having in view their welfare and happiness, William Senior would arrange the marriage of his slaves.

However, when he was confronted with the query posed by the Georgia Baptist ministry—"Whether, in case of involuntary separation [sale] . . . the [slave] parties may be allowed to marry again?"—wherein lay any genuine alternative? For himself, with his small and stable group of family slaves, it was in any event a remote problem, and as a man of affairs, who was he to judge of the needs of others whose business required different handling? Such being the practical situation, what sensible man could fail to concur in the foregone conclusion of the church's discussion? ". . . That such separation, among persons situated as our slaves are, is, civilly, a separation by death, and they believe that, in the sight of God, it would be so viewed. To forbid second marriage in such cases, would be to expose the parties not only to greater hardships and stronger temptations, but to church censure for not acting in obedience to their masters, who cannot be expected to acquiesce in a regulation at variance with justice to the slaves, and to the spirit of that command which regulates marriage between Christians. The slaves are not free agents, and a dissolution by death is not more entirely without their consent and beyond their control than by such separation [sale]."

Even so, the church was more generous than the law in blessing marriage, so long as the relationship could exist without impairment of the rights of masters. The law said that a "necessary consequence of slavery is the absence of the marriage relation." It assumed, "No slave can commit bigamy." It conceded, "A slave may indeed be formally married, but so far as legal rights and obligations are concerned, it is an idle ceremony." As for the slave child, one interpretation said: "A slave has no more legal authority over his child than a cow has over her calf."

Provisions like these, however, were never uppermost in the slaveowner's mind. It is safe to assume that my grandparents would have been relatively untroubled by them, as my father, a man sensitive to justice, was on the whole untroubled by many provisions in the law of our day, put there, he said, only for "rare and special contingencies," and in practice, little observed. It is certain that the law had its application in the case of slaves: "$50 . . . ran away from the subscriber, his negro man Pauladore. . . . I understand Gen. R. Y. Hayne has purchased his wife and children from H. L. Pinckney Esq. and has them now on his plantation . . . where, no doubt, the fellow is frequently lurking"; or, "$10 . . . ran away from subscriber, a negro woman named Sally, 40 years old. We have reason to believe said negro to be lurking on the James River Canal . . . where, we are informed, her husband resides." It may be these were the contingencies—rare or not as may be—against which the law was meant to provide.

Slaveowners on an old plantation like that of my grandparents might buy little and sell not at all, but if they were worth their salt, given the interests of their plantation, they kept an eye on prices. By their fellows both William Senior and Adoniram Judson Lumpkin were rated excellent business men. In their day slave prices were doing very peculiar things.

There had been an old rule, which practically all cotton planters went by, of pricing a Negro by the price of cotton per pound. Thus if cotton were selling at twelve cents, a prime field hand should be worth $1,200; if fifteen cents, then $1,500, and so on. This neat device, before the Civil War, had been going completely to pieces. In the 1850's Grandfather was finding that Negroes cost more with cotton at ten cents a pound than they had several years before when cotton sold much higher. When a brief financial crisis of the decade dropped prices of securities and commodities sharply, it affected slave prices hardly at all. "Demented speculators," as good, solid operating planters spoke of them, were playing havoc with customary rules.

Great-grandfather could remember when slave prices had been at their lowest figure. It was just at the beginning of his career, about the time of his first wife's death, and just prior to the Congressional ban of 1808 on slave importation. With the ban the spurt in prices started. Smuggling brought some importation of Negroes, but it did not meet requirements. Natural increase was a factor, but it could not begin to make up the difference. With the feverish rise in demand came the jump in prices. Some figured it was speculation pure and simple with a crash sure to follow.

More sanguine men said the demand for slaves in the Southwest "would keep up the prices as it caused their advance in the first place." "The Southwest is being opened by a great tide of emigration. The planter who puts ten hands to work on the prolific soil of Texas and Western Louisiana soon makes money enough to buy ten more, and they have to be supplied from the older States— hence the prices which rule in Virginia, the Carolinas and Georgia." This was said on the very eve of the war. All over the South, and more especially in old sections such as middle Georgia, men became increasingly uneasy, feeling in the wind premonitory signs of a gathering storm.

3.

GRANDFATHER was a heavily burdened man. There can be no doubt it meant this to be a resident cotton planter, whose plantation was a community and a business rolled into one. As children we may have dwelt in our minds on the "big house," and the life that went on there, as we heard of it and imagined it. Not so with Grandfather. Some absentee-owned plantations apparently got along without "big houses," merely providing dwellings where overseers lived. A man who lived on his place, as Grandfather did, would spend most of his waking hours and by far the greater part of his mental labor on the part of his place that centered in slave quarters, stables, and springhouse, and the work radiating out into the fields from this hub of all activity.

Down under the hill, almost a quarter-mile distant from the family dwelling, were the slave quarters. They were one-room cabins, strung out along a sort of lane, each with its rough chimney of native stone to furnish a fireplace for cooking. Conveniently near them were the stables and horse lot, both fenced in sturdily with rails, and both so located—the stock must be watered—as to be fed by the branch flowing from the never-failing spring. Stables they were called, but the word stood for all the buildings, outhouses, and pens, large and small, which were clustered around the stables proper to meet the dozen needs of a sizable plantation. Great-grandmother's inventory told us something of what was housed here and the work that went on in the structures; here the horses and cattle were kept when they were not in pasture; here the carriages and other family vehicles; here the farm wagons and ox cart; and for all these, harness and other gear for their several requirements, as well as for the plows and various farm implements; here also were the many saddles and bridles. Here were stored huge quantities of hay and other feed; and seed for planting. Adjoining were the structures of lesser size: the smokehouse for curing hams and bacon; the carpenter shop, neat and shipshape; the blacksmith's quarters, a sprawling place, big enough to hold a forge, admit the ungainly implements requiring mending, and let a horse or mule enter to be shod; and the sheds to shelter plows and threshers; and the smaller lean-tos for keeping hoes, rakes, mattocks, scythes, crowbars, pole axes, broad axes, and spades out of the weather. Near these were the pig pens, runs for the sheep when they were brought in, and chicken houses.

Also under the hill, but on higher ground, away from stables and quarters, was the spring that furnished all the drinking water. Nothing apparently was more a treasure on the place. It performed a major duty, to be sure, in providing a never-failing source of good water. But somehow, too, it held a special place in Father's nostalgic memories. We knew it as though we had seen it, welling up in clear coolness out of the hillside under a wooded rocky bluff, and the deep cache, long years before carefully walled around with flinty stones to hold the bubbling water; and the cold stream flowing from it, over which was built the sturdy, roomy springhouse; and the winding, shaded trail to the spring, worn smooth by generations of slaves' bare feet treading it or the shod feet of house servants going on their daily mission of fetching not just water, but overflowing crocks of milk and cream and buttermilk and butter for the family table; and how it was the master's custom regularly to inspect the spring, and personally to supervise its cleansing (with little Will—my father—always present to catch the minnows and tadpoles the men hauled out); and how Grandfather often went there in the heat of the day to have a drink of cool buttermilk.

While my grandparents' place was only moderate in size compared with really large estates, the conduct of any slave plantation was a complex affair. I do not know how many plows were put into the field, or how many of Grandfather's twelve hundred odd acres he planted in cotton, or what was his usual yield. A planter named Tait, who moved from Georgia to the rich Mississippi lowlands in the 1830's, on three hundred and twenty acres of cotton, with some fifty-odd slaves over ten years of age, and sixteen plow horses and mules, won a yield of nearly two hundred bales. As prices went, that brought him in several thousand dollars. Tait's might have been somewhat comparable to Grandfather's place in size. But he got nearly half a bale to the acre, which would certainly have been unheard of on the older lands of middle Georgia in the eighteen-fifties, except for the few men who had begun to fertilize. We have a slight notion of how much Grandfather had in stock, from what his mother still owned at the time she died. Susannah Lumpkin's inventory named fifteen horses and colts— "bald bay Tom," "bay mare Katy," "silver eye bald," "bay mare Nelly," and so on; also fifty head of cattle, more than a hundred head of hogs, twenty-two sheep, and some lesser items.

As nearly as possible Grandfather made his plantation provide for all his needs. On a place of this size he had to do so if he were to have any net cash income. He planted many acres of corn and some of wheat; he had a few Irish potatoes, but mainly sweets by the acre, as an item of slave diet. He had his hay fields and put in some grain crops. He kept up a large vegetable garden for family needs, but this was a small labor item compared with the demands of field crops and care of animals. Then, of course, above everything, he must raise his cotton. This last was the all-absorbing consideration. It was the source of all the cash he could count on.

Hence the season's farm round was a very complex one. In middle Georgia plows could be running in January if the weather was fine. In any event, fence corners should be cleaned, ditches opened, rails could be split for mending fences, and the poor work animals, hardly rested at all, be put at rail-hauling. This went on into February. In March the first corn could go in, and what plows could be spared from corn could be used for bedding cotton land.

Cotton could be planted in early April, though some men advocated waiting a little. "Nothing is made but hard work by planting summer crops in winter." In May the work mounted. "Action! Action! Action!" cried agricultural journals. "The campaign is now fairly opened." "Your enemies," the grass and weeds, should not occupy any good position. "Eternal vigilance" is the price of a good crop, they said. Hardly was cotton planting ended in May, but corn was ready for its first working. Now, they said, before the ground had lost its moisture from winter rains, might be the last chance to secure a deep, mellow soil against the summer droughts. Plowing and more plowing; hoeing and more hoeing. "From rosy morn to dewy eve the . . . plow and hoe must move. . . ." Into June would go on the same heavy labor: plowing and hoeing corn, plowing and hoeing cotton. Field peas had to be planted if they were to ripen before the frosts. Then July, and late corn waiting to get its last working; and cotton still demanding hoeing and plowing. Wise planters advised, "Don't let your choppers cut the roots by careless hoeing, for then the plants will shed their precious bolls." August: the main crops laid by, but still worries for the planter. Fodder should be pulled; everything made ready for cotton harvesting; the ginhouse and packing-screw put in first class order; baskets and bags mended to be ready for picking. And then that most prodigious task. Open bolls, long white fleece hanging precariously from them, would not grip the precious fiber for many days. In middle Georgia cotton could be picked in September, October, even a little in November. But meantime the other tasks must be sandwiched in. Corn should be brought in, fall oats sown. Cotton ginned and hauled to market. Hog-fattening must be pushed hard, for soon would come December and hog-killing time. Some planters might even start the round again before Christmas—at least "cleaning up" could be done —fencing and ditching.

This was the field end. In addition, Grandfather must grind his corn to have meal to feed his slaves. It was common to allow a quart of meal a day for adults, less for children. One man in Mississippi figuring his needs for seventy-five slaves, estimated them at seven hundred and eighty-five bushels—allowing a peck of meal a week per slave, and half as much for children. Also flour must be provided for the family's needs—for hot biscuit, "light" bread, rolls, waffles, cakes, and cookies. And beef, lamb, mutton, pork, hams, bacon, for the big house. Also chickens, turkeys, and geese. The slaves got pork for their meat. If each adult slave was furnished a half pound of salt pork a day—the basis for figuring on many plantations—it took many a hog to feed so large a company. Hence hog-killing time, when it came in December, was a major undertaking. It was something of a celebration too, for even the field hands might get a taste of sausage and cracklin' bread, and the family looked forward to fresh pork hams and spareribs.

To clothe the slaves, great bolts of goods must be hauled in from Athens or Augusta. The garments then had to be made for men, women, and children: trousers and shirts for the men, and dresses for the women, sturdy enough to stand up under heavy field labor. There was the mending also. Altogether the sewing could probably keep a few women busy practically all of every day.

Here were the tasks required to make the plantation pay. The problem was how to accomplish them wisely and most profitably. More than anything else, it would seem, this depended upon successfully handling the slaves.

From his father's estate my grandfather bought the "home lot," a piece comprising over six hundred acres, for about two thousand dollars. But the thirty-eight slaves who were appraised for distribution among the heirs, were valued at nearly twenty thousand dollars. On the open market, prices being what they were at the time, they would have brought much more.

Of course land values were an item to be considered. However, as one Virginia planter explained, given "the present value of slaves," he could not plant grain, but must put his acres in tobacco, even though tobacco required fresh land and exhausted his soil quickly. For the labor used, he said, it paid him, and if he was well paid for it, he did not know why he should not wear out his land. A traveler in Mississippi remarked on seeing abandoned plantations, hillsides gutted, stables and quarters falling to decay, places that not long before were said to have given the phenomenal yield of a bale and a half of cotton to the acre, or eight or ten bales for each prime field hand. They had exhausted the land, but what was their choice, asked they, when rich lands could be purchased in Texas at one dollar an acre, and prime field hands were selling at a thousand dollars a head? Everywhere masters had to equate the use of their land against slave values. On old plantations, such as Grandfather's, where there was little chance to expand, unless a man picked up and moved away, everything must be figured closely, including the use of his land.

Against property so valuable as slaves, land was therefore secondary. A master of sound economic sense and practical business acumen must weigh with greatest care the use of this, his most valuable property. One man put it thus, framing instructions for his overseer: "The effort must . . . not be merely to make so many cotton bales or such an amount of other produce, but as much as can be made without interrupting the steady increase in value of the rest of the property . . . There should be an increase in number and improvement in condition of negroes." Another owner undergirded his injunctions with his firm religious sense, not a little reminiscent of the pious nonconformists of R. H. Tawney's classic, whose religion so sternly reinforced their economic activity as they built the structure of early capitalism. It was "indispensably necessary" to successful planting, said this master, "as well as for reasonable dividends for the amount of capital invested, without saying anything about the Master's duty to his dependents, to himself, and his God . . ." to bear ever in mind the "health, happiness, good discipline and obedience, good, sufficient and comfortable clothing, a sufficiency of good, wholesome and nutritious food for both man and beast." I am sure this is much the way my devout Baptist grandfather would have explained his problem had he been asked.

Apparently, most planters were convinced that Negro slaves had a congenital dislike for work. As a clergyman of the time put it, "Slaves have no aspirations for . . . freedom of any kind, except . . . freedom to do nothing." Consequently, no problem loomed so large in a slaveholder's mind as how to induce a reasonable amount of labor from his involuntary servitors. Any number of devices were tried, depending upon the master's turn of mind or whether he left his problem to deputies. Some said they favored a strict, even harsh overlordship, despairing of the instant obedience they demanded unless it were enforced by the lash. Some went to the other extreme and instituted systems of rewards, saying it worked wonders. They would permit their slaves little gardens, or let them do handiwork, and even allowed them to sell their produce and keep the cash. Such planters said that to own cash would teach the slave to care better for his master's property. It would seem Grandfather went to no extremes in either direction, but followed what Father called "rules of common sense." This was so, unless we except the part Uncle Jerry played.

The matter of work assignments was very delicate. These must be handled discreetly to avoid a morass of discontent. At least, so it was said, and the notion seems reasonable. Some used the stint-system: this much of a cotton field hoed, so many pounds of cotton picked, and when the task was done the hands could quit. Some worked their slaves in gangs; when one field was done, the gang moved on to another, until the sun had set. Both ways might be used, depending on the nature of the work. Either way, the "lazy" men or women, the ones who tended to "shirk," those who were "smart at cutting corners," it was said, had to be watched, or the whole labor force would be demoralized by their irresponsible ways.

There were problems of age. An age would come at which children would be taken away from their light tasks of helping tend the "little darkies," or at small cleaning jobs, and be sent to do field work; not a full field hand's labor, at first, but probably starting at a quarter of an able-bodied hand's task; and later a half, until finally the child was big and strong enough to do the whole stint. Some plantations set twelve years of age when the child would begin in the fields.

Also, slaves grew old. A time would come when they were no longer considered "prime." Sometimes the age of fifty or thereabouts was set as the age for lessening the load. Some slaves became "old" earlier than others. Really aged slaves might have little at all required of them, if they had been kept, that is. On old plantations whose slaves had been in the family a long time, they would often keep the old people, instead of trying to get rid of the financial burden they entailed. The newer plantations and those in the newer, richer country may have tended to buy only prime hands or young people soon to become prime.

Besides this there was illness. Someone in authority—master, or mistress, or doctor, or overseer, or even, in slight indispositions, a slave foreman—must decide whether a hand was really ill or merely feigning, and as he grew better, when he was sufficiently recovered to take up heavy labor again. It would have been thought prohibitively expensive for a man of Grandfather's means to call in a doctor every time a slave complained. Usually the decision had to be made by somebody on the place and the doctoring done by him, except when the case was obviously serious. Be it understood, this matter of illness was not merely whether a given slave should or should not work, with no one to suffer but the slave if a mistake was made. A valuable investment was involved. Suppose one guessed wrong, as did a certain overseer who sent three women to the field with a fever, only to have them grow exceedingly ill in consequence and die? Little good would it do to discharge the offending manager; the loss had already occurred, and it was irreparable. At least these were the terms in which a slaveowner would naturally think, whose labor force represented his main capital investment.

More trying than almost anything, it appears, was discipline. It would seem Grandfather was in no wise a harsh man. True, according to Father, he felt as strongly as the next how firm an owner must be in requiring instant obedience. He was swift to curb any "rebellious" spirit, and hold "lazy" slaves to their tasks, lest they set demoralization loose in the quarters. But apparently he did not agree that slave management demanded unremitting sternness. On the contrary, his notions ran in this wise—if Father's mind was a reflection: "Look out for the planter who feels all Negroes are devils incarnate, responsive in the long run only to harsh measures. Such a man never could be successful managing slaves." And the argument continued: "They are like children, sometimes quarrelsome, sometimes out of sorts, ready to squirm to avoid a duty, occasionally disobedient." All this could be extremely annoying, men like my grandfather felt; master and mistress must perforce deal with a succession of petty disciplinary problems, but usually these need not become serious unless a master, or his overseer, aggravated matters by mishandling. Then indeed affairs could get out of hand. All in all, to Grandfather—or to Father at least, and we may assume he learned it by example—a good master was a just and kindly man, as well as one who was firm, maintaining in his charges a never wavering obedience.

4.

As a matter of fact, my grandfather did not have to bear his burden of management unaided. He was fortunate in having a slave who carried on his mighty shoulders a substantial share of the heavy load. It was not unusual for planters to own foremen who were themselves slaves. They might be very gifted men, such as one on a certain large Carolina plantation, whom his master called "the watchman," but whose duties were those of steward or manager. The man carried the keys to the warehouses where were all the stores of provisions, tools, and implements, also the produce before it was sent to market; he dealt out the slaves' weekly food allowances and the feed for the animals; he was himself a well-trained mechanic, who had oversight of the plantation's various craftsmen and personally ran the steam-engine on the place. In his general responsibilities he was superior to the overseer, dealing out his supplies to the latter. He himself owned three horses and, indeed, was said to receive more in gratuities from his owner than the overseer was paid in wages—a practice that had obtained since the time of the planter's father, whose favorite slave this mulatto watchman was said to have been. Few planters would have such a slave or treat him in this wise, but the practice was common to use a slave in a foreman capacity. Indeed, it could hold out obvious advantages to the planter, which a writer of agricultural aphorisms of the eighteen-thirties put in these plain words: "When an overseer puts a black man in his place [as driver] he gives a lesson to his employer. If 'Uncle Tom' is to manage, let Uncle Tom have the honor, and his master save the wages."

Grandfather's Jerry was allowed the honor together with the onerous duties going with it. Nor did the occasional presence of an overseer detract at all from his post of deputy to his master. Overseers would come and go, uncertain quantities that they were, and on all scores expensive. Uncle Jerry, the master could know, would always be with him, barring death or disablement. Indeed, he was, until his passing in 1864. As Father put it, "He never saw freedom."

On many plantations a bell or cow horn awakened the slaves of a morning. Not so on Grandfather's. Uncle Jerry performed the duty, and he did it in his own way. He was six feet, eight inches in his stocking feet, they said, and weighed three hundred and twenty pounds. At dawn his great form loomed more giant-like than ever in the dim light of approaching day as he would stand at the barnyard gate to peal forth his mighty voice, deep as organ notes, until it reached into every cranny of every cabin of the slave quarters and pushed far beyond, even until its echoes returned again from the red hills. The men vowed that on a frosty morning he could be heard for miles around. "Oh Yes! Oh Yes! Time to get up! Time to get up!"

Jerry's work had just begun when he called the slaves to labor at dawn; he sent them home again as the sun disappeared. He must apportion the tasks as Grandfather had assigned them, divide up the work-gangs, put the drivers—as slave sub-foremen were generally called—in charge, and see that all went about their appointed labor. He must fill in as driver on some particularly critical acres, where perhaps the weather had slowed down cotton chopping and the young plants were suffering with an excess of weeds. He must keep a constant eye out to see that animals, tools, implements, buildings, were at the level of care and upkeep which Grandfather strictly required. He must deal out weekly, under Grandfather's supervision, the field hands' allotment of corn meal, fatback, sweet potatoes, and any occasional extras that might be allowed them. He must oversee the slaughtering of beefs and lambs for the family table and, when hog-killing season came, be in charge of the gang assigned to this heavy task—and incidentally, select the best cuts of fresh pork for family consumption. He must report on any ailing slaves to his master, also on any recalcitrants who did not respond promptly to his own authority. Even sometimes he was left to handle disciplinary problems of a minor nature. Runaway Dennis himself was not exempted from Jerry's duties. It seemed to take everyone with any authority on the place to keep Runaway Dennis in hand.

So many plantations seemed to have their "runaway" Negroes. Grandfather's was certainly not nearly the problem some men had. Runaway Dennis earned the name because so many times he had "taken to the woods" when punishment for his misdeeds threatened. Dennis was a lone man; he could claim no wife or family of any kind; and while the other slaves seemed to feel sorry for him, his nature was so quarrelsome, it was said, and he so prone to get himself and whomever he quarreled with into trouble, that other slaves "fought shy" of him. When, at such times, Dennis was sent for by the overseer or by Grandfather, or when Jerry told him he must report him, he would simply vanish from the quarters. Nor, it was said, would he return from hiding until his one friend and champion in trouble, my grandmother, interceded for him. It seems Big Dennis touched his mistress's heart: for his shyness, his pitiful stammering, which made him the butt of teasing from his fellows, and for his incoherent gratitude to her, expressed in ways which she alone recognized. One part of the story always interested and slightly puzzled me. It appeared to be taken for granted that the other slaves—not Jerry, of course—knew where Dennis was. Jerry would be told to let the word trickle through the quarters that if Dennis returned he would not get his "deserved" punishment. There and then he would shamefacedly come in, to stand with head bowed before Grandfather for a stern reprimand before going to the fields to pick up his work again. No slave on the plantation could do a mightier stint than Dennis in that first week or two after he had "run away." Be it added, Jerry never approved of being thus lenient with Big Dennis. Jerry was known as a just man in his dealings with his fellows, but exacting in his standards.

Useful as Jerry was in helping his master to manage the plantation work, it would seem this was not the part he was most valued for. Not infrequently owners felt themselves seriously responsible for the manners and morals of their slaves. On some the duty might sit lightly, or be performed perfunctorily for purely utilitarian reasons, or even be carried out harshly with hardship the result.

But on Grandfather's kind it was an obligation, and a heavy one. What to do, indeed, about slave morals, when under law and custom, as it stood, slave marriages were readily terminated, either for monetary reasons or to be rid of a recalcitrant? And how to build up in slave parents a sense of responsibility for their children, who, as they perforce knew, were not theirs but the master's to dispose of at will—if he chose? And how hope to inculcate habits of honesty and responsibility, when in the first place one believed the black man innately had "thieving" propensities and was innately "irresponsible," and in the second, felt he should possess nothing about which to be responsible?

It was in this dilemma that many planters looked upon religion as a prime morale-builder and outlet, too, which could bear dividends in the sanctions it furnished for enforcing good conduct. A certain Bishop Mead of Virginia put the matter in this way in a sermon he specifically wrote for masters to use with their slaves. "Think within yourselves what a terrible thing it would be, after all your labors and sufferings in this life, to be turned into hell in the next life . . . to go into a far worse slavery when this is over, and your poor souls be delivered over into the possession of the devil, to become his slaves forever in hell, without any hope of ever getting free from it!" Of their duties to master and mistress, he enjoined them, "Poor creatures! you little consider, when you are idle and neglectful of your masters' business, when you steal, and waste, and hurt any of their substance, when you are saucy and impudent, when you are telling them lies and deceiving them, or when you prove stubborn and sullen, and will not do the work you are set about without stripes and vexation . . . that what faults you are guilty of towards your masters and mistresses are faults done against God himself, who hath set [them] over you in his own stead. . . ." He exhorts the slaves: "Remember that God requires this of you; and if you are not afraid of suffering for it here, you cannot escape the vengeance of Almighty God, who will judge between you and your masters, and make you pay severely, in the next world, for all the injustice you do them here."

Some slaveowners, to be sure, found drawbacks in religious observances. Some went so far as to forbid church attendance, finding a Sunday spent in this fashion too detrimental to Monday's work. There were those who seemed to fear any coming together of their slaves, even for group worship, for the opportunity it might give their chattels to air their grievances in company. Nor could their fears have been entirely unwarranted. As children we might and did pooh-pooh the idea that slaves ever "rebelled," but apparently the record showed something else. As did the unwritten history—of which I was unaware until later years—buried in spirituals such as "Steal away. . . ."

It was not for nothing that William Lumpkin, Senior, and Adoniram Judson, his son, were pious, God-fearing men, with a Baptist conviction about salvation. To be sure, they were concerned about good manners in their slaves, respectful conduct, self-control, honesty, and above all, obedience. They were sensible of these virtues and sought to have their slaves manifest them; and undoubtedly, in their minds, religion could be a main means to this end. They might even join in the argument, which white men of the time idly toyed with, as to whether Negroes, besides being a lower order of human being than themselves, really had "souls." They were certainly running no risks, however. For a long period of years Jerry served as preacher and pastor for their slaves.

As religious head, Jerry could sternly reprimand his fellow slaves who were "unruly," or "impudent," or "slovenly," or neglectful of their duty toward the master. Also he was their stay, whose mighty frame and steady spirit were the staff on which they leaned when trouble and sorrow overtook them—as it could overtake slaves. Master and mistress stood by as they could to give comfort when death visited a slave's loved ones, but it was Jerry who buried their dead, preached an eloquent funeral sermon, and gave them assurance of a happy hereafter over the River Jordan, where all who were faithful in the sight of God—and master—would some day go. It was he who saved their souls, converting them in the first place and then—a very slave John the Baptist—taking them down into the water of Syls Fork Creek each August at the annual baptism.

My grandparents were not alone in seeing in Jerry's influence an exceedingly valuable possession. Neighboring planters coveted it, with the result that three others joined with Grandfather to build a church on the Lumpkin place where Jerry could be preacher for the four plantations' slaves. It was a large wooden building, its

walls made of rough-hewn boards, three feet wide, riven out by
the slaves' hands with a "fro," as Father spoke of them. On Sunday afternoons slaves from the four plantations would gather in
this, their own church, for preaching. A few whites would also
attend, occupying the seats especially reserved for them. Father
told of going many times as a boy. In his recollection, they attended because Jerry was a strong and eloquent preacher whom it
profited any man to hear, whatever his station or skin color. It
seems to have been a rule as well, that slaves should not foregather
unless whites were present. Also, it may have been that, with all
their devotion to him, these white masters felt a trifle more secure
in knowing what Jerry the slave said as he preached so earnestly
the Word of God.

Jerry, it seems, suffered a single handicap. He could not read.
Hence he could not read the words of his Bible. It was contrary
to law, of course, for slaves to be taught the art. My grandparents
apparently obeyed the law to the letter. The story goes, however—
for what it is worth—that Jerry surmounted the difficulty by reason
of a phenomenal memory. Each Sunday morning my grandmother
would make her way to the back veranda, or in winter to her rocking chair in the dining-room. Jerry would be standing there waiting
for her. His bare head bent a little and listening intently, he would
watch her while she opened the Bible and read him a chapter. It
was his own Bible she used. She had once given it to him at his
urgent request, gladly complying with his wish, confident as she
was that the gift comforted him only by its possession. Having
read the chapter slowly and distinctly, she would mark the place
and hand him back his Book. That afternoon, standing on the
rostrum of his little slave church, having led his congregation in
song and wrestled lengthily with God in prayer, Jerry would open
his Bible at the place Grandmother had marked for him. Then, it
was said, there would pour from his lips the entire chapter his
mistress had read aloud to him in the morning. He would "read" it
word for word and from it take his text and preach his sermon.

5.

On St. Valentine's Day, 1859, my father reached his tenth birthday. Other birthdays had been eventful: his seventh, for instance, when his mother's father, who lived on a plantation near by, had presented him with a young riding horse which had been especially raised for him. The tenth birthday, however, had a special significance. It belonged not to Will alone, but to the plantation. February might be a busy season. Fields had still to be burned off, the pleasant acrid smell drifting with the smoke across the home lot. New acres had to be cleared of stumps and brush and stones so that the plow could be put through. A multitude of lesser tasks waited to be done preliminary to the plunge into full spring plowing. But busy or no, this February fourteenth was declared a holiday. The master had told Jerry, and Jerry had told the slaves that they need not go to the fields on this special morning.

When the family had finished breakfast—this is as Father told it —and Grandmother her absolutely necessary duties in her continuous daily round, then Jerry's voice boomed forth to the quarters calling up the slaves. All were to come to the big house without exception—babies, children, youths, adults, the decrepit. Father could clearly remember how they trooped to the backyard below the dining-room veranda; all but the house servants, that is, who clustered around Aunt Sarah at the kitchen door, and Jerry and his wife, Winnie, who stood apart as befitted their special station.

Grandfather, the master, walked out onto the veranda from the dining-room, leading William, his son. Behind came Grandmother, the mistress, and very probably with her were relatives, who had come visiting for the occasion. When all voices were quite still, Grandfather addressed his slaves. "This is your young master," he said. That was all.

But then Uncle Jerry bowed his great head in solemn dignity, and tiny Aunt Winnie curtsied to this, her child, whose "mammy" she had been and still was, both saying, "Howdy, young master." Aunt

Sarah, together with the other house servants following her lead, did their little obeisances and spoke the greeting. After them the field hands, whose voices rose in a volume of men's deep tones, and women's soft or high, and children's shrilly excited, "Howdy, young master!" Even the babies held in their mother's arms perforce were bobbed as their parents' curtsied, while the old woman, Big Sally, always one to put in an extra word, sang out in high good humor, "He's a mighty fine young master and sho' gwine to be jus' lak his pa."

Young Will expected it, of course. He had long known what his tenth birthday would bring. It had been the same for his father before him and for his grandfather. It was in the order of things thus to have his position of eventual master of the plantation and its slaves ceremoniously recognized at this early age. Nor was he unaware, even though it would weigh lightly on his ten-year-old shoulders, something of what it would one day entail.

The plantation and its prescribed ways had been filtering into Will's consciousness since babyhood. As soon as he was old enough to "notice things," hardly more than a year, so we heard it, Grandfather had called in Pete from the quarters, a fine-looking, eighteen-year-old slave, whom he had chosen with seemly care. The child was given into Pete's charge, to look after out of doors in his early years, and as he grew older to become his body servant. Reluctantly and with a dozen stern admonitions, Aunt Winnie would put her baby into Pete's arms for a daily outing. Even before little Will could walk or talk, said Pete in later years, the child would show where he wanted to go by "pinting." Then came a time when he could trot on his own two small legs at Pete's side, helped of course by occasional rides on his servant's strong shoulders. Later still, he could be lifted onto Old Mingers and, with Pete leading, would ride far and wide about the place. So they would spend hours together out of every day around the stables, or at the spring, or in the fields where "the hands" were working, or over watching the cotton gin.

It was as "gentleman," of course, that a boy grew up to own a body servant. In Father's rearing, being gentleman was counterpart to being master. These were two sides of the same man. To be sure, many masters were not gentlemen. Also some gentlemen had far more in possessions than had Grandfather and the many others of moderate means like him. The more exquisitely cultured, broadly traveled, luxuriously reared men and women of some of the low country estates, who were accustomed to city mansions and city ways, would have regarded as hardly commensurate with their standards of gentle living the simple abundance of Grandfather's hospitality: the sturdy pegged beams, hand-riven and unpainted, which supported his walls, the solid old pieces of furniture, the fine, unadorned, utilitarian silver on his table, or even perhaps his outspoken, unselfconscious piety, as he stood at the head of his long table at every meal whatever the occasion for his solemn words of grace.

It would seem that Grandfather and his fellows did not give a thought to what the gentry of greater estate and luxury thought of them. In their own eyes there were no grades among gentlemen. They had a sufficiency of worldly possessions to make them feel as secure in their rank as any man who could claim the title. In this respect they went about their lives in serene self-confidence.

It was in this same sense of confidence that Father was reared. He learned to think of himself as a gentleman by inheritance. If fortuitous circumstances deprived such a man of his wealth in land and slaves, or if he went into a profession instead of becoming a planter, no matter: his name was his. It would have been the same for Joseph Henry Lumpkin, older relative of Grandfather's, if he had remained a simple country lawyer instead of going to Princeton; and moving from his first law office in tiny Lexington to the larger, more sophisticated Athens; and after that to the legislature and by various stages to the State Supreme Court bench. Or Samuel Lumpkin, best loved of Father's numerous uncles, "as gentle as a woman," "the sweetest of them all," whose life ambition was surgery, for which his training at Jefferson Medical School in Philadelphia had fitted him. Then war came, imposing its will upon his sense of stern duty. He chose to enter the regular army at the head of a fighting company, whose final march led him up the slopes of Gettysburg. Indeed, dying young, he had little to leave behind but a few acres and slaves and his personal effects. The last, Grandfather sent to the girl who would have been his bride, excepting one keepsake, an embroidered vest, having in it a small sword-shaped gold pin which Uncle Sam's own hands had left there. His citations for gallantry, his promotion in rank to Colonel, 44th Infantry, C. S. A., his devotion to duty, his unfailing courtesy and gentleness, in the minds of his family and friends singled him out as Southern gentleman par excellence. Still more would name have been almost the only claim to title for Jabez Lumpkin, younger brother of Grandfather, who died before he was of age, and whose entire possessions came to a short list consisting of: Emily and two children valued at $1,250, Bill, his body servant, at $596, a watch, a banjo, a trunk, a saddle, a valise, and a note for $100 payable to his brother, my Grandfather.

At the same time, Father fully expected to have all the appurtenances in land and slaves. He expected to be "master" as well as "Southern gentleman." When the one was taken away, it may well be the other was enhanced. So that in after years, when all outward trappings were gone, he would teach his children very earnestly, "You may hold up your heads knowing no man is better."

There was a pleasurable side to ruling over a plantation. Indeed, my father seemed to remember this side with especial vividness. The men hunted and fished as a favorite pastime. They went up to town, to Athens or Augusta, to market their cotton and purchase supplies. They might travel even greater distances to attend conventions of church or political party, or go up to the legislature. More than anything else, they and their kinsmen and friends visited among each other. Lumpkin families, being numerous and living as they did in fairly close proximity, were staying at each other's houses much of the time. Then unceasing conversation would make up for the periods of relative isolation. The women would talk of housekeeping problems and county gossip and—so Father said—"fashions. Paris fashions, too." With the men the recurrent theme ever and always was politics. But also they told jokes, and when these began a volume of them would pour forth from their pent-up store; and surely they would find them more uproariously funny than would city folk who were so continuously in good company. Many of the hours together were spent at the overburdened dining table, the men talking hungrily even as they ate the lavish food from great platters passed to them by Fed and his helpers. (Can it be that Great-grandfather's drop-leaf table, now so seemingly frail, ever bore the loads of food that Father remembered or seated the many guests that were said to gather around it? If it was winter, he said, and hogs just killed, for breakfast there would be sausage and spare ribs, besides fried chicken and eggs and beaten biscuit and battercakes and also preserves and all kinds of cakes—yes, he said, cakes and cookies for breakfast.)

On the plantation, Christmas was chief among all the times of celebration. Even for the family it was true. Christmas dinner was the principal event. Then everything of food the place produced seemingly went on the table: turkey, chicken, ham, pressed meat ("souse meat"), backbones, tender beef, barbecued "shoat," mutton, light bread, every kind of preserves, brandy peaches, cake and pies, sillabub.

It seems, however, that Father's most haunting Christmas memories were not of the family celebration. They had more to do with the rest of his little world, the part in which slaves were participants, and of which, so he then assumed, he would one day be master.

For the slaves, Christmas was a time when the sun came up late and went down early. Of necessity it shortened the long working day. In any case December is a Southern farmer's slack season. Some planters permitted their slaves two or three days of celebration. Even nonresident owners, for morale's sake and because custom decreed it, saw to it that their chattels had something to celebrate. A Mississippi man of large estate was said by his overseer to send to his place at Christmas a thousand to fifteen hundred dollars worth of "molasses and coffee and tobacco and calico, and Sunday tricks for 'em," worth, the man claimed, eight to ten dollars a head. That is as may be. It was general practice everywhere to do something for the slaves.

On old plantations where the family lived the year around, much was apt to be made of the season. On Grandfather's, all would be up early, white children, as well as Negroes of all ages. The game was to catch each other at "Christmas gift!" He who was caught was in duty bound to hand over a present. Little Will played the game; he would catch his father and mother and even Aunt Winnie, his mammy, who made a point of letting him. But also, as he grew

40

older, he liked being caught by the slaves, just as his father and mother let themselves be. It was something expected of the master, and he as "young master" began to enter into it as was correct for his station and prerogatives.

Hardly a door in the big house but had one of the house servants behind it ready to spring out and shout, "Chrismas gif'!" Up from the quarters would flock all the field hands to hide behind a corner or tree and catch master or mistress or "young master." Grandfather would give each older Negro some silver money and the young ones an apple or stick candy; Grandmother would be ready with tea cakes or a slice of pound cake; among the visiting relatives the men folk would have small change handy in their pockets. It was a perennial game to see if Runaway Dennis could catch anyone, and how he would stammer and try and never get any farther than "Chr-Chr-Chr-." It seems all tried to help Dennis, so he would not have to say his disappointed, "Dar now!" It was all very boisterous and gay in Father's memory with a bedlam of noisy shouting, "Thank 'ee, master!" "Merry Christmas, missis!" "Christmas gif', young master!"

When night came, the slaves had a special Christmas supper at the quarters, though what they were served I never happened to hear. After that, there might be a wedding and, without fail, a dance. The family would go down from the big house to watch awhile. But Father said he could even hear it after he was at the house in bed. Far into the night until dawn, the banjo sounded, accompanied by rhythmic foot- and hand-pat and the feet of dancers thumping out the tune,

Thrumpety thrump, thrumpety thrump,
Thrump, thrump, thrump.

By the time young Will was ten he would know a great deal about the work on the plantation. He would be familiar with what was to be done as each season came around. In a general way he could have told when it was cotton chopping time, and when cotton picking. He would have a notion of how many acres were put into different crops. He would know the kind of care stock must be given, also farm implements, also something of the expense of upkeep for the slaves, perhaps the names of the merchants with whom his father usually traded for the goods for slave clothing, and the place he habitually bought their shoes. He would certainly know, because he had watched it so many times, how the work was laid out, how the gangs were allotted their tasks, and which of the slaves were good workers and which had especially to be watched. More plainly than anything else, he would know that in his circumstances of life on a slave plantation the white master did not do any farm work himself. His slaves did the actual manual labor. His part was to tell the slaves what to do. This was the very essence of arrangements. His part as white master would one day be to supervise and direct and issue orders to his slaves.

A boy of ten could even realize that his responsibilities as master would not be light ones. He could sense very early how much time and worry his father put into making the plantation pay. He did not understand, it is true, until much later—indeed, until catastrophe was almost upon his family—how poorly the old place was paying in the years leading up to the Civil War; or how its land was being worn out by uneconomical use of it; or how financially serious it was to have many of the family slaves passing their "prime." Yet in spite of the times he lived in, which were not such as to breed a feeling of quiet serenity in men whose major capital was in slaves, young Will would quite naturally assume throughout his boyhood that all would remain as it had been, that one day he would have to carry the duties which his father early in life was beginning to teach him.

Believing this, he would all the more surely believe all he learned from teaching and example as to the nature of his slaves and what their attitude should be towards him. He would know as a fact beyond argument or question that his black slaves deserved and needed their slavery. Undoubtedly he heard the point argued and proof offered for it. This was not because any doubts lurked in his elders' minds. It was a time when abolitionist talk was rife. Southern slaveowners had become very sensitive. They did not believe the criticisms of their "peculiar institution" to be justified, and of course they answered back. But when it came to the quiet conversations of their firesides, the tenor of their jokes, the worries of management, the problems of what they regarded as their chattels' innate vagaries which made them different from white men, in all these their minds moved back again into the familiar grooves.

There was also the other side to the matter. It was in the very nature of slavery that the chattel should render the master unquestioning obedience. This lesson was instilled into Father almost from babyhood. To be sure as a boy he could not indiscriminately order his father's slaves around. He quickly learned his limits. He could give orders to Pete, his body servant. Pete belonged to him. Even in Pete's case, if he disapproved of what his young master wished, there were courts of appeal in Aunt Winnie and his mistress. Father, as a little boy, might get angry with his mammy, Aunt Winnie, and try to order her around because he felt she was black and he was the young master. Winnie, however, would not have been greatly troubled by this, except that the child she loved was being extremely naughty. His parents, she knew, would uphold Aunt Winnie, at least while their son was very small. He would never dare speak other than respectfully to Uncle Jerry. Actually, while small, he stood in awe of the slave foreman's imposing presence and his obvious authority among the slaves. But he would most certainly know some day even Jerry would have to obey when the young master spoke. He was even "scared" of Runaway Dennis, he said. Aunt Winnie used to frighten him into being good by saying, "Runaway Dennis will get you." So Father told us, "As a little boy I was always afraid of runaway Negroes." But as a boy would, he probably had ideas as to how he would handle a runaway Negro when he was master. He could "order" the "little darkies" to do this or that. No doubt he did upon many occasions. But if he were too arrogant and "bossy"—and what child would not be under similar circumstances?—they had ways of refusing to play with him; if necessary they could invent something Aunt Winnie had "ordered" them to do to get away from a quarrelsome "young master." With all these "ifs" and "buts," however, young Will grew up knowing in his conscious mind that these black people on his father's place belonged to his father, and would one day belong to him. He was their "young master" and someday would have the authority to elicit from them the same obedience his father commanded. He would know in his very bone and blood as a court decision once put it, "The power of the master must be absolute, to render the submission of the slave perfect. It would not do to allow the rights of the master to be brought into discussion. . . . The slave, to remain a slave, must be sensible that there is no appeal from his master."

My father had only a few years to live as "young master" among his slaves. There were five at best after his tenth birthday, and the better part of these were spent during a raging war which patently threatened his heritage. Nevertheless, until the very end, he went on expecting to be even as his father had been. He continued to think of himself as one day riding over his own acres, knowing every field, stream, hill, and pasture, as he knew the palm of his hand. He would look on every building and fence and know it had either come down to him, built by his forebears, or had been planned by himself and constructed under his direction. He would expect to know when an animal was ailing, the poultry had a disease, the gin required a new part for its running, or rust had formed on the threshing machine. Above all, he would know his slaves, each by name, and each for his good points and his foibles, most of them being inherited, or the children of those who had been handed down. He would expect constantly to guide and discipline and keep them contented by skillful handling. First and last, he would know that every plan, every decision, every quandary nagging his mind, save those of marketing his cotton and purchasing supplies from the outside, resolved itself into a human problem, if it could be so called: the problem of managing his black dependents. He would know he was master in all things on his plantation, everything, nothing excepted, including the life of his slaves. With it he would know that his station was secure as a Southern gentleman.

It would seem it left a special stamp on men who lived this life. But more particularly in a special way it stamped their sons, who were reared to expect it and then saw it snatched away.

BOOK TWO

Uprooted

1.

At the outbreak of war in 'sixty-one, Father was twelve years old. In after years he could easily remember how one kinsman after another had come to bid them goodbye. There were eleven such goodbyes to members of Grandfather's immediate family—sons of William Senior or sons-in-law. Nor did this count the cousins, near and distant, for all went who were physically able. Few days passed in that first month that did not see a relative come riding in through the gate and up the long tree-lined roadway to the old home.

In Lexington where the companies were assembled it was gay and lively and exciting. Flags were presented and speeches made and little parades went down the street between a line of cheering women and children and older men. There was bustle and exhilaration in tiny Lexington.

Out at Grandfather's plantation also the war had its gay aspect when their kinsmen rode in. They would shout a greeting to young Will and tell him laughingly that they would "lick the Yankees in no time" and be home again before Christmas. But there was also a serious, practical, business side. When one of the men and Grandfather would turn aside together, Grandmother would shake her head at Will not to follow them. Grandmother knew, if Will could not, that another relative had come to ask Grandfather to do for him what needed to be done in the event—then so suddenly possible—that he should not return; and in any case, in his absence keep his eye on his family and place. Their farewells could be light and cheerful, but never their eyes; one may believe least of all the eyes of William Senior's sons, who were riding away from the old home where they had come into the world and had spent their

47

peculiarly carefree boyhood years as sons of a slaveowner on the old plantation.

They were difficult farewells for Grandfather for another reason. He was contemplating giving up the place. Even before the war, it seems, he had vaguely considered a move. Like other plantations around him which had not yet begun to enrich their soil with fertilizer, each year Grandfather's yielded less and less cotton per acre. There was no new, more fertile land he could turn to in the county. Cotton remained the all-important cash staple, so that he must continue to plant it. He could not have afforded to replace his aging family slaves, prices being what they were, even if he had wished to. It was a saying also, that many a planter was literally "eaten out of house and home" by his open-handed hospitality. Grandfather had special obligations in this regard. He was his father's successor; he lived in the old home; in this sense he was head of the clan of Lumpkins who were sons and daughters of William Senior and to whose numbers were now added their wives and husbands and sons and daughters. Besides this, there were my grandmother's relatives. She too was of Oglethorpe. Her parents and brothers and sisters lived there. On no account would my grandparents have had less of the comings and goings of their numerous kinsmen or of the visits of friends in a country where hospitality was so revered.

Becoming aware of his dwindling resources, Grandfather had made a plan just before the war. It never was fully formed, but the general notion was to follow in the footsteps of many Georgians of an earlier, more prosperous migration. He would sell his place, pick up family, stock, and slaves, and move to better lands in Mississippi or further westward. His heart was not in it, but his situation was critical. This was around 1860. Before he could go west to investigate, national events had taken their course. The war had begun.

As each year passed, the burden on my grandparents grew heavier. Not only would news come of a loved one wounded or lost in battle—an event that, besides its sorrow, involved new business cares for Grandfather—but running the plantation under wartime conditions became more and more impossible. This was true even in middle Georgia which until Sherman came was not directly touched by the actual inroads of the fighting. Many goods that the family had formerly bought could not be had. There was practically no outlet for their cotton and hence little cash from it. What cash they could get was in a fast depreciating Confederate currency, which bought only a fraction of what the same sums had formerly purchased. Their older slaves were growing older, and their younger ones restless and more irritable and poorer workers, so they said. Moreover, it was harder all the time to feed and clothe them properly. Mounting demands came in from the army for horses and mules, for corn meal and meat, for every kind of supply which would serve the needs of their fighters. A patriotic man, such as Grandfather was, strove to send everything he could to the front. But then transportation, inadequate in any case, became more tangled. In some of the most critical periods this great middle Georgia "bread box of the Confederacy," as it was called, could not get its abundant agricultural stores to the points of acute need, so that they remained dammed up there.

Toward the end of the war Grandfather decided to take the drastic step of leaving his plantation. Two events precipitated his decision. Jerry died, who had until his passing remained the family mainstay in plantation management. It was like having the strongest prop removed from the already tottering little community. Also, with Sherman before Atlanta, Father, just turned fifteen and already becoming a right hand to his father in running the place, asked permission to enter the army.

No informed Southerner but knew the desperate straits the Confederate Government was in for recruits for its forces. As early as 1862 its first conscription bill had been passed, much as it was deplored by many Southern patriots as contravening all the South was fighting for of "state sovereignty" and "individual liberty." Additional, more stringent conscription acts were later resorted to. Desertions from the Confederate forces reached alarming proportions, it is said, totaling one hundred thousand by the end of the war. Patriotic Southern men could not wait to be forced into fighting, not if they were inheritors of Father's tradition. They wished to do their duty without any stigma of coercion. Moreover, the enemy was beating at the very doorway to middle Georgia. Other boys of fifteen were becoming soldiers. Grandfather might be exceedingly reluctant at the duty laid upon him. He could not shirk it, however, when his son made the request. Apparently, with his son's going imminent, the last reason was removed for continuing to struggle to keep up the plantation.

Grandfather moved his family to the town of Union Point in Greene County. He readily secured the pass which let him move about freely, stamped by Greene County with the words, "Loyal to the Confederacy." Greene lay just south of Oglethorpe. Union Point was perhaps thirty miles distant from Grandfather's place. We heard very little about that move as children. As to why Union Point was chosen we can only guess. It was something of a center of manufactures for the army. It may be that a business opportunity came whereby Grandfather could do something to aid the Confederacy and at the same time provide for his family. We know he closed down the plantation "lock, stock, and barrel," as they said. He took some of his slaves to his new home. Some he may have put to work on other plantations or in the factories. At most he would need to keep with him only his house servants, his coachman, a gardener or two, and a few others.

The day came finally, when wagons were loaded with what supplies of meat and meal and flour and potatoes and other edibles they could take with them. The slaves were sent ahead to be placed in their new surroundings. Disposition had been made of any bales of cotton that should be stored. What horses and cows they planned to keep had been started on their journey. The big house itself was dismantled for leaving it. Window shutters had been closed and nailed down.

To be sure, they did not consider this a final leave-taking. They expected to return at a later, happier time. Yet surely the old place, which for three-quarters of a century had been the home of their family, must have seemed gaunt and sad to them on this bleak February day. For the last time Grandmother's carriage was brought around. For the last time Grandfather, his wife on his arm, came through the old door, and down the familiar steps. Then Grandfather went back again and closed the door, turning the great iron key to lock it.

His family settled in Union Point, Father, with Pete his body servant beside him, rode away to join Wheeler's Cavalry.

The months that followed were wildly active and exciting for Father. Wheeler's Cavalry must be everywhere in this time so perilous to the Confederacy. It must be in a dozen places and, in so far as it could do it with slight numbers, harass and confuse the flow of Sherman's inexorable march. Johnston had been withdrawn from command of the Confederate forces before Atlanta. Hood, dashing and brave, so men said, but lacking Johnston's acumen, lost the battle of Atlanta, thus letting the gate be opened wide for Sherman to begin his Georgia march. Near Chattanooga, in Alabama, before Atlanta, along the entire stretch of Sherman's forces, Wheeler's men must spread themselves, each man if possible doing the fighting of ten.

Private William Lumpkin, my father, was courier to his captain. He was big for his age, it seems, tall and lean, with wartime experience each day laying a new maturity upon him. He was a keen wit, a fine teller of tales and singer of songs around the camp fire. Outstandingly, they said, he was one who never shirked his part, whatever was called for. It seems certain his comrades liked him, for the story goes that when a young lieutenant fell, leaving a gap among the officers of his company, his fellows wanted him to be promoted despite his youth.

He was hardly a year in the war. In early 'sixty-five came the sudden debacle. Lee surrendered to Grant at Appomattox; Johnston to Sherman in North Carolina and with him General Wheeler with those of his troops that were there. In Georgia, General Howell Cobb, commanding militia troops at Macon, received word from Johnston to ask for an armistice. Others in the scattered southwest sections began laying down their arms.

So it was, on an evening in May 1865, Father came home from war. Beside him rode black Pete, his body servant, who had gone away with him and stayed by his side during his soldiering and now was returning, still by his side. But not to the old place in Oglethorpe. Home for him was in Union Point, as it continued to be for many years.

Almost to the day that young William Lumpkin was bidding farewell to his parents in Union Point, Georgia, to go away to war, a little girl of eight years, Annette Caroline Morris, who a decade later would become William's bride, was boarding a train in Griffin, Georgia. It was her first train ride, it seems, when she made this long, trying trip to the city of Augusta. She too was leaving all that was dear and familiar. True, her grandmother had assured her many times that she was going to the home of dear friends who loved her mother who had recently died and who would care for the child as their own. And so she learned in good time, spending her full, happy girlhood with them. Now she was leaving the known and cherished, in which so many ties had suddenly been broken, to launch out into the unknown, only one sister beside her, and she younger, to share the uncertainties.

Mother, also, came of middle Georgia people. But whereas Oglethorpe County was near the Carolina border, Meriwether, where her parents and grandparents lived, was over near Alabama. In minor ways Meriwether differed from Oglethorpe. It had a larger total population, with its whites outnumbering Negroes slightly— Oglethorpe had just the reverse. Its land may have been more productive; at least, more cotton was raised in proportion to the number of slaves. However, when it came to essentials in the backgrounds of William Lumpkin and Annette Caroline Morris, these were distinctions without any real difference. So inconsequential were they that Father and Mother might as well have been reared in the same county on neighboring plantations.

During the war Mother went to live on her grandparents' plantation. These were her maternal grandparents, Henry and Nancy Du Pre Patillo. It had been the latters' custom each summer to gather their children and grandchildren around them. When the war came, sending many husbands away, Mother's father among them, Mother, with her mother and sisters and brother, went to stay again at Great-grandfather Patillo's.

All during the war they lived there, as they had done each summer, in a cottage my great-grandfather had built for them in a grove of chestnuts near the big house. As Mother's memory went, she spent 1862 and 1863 almost in happy oblivion of the bitter war, except that she knew her father was away. It seems that she was quite content, as children can be in country life where it holds abundance for them, and peculiarly secure, as it may be for children, where their lives are wrapped in a warm sense of close, protecting family.

Certainly my mother remembered with persistent vividness her pleasures on the plantation, the places she loved there, its sights and sounds of leisurely, never-ending activity. There was the dairy, "delicious" in memory, so good was its smell of fresh warm milk brought from the milking to be strained and cooled in the spring, of sweet butter, dipped out of the old cedar churn to be kneaded and worked until it could be put aside in stone crocks ready for the table, and of rich, thick cream in great white bowls especially reserved for it. There was the carriage house, in a grove of fine old trees, a white roadway winding up to it, where no game was better than playing at journeys in Great-grandmother Patillo's carriage. For high adventure, there was the kitchen and spinning house under one roof and connected with the big house by a long board walk. It was worth the trip, to watch the spinning wheels reel off their yarn and in the kitchen to see the great roasts and fowls go into the ovens, but entailed some risk, because of a certain huge turkey gobbler, whom even older people held in awe. His size was immense, his age fabulous (if tales could be believed), his ire quick to rise when bright-colored garments were flaunted near him, his fierce lording over the premises a thing to beware.

At almost any time in summer there were some kinds of enticing fruits on which were no restrictions so long as the choice was of ripe ones. Apple and peach orchards could be visited every day in season and before season to investigate when they would be ready. Three plum trees she remembers as growing near the kitchen building, tall as its roof: one a damson, another a big blue plum, another a mogul, the mogul being best of all. All manner of wild fruit trees and berries grew in the fields near the house. Chestnut and pecan trees shaded their cottage, dropping their nuts almost into the children's hands.

There was the cider press behind the big house and across the beautifully kept yard, where one could watch the Negroes working. The apples, Mother said, were put into a long, clean wooden trough and beaten into a pulp with wooden mallets made of hickory; then they were emptied into the old press, where a screw with long arms would be turned by slaves' hands to force the juice; then—overflowing reward if one had waited—a cup was filled and filled again, as much as any child could ask for, of the newly made sweet cider.

There was the arbor. The hum of bees sang through all Mother's memories, and little wonder. The hives were in a bower of yellow roses and honeysuckle, where to stand cautiously outside was to sniff the delicious overpowering fragrance and see the busy honey-makers come and go. Near the hives was Great-grandmother Patillo's old fashioned flower garden where something or other was blooming throughout spring and summer and fall.

Personal disaster began late in 1863. A long and ominous silence was broken by the news that the child's father, who was of the Intelligence Service of the Confederate Army, had been killed in action. Soon thereafter, first her grandfather, then her mother, then her oldest sister, were stricken with typhoid fever. All three died in quick succession. Thus was my Great-grandmother Patillo left with five grandchildren who were fatherless and motherless, the slaves to supervise and care for, the crops to bring in, the cotton to be marketed, all in the midst of war, and all with no man to help her. It was no more, indeed, than many another woman left alone on the plantations had to undertake. But Great-grandmother Patillo was far from young any more. The loss of her loved ones had been staggering.

She carried the burden into the fall and early winter of 'sixty-three. In the midst of everything she even found time to teach the little girls, her grandchildren, how to knit and make other useful things for the army. Some duties, it seems, she simply let pass, such as the great task of hog-killing. Mother remembered the latter omission because of the care they must exercise in using candles since no new tallow was being made. Two of my great-grandmother's married daughters, their husbands at war like the others, had come to be with their bereaved parent. It was but a temporary arrangement. Great-grandmother Patillo could not face another farm season with such a heavy load. So she left the place in her daughters' care long enough to take her little grandchildren by carriage the thirty miles to Griffin. From there they went to the family friends who had asked to care for them.

Annette Caroline never was to see the plantation again, or her grandmother, or, for years, her sisters, save the one who was her companion on the journey to Augusta. Of her mother's estate—what her father had left—nothing came down to them. It was sold to net something for the children, but in Confederate money, which soon became valueless. We assumed that a like fate came to Great-grandmother Patillo's plantation.

2.

To MEN of property in 1865 the chaotic devastation left by war would of itself have been sufficient to cause severe confusion and anxiety. It is true, in middle Georgia, they were spared some of this for a while. Throughout the war they had done without; they had lacked many commodities which formerly had been abundant; they had sometimes lived in crowded quarters as "refugees"; they had labored night and day as they had never worked before for the needs of the army; they had run deep into debt, worrying constantly as to how they ever would climb out. No doubt, to them, what they experienced in many instances was poverty, but it was not the privation they finally knew. Moreover it is certain they were always upborne by hope of a better day. So long as they believed it possible for the Confederacy to be victorious, they need not despair at some day mending their fortunes. This was so for my people and many others like them, until the March through Georgia.

Then Sherman came, and after Sherman, the surrender. The values propertied men had thought to possess once victory had come were now practically worthless. Probably few were like the sagacious Georgia woman, who being left a widow early in the war, besought her brother-in-law, her executor, not to invest in Confederate securities. But he only ridiculed her little faith and thereby lost her half a million dollars. However, on her own part, she converted every cent she could muster into gold; and when

Sherman's armies were moving on Savannah, she studied her maps and decided he would next go to Columbia (though many were guessing otherwise). She loaded railroad cars with all her possessions, astonished her broker by giving up her last Confederate notes for gold at sixty-to-one, and made her way to the mountains and security. More were like my great-uncle, who, in settling my maternal grandfather's estate during the Confederacy, found himself at the end holding in his hands so much worthless paper to hand on to his sister's orphaned children. Naturally many men in patriotic fervor as well as in their belief in Southern success had thus sunk their funds in Confederate securities.

Many had their land still, it is true, and some in time came to use it again or continued to use it where their families had remained on the plantations. But others, like my grandfather, who even before the war had drifted over into the large group of planters whose resources were diminishing, could hardly swing the heavy financial burden of restoring a plantation to productiveness, not with the loss of their main investment, which at the same time was their labor force. In Greene County alone, with slavery passing, more than half the taxable wealth had melted away from the hands of erstwhile slaveowners. It was this that constituted the major loss of capital attendant on the war.

For these men of property, however, loss of their possessions was not the final nor even the foremost disaster. If they possessed to a moderate degree personal resiliency, to lose everything material, or almost everything, would not necessarily have been shattering, so long as the foundations of their order remained calm and secure. But the end of slavery, when four million Negroes became free men, meant to them the end of the old order. They had not merely sustained a property loss. They had sustained a shocking change in the relation of white to black.

Thus it was, with the thousands of gray-clad paroled soldiers— if gray it was any more, they would tell us, behind the rags that had been uniforms. They were not alone weary in body but extremely anxious in mind as they straggled back along every means of sparse transportation men could find in a countryside gutted by war's devastation. They saw the old order had collapsed, which had been but tenuously held together during the final stages of the

Confederacy. Nothing apparently gave them so acute a sense of finality—this was true of the men of property among them—as the freedom of their slaves.

It would seem that Southern slaveowners did not question emancipation—once the war was over. They assumed that the issue was settled. Successful force of arms left no alternative to their minds. Men would say to one another, men who had been slaveholders, "Emancipation is a fact. I have sworn to uphold it, and I will keep my oath. Sambo is a freeman. . . ." Some planters made it their first act after news of the surrender to tell their slaves, as did Colonel Dabney, "riding to the fields with his son beside him, that they were now free"; and a Mr. Clayton: "You are not bound to remain with me any longer. . . ." This was certainly true of men who adhered strictly to their code of *noblesse oblige*.

At the same time it would seem that one-time slaveowners everywhere were profoundly agitated, until men were saying, "The heart of the South is beginning to sink in despair. The streets are full of Negroes, who refuse to make contracts to labor the next year." Labor, Negro labor, which heretofore they had owned, now was free to come or go as the individuals pleased. For the time being it was true. They had to be dickered with, made contracts with, paid wages to, or other means found to keep them on the land. Here was certainly what most gave ex-planters pause, men who had left their land temporarily and were contemplating a return to it.

1865 was not ended before all over middle Georgia men were telling of the "want of labor throughout the cotton country"; of "none of the plantations in this vicinity . . . fully stocked with hands"; of "more laborers in this neighborhood" last year than we have this year "and nobody knows where they have gone"; of the ". . . rising generation of negroes [who] as far as possible, are shunning labor in the field; the female portion have almost entirely abandoned field labor . . ." and the men left are performing only "from one to two-thirds of their accustomed service"; of black men ". . . retiring from plantation service to any and all other avocations they can gain even a meagre support by"; of "Negroes—the *'vexatio questio'*—the *'pons asinorum'* of all beginners. What will become of them and us!"

Everywhere it was much as it was in Greene County. Some Negroes went away, never returning. Some came back to their old quarters on plantations and settled there. Many drifted into the towns to eke out a meager livelihood. Shifting around went on in the first months as families became reunited; a man would go looking for his wife who had belonged to another master; husband and wife and children would seek each other out and settle down in a common home; strange weddings were celebrated—men called them strange—of couples who had been "married" for many years but due to restrictions imposed by some masters had never had a legal ceremony. There was much talk of the "restlessness" of the Negroes, an unwillingness, so it was said, to tie themselves to any employer, a readiness sometimes to promise to work but a light regard for the promises. There was much bitter talk, also, of the hordes of Negroes "flocking to army camps" of the occupying Federal authorities: here they were in want of labor, while their former slaves were handed out relief. It was not, they commented caustically, as Carl Schurz reported to President Johnson, that Negroes went to these camps "to obtain certainty of their freedom." Rather they went because they could be fed without working.

Nothing was more disturbing to Southern planters in the midst of all this confusion, than the rumors persisting—among the Negroes, that is—that there would be land distribution, that each former slave would be given a piece of land of his own to farm and the necessary equipment. A Northern newspaper man said country Negroes would ask him when the land was going to be divided. Some were sure the land in the coastal area would come to them. (After all, the famous Sea Island plantations, given to the Negroes by General Sherman, were still in ex-slaves' hands.) Others thought the plantations on which they were slaves would be theirs; some that the whites would be driven out from the coastal area so that the Negroes could have it. A very general "absurd notion" had it that freedom could only be found "down country," that is, where the main Union armies were stationed. Tales were told of how unscrupulous individuals would go about perpetrating the famous painted pegs on ex-slaves. These were pegs with red, white, and blue stripes painted on them which these men sold to Negroes for a dollar each, so went the story. Four were needed, the buyer was told, to stake out a man's forty acres. He should stick one peg down at a corner, then walk so far and stick another peg down at another corner, and so on, until all four were planted. These pegs assured the Negro of his new property; he could stick them down anywhere, and no one could gainsay him, for the Government was issuing the pegs especially for the freed- men. Only, so advised the wily salesmen, the man would do well to take half woodland and half clear acres. Southern white leaders declared that Radical speakers were going about the countryside agitating the issue. They were saying, "All this property that you see, these lands, were cleared by you; you made all these fences; you dug all these ditches; and you are the man they belong to." The Negroes, they said, were being "taught to believe that this [land distribution] would be done; that all those immense farms would be hashed up into small pieces and divided among them, provided they would support the Republicans, and keep down these bad men called 'rebels' and 'secessionists.' "

When we were children we used to ridicule the slogan "forty acres and a mule" as a stupid deception used by the Yankees to get black men to vote for the Republicans. Actually, it would seem, Southern men of the time really felt some alarm. They argued that their slaves had been taken "without compensation." Surely, it was not inconceivable, therefore—especially, once the Radicals got con- trol in Congress—that their land might go also. It did not still their uneasiness when Thaddeus Stevens introduced his "confiscation bill" in Congress. It would be hard to say which drew the harsher note to men's voices, as I used to hear it in my childhood, the name of William Tecumseh Sherman or that of Thaddeus Stevens. Al- ways they spoke stingingly of Stevens's "vindictiveness." In a pro- posal like this one for land confiscation, for instance, how he wrote in it: ". . . It is due to justice . . . that some proper punishment should be inflicted on the people who constitute the Confederate States of America. . . ." The measure provided that the Congress should confiscate the land of all who owned over 200 acres in the Southern States, and distribute it to landless freedmen, "in each case . . . forty acres, to be inalienable . . ." and with it, fifty dollars for each man, to be used for erecting buildings. Stevens, it seems, figured that only 70,000 persons would be thus deprived of their property; this number, he estimated, owned 394 million acres of the nearly 500 million in the "rebel" states. Thus, he argued, the vast majority of the Southern people would remain unaffected, save as they benefited by his program. As time passed, in their own Southern state bodies, Negro representatives began to urge land division. Francis Cordoza did in the South Carolina Reconstruction Constitutional Convention. "One of the greatest of slavery bulwarks was the infernal plantation system . . . our freedom will be of no effect if we allow it to continue. . . . Let the lands of the South be similarly divided," although he did add, conciliatingly: "I would not say for a moment they should be confiscated. . . ."

It is true there was much to diminish men's anxiety. President Johnson early declared himself in ways to comfort Southern uneasiness. He insisted on the return of temporarily confiscated estates, the ousting of squatters, and even the return of lands where the people had settled supposing it to be lawfully theirs, as on the Sea Islands. Thaddeus Stevens's influence was waning, so of course his proposed confiscation bill got nowhere. His own party rejected it outright. In the South itself the Freedman's Bureau, the agency so despised by all Southern propertied men, yet threw its influence and resources into the effort to convince the freedmen that land distribution was a myth. In Georgia the Bureau sent out an urgent order to all its officers and sub-agents with a plea to occupying United States armed forces to cooperate to convince the "freed people that they are utterly mistaken . . . no such distribution will take place at Christmas or any other time. . . ."

As time passed, landowners became very impatient with their helpless dependence upon their former slaves. There was but one answer, some men said, to "unreliable free Negro labor": to supersede it. German labor, some argued, would be vastly superior to the Negro; "I should say to the free Negro," they added, and landholders "cherish a fatal delusion" if they are basing their future upon Negroes. To those who urged that German laborers were not accustomed to the kind of labor that was required; they would not be satisfied with the wages the South was accustomed to pay; "living quarters we now have will not satisfy them—hence millions we have invested in these would be wasted— . . ." to such objections the proponents answered, if the immigrant finds wages paid by Western grain planters sufficient inducement to go there, why cannot the Southern cotton planter pay as well? And when it was objected: "If the white man does not receive them on terms of equality, will they not be forced to affiliate with the negro?" the proponents cried: this was a gratuitous insult to these immigrant white men. One had but to circulate among German laborers, and "see if he will find them likely to degenerate in any such beastly fashion . . . we will find them true to their blood and their instincts." Indeed, it was said, "What possible objections can there be to our receiving them on terms of equality? . . . I should treat them in like manner as I do all respectable people." On the contrary, cried those who opposed immigration, there would be "no escape from a mongrel race in the South, except by expurgation of the negro. . . . During slavery . . . this was avoided, but it will not be so with the freedmen." No one feared that "a respectable white woman would ever intermarry with a black negro . . . but some . . . not respectable . . . will. While not over-nice white men, alas! cohabit with negro women . . ." whence in a generation or two persons of the color of skin of Spaniards or Italians would have no difficulty in "forming alliances with genteel people. . . ."

As for the fear of "strikes" among white immigrants, the remedy could be found if the planter would take the precaution to bind his laborers by written contract. This was the proponents' argument. One man sarcastically reminded his fellows that in any event, "We are already blessed with what we may call quits, under operation of which a man wakes up some fine morning to find half his [Negro] hands, or perhaps all of them, without warning on their part or sufficient provocation on his, have gone into the employment of his neighbors. . . ."

Some proponents of immigration, rejecting "Caucasian" labor for some of the same reasons as did their opponents, favored yet another solution. "On the great Asiatic plateau" Chinese laborers "even now with eager feet are hastening to press our inviting shores. . . ." Here is a race "not affected by the sun" of the cotton fields as are Europeans. "They are early risers, industrious and intelligent. . . ." Among them are carpenters, and all description of mechanics. By competition they would operate "in preventing the industrious Negro from relaxing from industrious habits," when, no longer "commanding the labor market," he must work or starve. Are we not, they would chide, in danger of-adhering to the idea that "old things are best"? They had been doing it with but indifferent success since the war, "and the reason . . . may be found in sambo's thickness of skull and settled aversion to being enlightened in any regard, having prosperity, through work, as a medium."

It would appear that most planters saw only hapless dreaming in these proposals. They asserted: "The negro is among us—he is here, and we cannot help it, and the destiny that placed him here, has placed him here for a wise and good purpose." Sensible men should deal with matters as they found them, they said. "Is it wise at this juncture . . . when society in the South is upheaved by recent social and political convulsions of the most trying character, to introduce among us an element which it may be difficult to control?" Moreover, look how the difficulties multiply. There was a very wealthy planter over in Texas, so the story went, in the old Caney River region—"richest in the world." But at the surrender, when the Negroes knew they were free, everyone had an "Aunt Sallie" or an "Uncle Josh" or a former husband or wife to hunt up back in the old states where they came from; and every ex-slave who could "raise the wind" took his line of march to the East. This planter, at the prompting of labor agents, went in person all the way abroad to get some Scottish cotters to work for him, paying their passage money. On their arrival at his plantation he took them to the former slave quarters, told them to make themselves comfortable, and went back to the city where he resided. In a week every Scotsman had left. When the planter in dismay hunted them out, they told him that they were disgusted with the state of the quarters. The planter whitewashed the cabins, spruced them up generally, paled off a garden space for each one, and got his cotters back. In a week or two they were gone again—"Not content to live on cornbread, beef and milk—must have biscuits and coffee." Again he got them back, bought flour and coffee and added butter. In a short time most of them were gone once more. At last accounts, the planter had some of them in jail, "trying to get the Yankees to help him make them stick!"

Planters, in blunt language, added their moral to such tales.

Uprooted

"Give me cuffee, and I can give you cotton," they said. "No set of laborers on earth, save the sambo's, can make a cotton and corn crop, on three pounds of bacon and a peck of meal a week. . . ." As for a German laboring man on such diet, "he would shrink up so promptly that a cut gourd vine would not even be a parallel." Nor would Chinese be like the Negro, "satisfied with plenty of 'hog and hominy,' and a shelter to turn out the rain." They should not be taken in by these "Yankee Coolie speculators." "Badly spoilt" as Negroes were, they insisted, "they are the *cheapest labor we can get*," the writer emphasizing it. And they will improve, men believed, "if the carpetbag politician and puritan school marm will only 'hands off' for a while."

Middle Georgia's leading progressive agriculturist, a Mr. David Dickson of Sparta, was a main opponent of immigration in this section. He was convinced it would "prove destructive to the cotton interest." Mr. Dickson said the answer to the local labor problem was to give the Negro employment, "full employment." Then, he said, they will "steal less, be more law-abiding, and less nuisance in every way." He advanced the astounding notion that it was to the planter's advantage to have a scarcity of labor. "Your prosperity depends upon a scarcity of labor and a high rate of interest," he said. "The value of your labor being fixed by the value of cotton in Liverpool where interest is low. . . ." Where are laborers best fed and clothed? Where does land pay the best profits? "Where labor is scarce, and the reason is, the products of the farm bring the best prices, under the circumstances." Some planters were aghast at Dickson's reasoning, while admitting his own success. One man, who was well-read in political economy, said: "He erects the standard of revolt against the authority of Hume, Ricardo, Matthews and Adam Smith. . . ."

Mr. Dickson pressed his argument. "Cotton planters!" he exclaimed, "the whole capital of Europe, including money and machinery, together with that of the North" is striving to increase the quantity of cotton, and to reduce the price. . . . Your only remedy is to make only what is wanted at *paying* prices. Keep out of debt, be the creditors, make the most of your supplies at home." "Then, and only then, will you have power." "I am no apologist for the Negro," he said to them. "I would be glad to have him feel the

63

stimulating effects of immigration, if it could be done without injuring the white race."

Curiously, perhaps, planters seemed not to turn to native white labor, although it was certainly all around them in abundance. When the time came and owners were seeking factory hands to work in their cotton mills, their agents had but to go out into sand hills and pine lands and mountain country, and tell a story of a dollar a day for men, women, and children, to start a migration of these people. Apparently too in the sixties, there was much suffering among them. Even the small farm owners and artisans and other working men in the towns suffered serious hardship during and after the war. In the Atlanta area in 'sixty-five, relief establishments of the Federal Government, of which there were many, handed out rations to some thirty-five thousand people during that one winter. Some were refugees, some just folk of the countryside rendered destitute by war and a broken economy, who straggled miserably into town, hundreds at a time, looking somewhere for succor.

3.

FOR THOSE who were planters it was not merely a question of each man on his own land fumbling at some kind of reordering. The matter was more complicated, as both practical men and statesmen fully realized. General Howell Cobb of Georgia, himself a planter, reminded his fellows: "So completely has this [slave] institution been interwoven with the whole framework of our society, that its abolition involves a revision, and modification of almost every page of the Statute books of the States where it existed." Men were fully cognizant of their central problem, which one man despairingly summed up: "Once we had reliable labor, controlled at will. Now we depend upon chance for labor at all." A first task undertaken by men of affairs after the surrender was to rewrite the laws governing this labor force. They did so prior to reconstruction, in that brief interval when the old leaders were still functioning in Southern state governments.

South Carolina, with its usual forthrightness of action, had its so-called "Black Code" written and ready for operation by Christmas of 'sixty-five. In it, it appears, former slaveowners put down what they believed should obtain in the new era. With "slave" gone as a legal term, new language must be substituted. "All persons of color," South Carolina said, who contracted for service would be known henceforth as "servants," and those with whom they contracted, "masters." There would be "household servants" and "servants in husbandry," and a contract form was carefully provided for both. The code allowed a system of apprenticeship: colored children could be apprenticed to white masters to the age of twenty-one by their parents; or by the court, for specified cases, such as of children "whose parents are not teaching them habits of industry and honesty." The master could chastise his apprentice and could "recapture him if he depart from his service." The code strictly regulated labor on farms—"servants in husbandry." For these, hours of labor were set ("sunrise to sunset" with a suitable interval for breakfast and dinner). Duties were enumerated ("servants shall rise at dawn . . . feed, water and care for the animals . . . do the usual and needful work about the premises, prepare their meals for the day . . . and begin the farm work or other work by sunrise"). Lost time, not the fault of the master, could be deducted from the servant's wages. The servant's behavior was indicated (". . . quiet and orderly in their quarters, at their work, and on the premises; shall extinguish their lights and fires, and retire to rest at seasonable hours"). Tasks of work could be set by the master "which shall be reasonable." Upon making a contract, servants shall rate themselves a full hand, three-fourths hand, etc. Servants might not have visitors nor be absent from the premises without the master's permission. A servant departing from his master "without good cause" would forfeit his wages, and he must obey all "lawful orders," be "honest, truthful, sober, civil and diligent in his business." The master could discharge his servant for enumerated causes ("willful disobedience," "habitual negligence or indolence," "want of respect and civility to himself . . . family . . . guests," and others). Servants could depart from the master under certain circumstances ("insufficient supply of . . . food," "unauthorized battery" upon his person, invasions by the master of his "conjugal rights," were some of them). Much the same laws applied to house servants and others not in husbandry save that house servants "shall, at all hours of the day and night, and on all days of the week, promptly answer all calls and obey and execute all lawful orders and commands of the family. . . ."

The code allowed persons of color to become mechanics, artisans, and shopkeepers under certain conditions. They could pursue these trades if they had obtained licenses to practice from the District Court and paid the required fee for it, "which license shall be good for one year only." To care for indigent colored persons a per capita tax on persons of color was allowed by the code. "Vagrancy" and "idleness" on the part of persons of color was guarded against by severe penalties.

It was made a serious crime to deprive a master of his servant by "enticing him away," or otherwise detaining him. Any man doing such a thing was liable to a large fine and even to imprisonment at hard labor at the Court's discretion. The Court also provided for full enforcement of contracts: a master holding a "valid contract" with a servant could compel the latter to observe its provisions or receive punishment or fine, by order of the District Court.

It took Georgia longer by several months than South Carolina to work out its code. When the laws were written they were much less detailed and thorough. Some said former Governor Joseph Brown's influence had tempered them. It is possible. A year or two after this he was to turn Republican for a brief time. Even during his Republican period, however, he plainly never forgot how it felt to be a former slaveholder. He was able to explain, "Emancipated suddenly . . . it was very essential that we should do all that was possible to cause them to engage in labor and not turn to idleness and dissipation, and thieving . . . They have always lived under the control of somebody to direct them; and being turned loose at once . . . it was very natural that we should do all that was possible to direct them in such a channel as would secure their labor. . . ."

In essentials, however, the Georgia laws were much like other Black Codes. An apprentice provision permitted persons to be bound out until twenty-one. The vagrancy law was made very stringent and carried heavy penalties including in the term "all persons wandering or strolling about in idleness, who are able to work, and who have no property to support them. . . ." The "enticing" of labor was made a criminal offense: a man could not employ another man's servant during the term of the contract or induce a servant under contract to leave his employer.

As it turned out, these codes were not allowed to answer the landowners' problem. The Congress at Washington very quickly abrogated the laws and shortly thereafter undertook its own mode of reconstruction.

Southern men who but two or three years before had owned their labor now felt themselves at their wits' end. They were subjects of an occupying army; to make a labor contract they must submit its terms to an occupying Freedmen's Bureau; if they were accused of breaking the terms, they could be haled before these local bureaus for breach of contract; let their hands become "inefficient" or "unruly," and they try to manage them, their only recourse was to a court where, in their view, "justice is generally administered solely in the interest of the laborer." They might say, as middle Georgia's agricultural journal did: "We don't believe that, with a great many negroes, *anything* will ever take fully the place of the lash as a stimulant to labor. . . ." They might believe that their ex-slaves would "prefer to be punished with stripes, as under the old system . . . to going to law and having the law administered upon them. . . ." They could say and believe these things, but it little profited them. For the time being at least, they were unable to deal with matters in their own way. Some said that reconstruction conditions ". . . have naturally produced in the minds of the Southern people, a feeling of temporary antagonism to the negro. Hence we are disposed to separate ourselves from him, and, as far as practicable have nothing to do with him. . . ." Others soon began to tell one another that they must make no such mistake. The Negro, they said, "has been, is, and must continue to be the instrument in the hands and under the control of the intelligent white man of the South. . . ." It was simply a matter of how to accomplish it, how in particular to secure a stable labor supply for the immediate needs of agriculture. All questions of ultimate policy aside, this was the pressing issue.

This was the problem they must without delay find some solution to, or they could not go on planting.

Under the new conditions the laborer must of course be hired. But once hired, which in itself was problem enough, they said, everything being so unsettled, how hold onto one's laborers? How be assured another employer would not draw one's Negroes away, or that just out of whimsy, so they believed, these freedmen would not pick up over night and go away precisely when they were most needed?

Many tried the obvious method of offering cash wages. But this system was severely criticized. Perhaps men who never before had been obliged to pay out cash to their Negro labor had a natural shrinking from it. But also, they said, "If we paid them wages, the first five dollars they made would seem like so large a sum . . . they would have imagined their fortunes made and refused to work any more."

Some ingenious men devised their own special plans. A Captain Hazard, who had large plantations in South Carolina, did this. He did not like a cash wages system, being as convinced as anyone that it meant losing one's laborers, contract or no contract. But neither did he approve of the new scheme, then coming into vogue, of hiring on shares. Nothing, he said, could prevent heart-burning under year-end division, or the laborer's share from appearing "very small as the result of a year's toil."

Hazard signed with his laborers a detailed contract covering everything of importance touching their work. It retained the ante-bellum system of rating hands—full-hand, half-hand, quarter-hand —save that the laborer, upon being hired, must rate himself. It carried over the task system providing that laborers who failed to do their full task got no pay, and those overperforming were paid more accordingly. He put a foreman over every twenty-five laborers, allowing him double pay but docking his wages if his gang fell short of their prescribed task. The heart of his plan, however, was his method of payment. Hazard's laborers were paid off every Saturday, but not in currency. He devised a system of "due-bills," and to make these function, he set up his own plantation store. Here his laborers could go any day they wished between the hours of two and nine p.m. to purchase supplies, provided, that is, they

68

had due-bills with which to buy. Absolutely no credit was allowed. At the end of the year he would redeem in currency any due-bills his laborers had not expended.

Hazard made his plantation store something quite extraordinary. He deliberately set it up on the public road, "remote from the barn and its associations." Likewise, he deliberately stocked it with goods which would be tempting to his field hands. It had in it bacon, fish, grist, lard, molasses, wheat, flour, sugar, soap, candles, cheese, pilot bread, crackers, sweet biscuits, tobacco, candy, shoes, ready-made clothing, blankets, cloths, calicoes, chintzes, shirtings, sheetings, crinolines ("why not?"), and gunpowder. "The greater the variety," reasoned this planter-economist, "the more their wants are multiplied, and their industry stimulated, in order to procure means of satisfying those wants. . . ."

Probably few planters could have attempted anything so elaborate, if they had wanted to. It took too much capital, and capital was precisely what they lacked. More and more cotton growers began to try out the share system.

The advantages to be seen in it were much talked about. Men felt it gave the laborer some motive for protecting the crop; also the planter was relieved of some of the loss in crop failure or decline. Some claimed it stimulated industry in freedmen: it gave them an interest in producing more, since their share depended upon the total. It was generally believed that the ex-slaves preferred it, seeing it as a higher form of contract than wages. Critics of the time, however, said it was for this very reason that the share plan chanced to be begun. It was a "concession" to Negroes, they complained, who felt that to be a "tenant" and "rent" land was better than being a mere field hand. (This was only two or three years after the surrender.) "The colored laborer, in the first flush of freedom—ignorant of his labor and of its dependence upon capital—seemed disposed to withdraw altogether from hire." Planters were frantic, cotton was at a high price; they were eager to grasp at this advantage, so they hit upon crop-sharing as a means of inducing freedmen to work for them.

Several share plans emerged. If a laborer could furnish nothing but his labor, then the landlord, besides providing the land, advanced him tools, seed, whatever else he needed to farm the plot, and also a cabin and food and clothing for himself and family. Such a laborer got one-third of the crop. If he could furnish something, he got one-half; if he furnished everything, except the land of course, he received two-thirds. Large-scale planters very often hired all three types of laborers simultaneously.

Just because more and more landowners were using the share system, did not mean it took the Black Belt by storm. Many objections were raised. The matter was debated back and forth. Everyone admitted, it seems, that having to divide up the place and divide up the crop involved a multitude of difficulties. They said a man had to split up his plantation into small plots often at a loss and always at inconvenience. When it came to dividing the crop, even worse problems ensued. They even thought he must divide up his gin-house into separate small rooms to house each laborer's share, with much resulting confusion in ginning and packing.

One story going the rounds in the late 1860's told of a rice planter who gave up the share system because he could find no way of keeping his laborers satisfied. He arranged to go halves with them. He would advance them seed and provisions which they were to repay out of their share of the crop. "The harvest being secured and the grain threshed, every precaution was adopted, not only to comply exactly with the terms of the agreement, but also to satisfy the minds of the laborers that this had been done." Two large bins were set up. In each was put one-half of the crop. "The laborers were permitted to take their choice of the two." But then the landlord must take from the laborers' bin what they owed him for his advances to them in seed and equipment. "This made a great difference in the size of the two piles, and at once imparted an aspect of inequality in the distribution. When this process was continued into payment of advances made for provisions . . . one bin was piled up nearly to the ceiling, and the other lowered almost to the floor. . . ." "The great pile," went on the story-teller with emphasis, "was seen to be the portion of *one* man, and the small one that of *fifty*, no logic known to the human mind was capable of persuading the fifty men that they had not been cheated."

Many men complained that under share hiring they could not get the general work of the plantation done. They said laborers refused

70

to do this general work, saying it was not part of their contract. It was put in this way: If a planter says, "The working stock must be taken care of and kindly used; the lands must be prepared carefully and thoroughly; manures must be made; fencing . . . put in good condition; ditches . . . dug, and the old ones cleaned out," he may be told by his laborer: "My business is to plow and hoe enough to get the crop in the ground. . . ." When the crop is planted and the laborer is told to plow and hoe carefully, he may reply: "My business is to plow and hoe enough to keep the grass from taking the crop." Grass begins to grow, grass is going to take our crop; but the laborer says: "If grass is growing, crop is growing also. . . ." The planter says: "If we don't be sharp, we won't make enough to do us"; laborer says: "I will make enough to do me, and if I want to go fishing in the morning or hunting in the evening I will go." With such a system a farmer must be sharp, very sharp, to make anything clear.

There were those who felt uneasy about crop sharing because they feared it would increase the Negro's disposition to wish to own land. It would make them "landholders, and not hirelings"; it but catered to their seeming desire "to rid themselves of supervision on the part of the white race, and to look upon it as a sort of continued badge, or remembrancer, of their former condition of servitude." It was thought this might be due in part to "Loyal League teachings." On the other hand, it might simply be, they said, a "native disposition to avoid all manner of persistent physical effort, outside that required to eke out a bare subsistence. . . ." They feared the tendency was toward "these thriftless blacks" becoming the South's cotton growers, leaving the planter no alternative but to rent or sell his land to them. "Soon there will be no laborers, but all proprietors." "What an idea!" exclaimed a man writing to the paper. "Profound ignorance associated in business with intelligence!" Some went further, warning: "What will become of the present landholder, the upper strata of society? They will suffer degradation commensurate with the elevation of the lower orders." "And who will dare to say," one landholder put it, "that because the hewers of wood and drawers of water are elevated, at the sacrifice of intelligence and refinement, that civilization has achieved a triumph?"

Despite any drawbacks, hiring on shares took hold and began to spread. Apparently the reason lay not so much in whether it was efficient or not, or what it would or would not lead to, as in something else. If what mainly troubled propertied men's minds was how to have something of the old control over their labor, then they had found at least a partial solution in the post-bellum share system. Naturally those who had been slaves scarcely a year or two before would seldom possess anything beyond their ability to labor. If they hired themselves out on shares, they must at the same time be "furnished"; in most instances the landlord must advance them everything they required, both for farming and for existence, until the crop came in. Georgia's very first postwar legislature of 1866 (the same one that enacted the Black Code) passed legislation—and it remained in force—to protect the landlord who advanced supplies to his tenants. It permitted him to have a lien on his laborer's share of the crop to cover the advances he had made.

4.

RAMPANT DESTRUCTION was what my father had seen, riding home along the road from Atlanta to Greene County after the surrender. Here Sherman's army had cut its broad swathe through the countryside. Father had looked on the devastation each day he rode, heard the tales of woe, learned at first hand how the country but a few short months before had been denuded of everything—foodstuffs, goods, supplies, stock, stored cotton, both on plantations and in towns. He had seen burned-down buildings, some of them dwellings. He had traced his weary way along the route of mutilated railroads: seen burned depots, stark scorched sticks where water-towers had stood, looked on rails turned and twisted in grotesque shapes around trees—"Sherman's hairpins" they were called—which had been melted on the fires of burning ties to make them pliable and useless. Before Sherman's March Jefferson Davis had said that Georgia alone, from its abundance still secluded from war, could feed the Army of Virginia. Sherman's March had made short shrift of this possibility.

The worst of it to Father, as we heard it in childhood, was not mere destruction of military objectives. Rightly or wrongly, he believed the stories of silver and jewels taken, of clothing and books and furniture wrecked, of insults to helpless women and old men, of slaves enticed from their owners. He was a boy of sixteen then. These stories deeply affected him. He could still feel anger when he told us of them. He may or may not have heard of General Sherman's explanation: "This was a one-sided game of war and many of us . . . kind-hearted, fair, just and manly . . . ceased to quarrel with our own men about such minor things, and went in to subdue the enemy, leaving minor depredations to be charged up to the account of the rebels who had forced us into the war, and who deserved all they got and *more*." Perhaps, had he heard it, he would only have said: "I told you so." He certainly saw no slightest merit in the Unionist plea that Sherman's March was a brilliant military exploit, a means of quickly ending a terrible conflict. Nor would it have assuaged his feelings that Sherman's hand only helped to cut down an already tottering Confederate economy. The General estimated the damage done by his forces in Georgia at a hundred million dollars, twenty million of which, he said, "inured to our advantage, and the remainder is simply waste and destruction." Before that, of course, people had been well-nigh stripped bare by taxes, requisition of supplies, displacement of cotton, the cash-producer, by food crops needed for the army, the depreciation of currency, and the wildly rising prices. It was not these matters, however, but the destruction wrought by the enemy that had impressed Father.

On top of this, when Father reached home, was the uncertainty and fear he found plaguing everyone. Besides being worried about how to deal with free Negroes, ex-slaveowners seemed to feel something resembling disappointment at the behavior of their former slaves. They had said and believed the black man was happy as a slave and that he never wanted freedom. Occasional insurrections or runaways were to them merely signs that some individuals were disobedient or disgruntled or simply very bad. They had said and believed that the black man had not the qualities for freedom.

They still saw abundant evidence of this. The way free Negroes behaved, according to Father, merely showed they were even more "ungrateful," "irresponsible," "childish," than slaveowners had thought. Where indeed was the "gratitude" they should feel for their former masters, who had fed them, clothed them, cared for them when ill, borne their idiosyncrasies in patience, comforted them when troubled, "taken care of them" in every way? Where the loyalty and devotion so many had shown in the hard years of war, when the master and his sons were at the front and only women and old men were left to manage the plantations?

Of course many did stay by their masters. Father would tell us of his own black Pete. Back at Company D's last bivouac, Father had said to his body servant, "Pete, you are free now." He told him he could go or stay as it suited him. And of course Pete stayed. Indeed, although Pete came and went as a free man, in the two decades that followed, he never really left the roof of his none too affluent former master nor broke the peculiar tie which their upbringing had forged. So that Father would say to us, "I was a grown man, and he was black and I was white—but I cried when old Pete died."

More than once in the years following the surrender Grandfather considered the possibility of returning to the plantation. He still had his lands stretching away for a thousand or more acres in Oglethorpe County. His home still stood—and his barns and stables and springhouse and smokehouse, his cotton gin and slave quarters. None were in the best of repair, but they still remained.

Now and then in those years, Grandfather would mount his horse and ride over to Oglethorpe. He would lodge with a kinsman and when morning came would make his rounds of the old place. There he would check the stables and barnyard and quarters for their state of preservation and any crying need of repairs or any signs of vandalism. He would turn to the big house, try its doors, and test the nailed-down shutters to be sure all were snug and nothing tampered with. He would even open the front door with the iron key and look about the interior, with what poignant feelings we can only guess. While he was in the county he would sound out his friends and relatives as to the state of affairs and "how the Negroes were behaving."

He was always disturbed lest he find on his place what men were saying had happened on other deserted plantations. A man would go back to look things over, and there from a chimney of one of the quarters cabins smoke would be pouring out. When he rode up and shouted to know who was there, out from the door would tumble Negro children, yelling in shrill voices, "It's master! It's master!" And behind them would come a former slave and his wife. Their explanations were reasonable. They would say they wanted to come back to the old place. They had thought maybe the master would return some time and give them work. Meantime they had a little corn meal and fat back. And they planned to scrabble around for a little corn to plant next season and a pig to fatten and perhaps some chickens. They had found an old spade and hoe down by the stables and already turned over a little ground. They were glad to see "old master." It was plain these particular ones had no notion of "trespassing." Still, it made owners feel nervous. They could not rest content until they had made other arrangements for their former slaves—moved them to a neighbor's plantation, for instance, where they would be given work and especially oversight. Apparently, they never could feel sure that these returned ex-slaves were not touched by the rumors afloat about land-division and had come to claim their share.

Another fear made Grandfather reluctant. A man must think of his wife. Conditions in Greene County might be no better, but in Greene, at least, his family lived a town existence with the added feeling of protection close numbers afforded. He could not make up his mind to have his wife alone on the isolated plantation on those occasions when the men of the family must be absent: not given the course county affairs had begun to take; not given the fears he as a Southern man and former slaveowner entertained. As month succeeded month and conditions worsened, men were more than ever troubled by fears such as these.

The dominating consideration in Grandfather's mind necessarily was financial. If he were to go back to planting after being away from his place for years, it would demand a substantial amount of capital. He did not have this. He had lost his principal holdings when his slaves were freed. He would have to borrow. He would have to restock his place with work animals and hogs and poultry.

He must lay in new agricultural implements to supplant the old ones. His would have badly deteriorated—those he had not sold. Many new types had come into vogue in recent years. (Agricultural experts were urging: get a good revolving harrow; have a planter and guano distributor to save labor and do the work more efficiently; get a seed drill for small grains, as it soon made up its price in seed saved; have a good cultivator; and a good light harrow.) Grandfather would also have had to bring together laborers, not less than twenty field hands perhaps. His old slaves were scattered. Some Negroes he might get back again, but many of his hands would be new, who did not know him and with whose qualities he was unacquainted. Here was grave risk to the mind of a man who in the old days had managed an inherited labor force. Very probably his laborers would have nothing but the clothes on their backs, and these in poor condition. Shelter was simple—the old quarters would do after a few repairs had been made. But then there was clothing and food. The first year, at least, he would be obliged to purchase these for his laborers. This meant more credit. Indeed, the prospect was such a heavy plunge into debt as Grandfather's orderly, careful mind verily shuddered at.

This much we know. The final decision was delayed, and meantime it was arranged for my father to begin his preparation for the practice of law. There was one person above all others that Father wished to read law with. Mr. Alexander Stephens, whose home, Liberty Hall, was in nearby Crawfordville, had lately returned from his brief imprisonment up North as former Vice-President of the Confederate States. Mr. Stephens was well known to Grandfather. He had been a family friend for many years. As a boy, Father had learned to have the greatest admiration for him. If they had ever disagreed with some of Mr. Stephen's politics, as I imagine was the case, Father had certainly forgotten it by the time of my childhood. Even at the time men who disagreed never needed to doubt the aged man's loyalties or basic sympathies. Stephens himself explained the matter carefully to his fellow citizens. "It is . . . true that I opposed secession in 1850 and 1860, as a question of *policy*, but not as a matter of *right*. When Georgia seceded in 1861, even against my own judgment, I stood by her act. To her alone I owed ultimate allegiance. . . ." Not a few Southern men had felt this way, and few went on blaming them so long as they came around in the end. Also, men knew how Stephens stood on the question of slavery. He owned slaves himself, of course. "Slavery—so-called—" as he once put it, ". . . was with us, or should be, nothing but the proper subordination of the inferior African race to the superior white. . . ." Grandfather certainly looked on Mr. Stephens as a trusted Southern statesman and brilliant lawyer, under whom it would be an honor for his son to read law. When I was a child Father always spoke of "Mr. Stephens" with something like reverence. It was Mr. Stephens's way, apparently, to take an interest in young men, to help them with an education, and to make a start in the world. So it was that Grandfather and Father made their way to Crawfordville in the late sixties. There Father was established, to sit with two or three other youths on the porch of Liberty Hall, keeping their noses supposedly buried in the pages of Blackstone, with Mr. Stephens now and then instructing and interpreting.

Meanwhile their world was turning upside down. At first the political situation in the state brightened, as Georgia leaders saw it. President Johnson appointed a respected Georgia Republican as governor; a constitutional convention fulfilled the requirements laid down for Georgia's readmission as a state; to be sure, it also limited the franchise to "free white male citizens"; a legislature with many of the old leaders in it, besides enacting the Black Code, rejected almost unanimously the Fourteenth Amendment. After that began the overturning. Congress had passed its series of measures for dealing with the former Confederate States: a Freedman's Bureau Act, the Civil Rights Act, the Fifteenth Amendment, and in early 1867, the reconstruction measures. These were put into effect in Georgia. The state became a military district. A second reconstruction constitutional convention was held, and another election for state offices. The franchise could not be limited on account of race or color. In the bitterly-fought election of 1868, with the Democrats participating under the name of "Conservatives," a Republican administration won a majority of places. For two years affairs were chaotic; charges and counter-charges were hurled; each side tried to wrest control from the other; the Federal government recognized Georgia's statehood, and then withdrew its recognition; it was recognized again under the Republican administration, but then when a Conservative majority in the senate unseated its Negro members on a technicality, Congress refused to seat Georgia's delegation. Then in Georgia's legislature Republicans once more obtained the upper hand, unseating a number of Conservatives. Once more the Negro members were reseated; the legislature fulfilled Congressional requirements, including ratification of the Fifteenth Amendment; the state was again readmitted. Georgians called this latter period "Re-reconstruction."

The events in the state were reflected in Oglethorpe, as reconstruction policies were carried out locally. In the 1868 elections with Negroes enfranchised, the county went Republican by a substantial majority. It was claimed by Republicans that several hundred whites voted their ticket. In any event a white Republican "scalawag" named Robinson was elected to the office of County Ordinary, despite every effort on the Conservatives' part to defeat him.

Soon Oglethorpe's roads began to know the thudding horses' hoofs of strange, white-clad figures. Negroes were beaten; so were white Republicans; white Democrats were hauled before the county court to be accused of these misdeeds, although it would seem there never were any convictions, since the men seemed invariably to have strong alibis. Robinson himself was one day beaten on Lexington's streets in broad daylight. A furious planter's son thrashed him with a cane, alleging that the man had insulted his father.

Little wonder, then, that Grandfather put aside for a while any thought of trying to settle again in Oglethorpe. Thus, the old place, like many others, was left to lie fallow. Gardens grew up in weeds; arable acres became a sea of sagebrush and scrubby growth; stables and barns and outhouses began to sag at the corners. Each year the pleasant home seemed more forsaken and run down at heel.

Uprooted

5.

AFFAIRS in Greene County were worse in some ways. On the soil of Greene was planted the Eighteenth U. S. Infantry, Captain Kline commanding. It would appear that Greene County people were courteous to these troops of occupation, who had no choice about being there: at least one of the officers so reported—coldly courteous; harsh remarks, when made, he said, were not directed at them, but only in their hearing, and this not by people of the "better classes"; nor did the soldiers suffer any indignities. They knew, however, that they were resented. They knew that their role was a despised one. To U. S. troops could go complaining Negroes and renegade white men, and the next thing a man knew, young Lieut. George S. Hoyt, aide to Captain Kline, would appear at a Greene county white man's door, holding military authority to demand an explanation. Worse than this, however, to local whites, was the part troops played in the elections. Armed Bluecoats at their polling places! They were outvoted by the Republicans. A Negro had been elected to the legislature. Such an event must surely have made Greene's case seem to them worse than Oglethorpe's.

As in Oglethorpe, so here men had taken steps, hoping to bring about a different outcome. The *Greensboro Herald* spurred them on before the election: "People of this great country, wherever they have been permitted to speak their sentiment, have declaimed that the Anglo-Saxon race shall rule according to the Constitution. . . ." The county's white men, by every known means of persuasion, tried to woo the Negro away from voting, or at least, to get him to vote Democratic. Their most impressive public act was a large mass meeting, held in the Courthouse, followed by an eloquent manifesto to the Negroes of the county. "Now we don't want you to go with these people [scalawags and carpetbaggers]. We want you to come with us . . . then we who live together can all be friendly together. . . . We remember how faithful you were when you were slaves. . . . We know that we are the stronger

79

party . . . we can afford to be magnanimous. . . . We do not think you are qualified to vote. We know you are not qualified, and so do you know it. . . . We wish to live in peace. We wish to be like one family. . . . When voting time comes you had best go to your old master and get him to get you a ticket, that is the little piece of paper, and he will tell you what to do with it. You had best get your old master to go with you to the voting place. For if one of these stealing Yankees gets hold of your ticket, he will take it away from you and give you another in place of it, which will not do so well. . . . It will be impossible for the white people and the black people in Georgia to get along together if they are voting in a body against each other. . . ."

These efforts seemingly had little effect. Strangely, as it appeared to former slaveowners, who had been accustomed to obedience from Negroes, the Negro vote had gone almost solidly Republican: the whites could muster less than a thousand ballots against the Negroes' nearly two thousand.

There were exceptions, to be sure. A few Negroes did vote Democratic. Such a one was my family's Big Dennis, he of onetime runaway fame. At Grandmother's instance, so Father told us, Dennis had heeded the white man's manifesto and secured his ticket from his old master. Dennis, certainly, was a very special case. He was in any event more or less outcast. Friendless in slavery, he was still friendless in freedom, a lone man, who knew but one source of kindness—his former mistress. He would be unusually immune to the social pressures which, so white men said, were largely depended upon by the Negro community to hold in line any of their kind who showed a readiness to do their former master's bidding. Whites complained that the epithet of "traitor" was hurled at hesitant black men who were ready to "go over to the other side." It was said they were threatened with ostracism. General John B. Gordon told how his coachman said to him, "I want to vote the democratic ticket; I want to vote like you vote; but I am afraid to vote that way." Asked why, he replied: "My own color say that they will handle me if I do. . . ." But chiefly, Southern men cast the blame for the solid vote against them and the changed behavior on white carpetbaggers and scalawags, and especially on the Union or Loyal Leagues. "The negroes, left free from this influence, would have been exceedingly peaceable. . . . Our people would never have had any conflict of any sort with the negroes but for the introduction of this disturbing element." It was this class of men, they believed, whose very object was to stir up strife and create animosity, who were causing the trouble. "And they did succeed to some extent," General Gordon later remarked. "They did win the colored race away from the white race in a very great measure. . . ."

Greene County apparently had an active "scalawag" element, native white men who had turned "renegade." At least ten of them were well-known in the area. Against these men was directed all the pressure their white fellows could think of. "Flee from the wrath that is coming," was the warning given them. "We appeal to them," said the local paper, "to retrace their steps and save their honor." When it was expedient they did retrace them. However, before that all ten of them, by "bidding for Negro votes," as men put it, were elected to some kind of public office.

The Loyal or Union Leagues—they were called both—were especially looked upon by whites as their bitter antagonist. This was so all over Georgia. ". . . A great many northern men coming down here, forming Leagues all over the country. The negroes were holding night meetings; were going about; were becoming very insolent; and southern people . . . were very much alarmed." It irritated them, made them fearful, to know so little about this spreading organization. "We knew nothing more than this [about it]: that the negroes would desert the plantations, and go off at night in large numbers: and on being asked where they had been, would reply, sometimes, 'We have been to the muster'; sometimes, 'We have been to the lodge'; sometimes, 'We have been to the meeting.' " Now these might seem harmless enough answers. They were not, however, harmless to onetime slaveowners, to whom it was exceedingly strange behavior for their field hands not to tell them precisely where they had been when they went abroad. Hitherto, Negroes had moved about at night always on passes; hitherto, it had been the master's duty to keep informed of his chattels' doings; hitherto, it had been the master who had decreed what organizations a black man could belong to, what meetings he was allowed to attend. "Apprehension took possession of the entire public mind. . . . Men . . . were afraid to go away from their homes and leave their wives and children for fear of outrage. . . . There was general organization of the black race on the one hand, and an entire disorganization of the white race on the other." So spoke prominent Georgia men. More particularly, they explained the solid Republican vote of the Negro by these Loyal Leagues. White men said, and no doubt believed their own words: ". . . All the intimidation . . . ever seen . . . or heard of being exercised at the polls, has been by black men on black men, for desiring to vote 'against their race' as it is called." This influence was exercised, they said, at the instance of the Loyal Leagues. "They are secret societies, meeting for political purposes," said one Southern man. Those who "intimidated," they believed, were "for the most part, bold men of that organization."

In some such way they explained to themselves the election of Abram Colby to the legislature. Colby, by his own statement and obvious appearance, was half a white man. He was born in slavery, but set free upon his master's death. The master was not a Southerner but a Northern man who had settled on a Greene County plantation long before the war. He had willed Colby a nice farm with a house on it a few miles outside the county seat of Greensboro. Besides this, Colby plied the trade of barber. Since a decade before the war he had been a free man, and as time passed became well-to-do, as free colored men went. True, he himself never had any education, being able neither to read nor even to write his name. However, his son William, who had come of age in the late 'sixties, had been given some schooling, as well as being put at the shoemaker trade by his ambitious father. William became his father's standby. "I keep him with me all the time," said Colby, "make him read all my letters and do my writing." This was after Colby went into politics.

At the surrender Colby became a Republican and very soon a recognized leader of the freedmen. He could dare to do it, no doubt he would have said, because Federal troops were stationed in Greene County: Negroes felt really free to enter politics, they said, where there were U. S. Army units. The elections of 'sixty-eight found Abram Colby installed as representative to the lower house of Georgia's legislature.

Colby was not the only Negro official from the area. Another, Monday Floyd, had been elected from the legislative district in which Greene was located. Floyd was born in Greene but in 'sixty-eight lived in Morgan County, where he plied his trade of house carpenter. Unlike Colby, Floyd was dark of complexion; although he had been a slave until the surrender, he could read a little and write his name. Floyd could not nag Greene County men as Colby did. He lived elsewhere. They knew him only by hearsay. It was Colby, large of frame and lame in one leg, who walked the streets of Greensboro as one who had a right to; moreover, he was a "yellow" man—his part-whiteness flaunted itself, as they beheld it; he was also a landowner, something they could not feel easy about; and now he was a Republican and Georgia legislator. In his person he symbolized to white men of standing nearly everything that had become so intolerable.

Some say it was just before the 1868 elections that General Nathan B. Forrest paid a visit to Atlanta—"on insurance business," it was claimed. There, we are told, he went into quiet conference with General John B. Gordon and certain other prominent men. General Gordon at the time was Democratic candidate for governor opposing Rufus B. Bullock, carpetbagger Radical. Bullock won the election, as did many Republican candidates all over the state. And why would they not win, protested the state's white Democrats, with U. S. Army troops hanging over the ballot boxes and guarding the doors where votes were counted?

It was after Forrest's visit that a rumor sprang up, coming simultaneously from a dozen different places—a very strange rumor, in the way it was met by Southern white gentlemen. For if they were questioned by one who knew no better, they were apt to turn a blandly courteous face to the questioner, saying in substance: "Yes, I have heard such rumors, but I put no credence in them. We are living in a time so troubled it can breed a thousand far-fetched tales." If the persistent questioner had ventured to hold under the courteous gentleman's nose a copy of a local newspaper, saying: "But what do you make of this?" it is said men had a way of perhaps smiling faintly, as at something of no consequence, and replying in some such language as this: "Surely, you would give no heed to what is so obviously a mischievous boys' prank?" The notice might have read as did this one from an Alabama paper:

KU KLUX

> *Hollow Hell. Devil's Den. Horrible Shadows. Ghostly Sepulchre. Headquarters of the Immortal Ate of the K.K.K. Gloomy Month. Bloody Moon. Black Night. Last Hour.*

General Orders No. 3.

Shrouded Brotherhood! Murdered Heroes!

Fling the bloody dirt that covers you to the four winds!

Erect thy Goddess on the banks of the Avernus. Mark well your foes! Strike with the redhot spear! Prepare Charon for his task!

Enemies reform! The skies shall be blackened! A single Star shall look down upon horrible deeds! The night owl shall hoot requiem o'er Ghostly Corpses!

Beware! Beware! Beware!

The Great Cyclops is angry! Hobgoblins report! Shears and lash! Tar and Feathers! Hell and Fury!

Revenge! Revenge! Revenge!

Bad men! white, black, yellow, repent!

The hour is at hand! Be ye ready! Life is short!

. . . .

All will be well!!!

> *By order of the Great*
> *BLUFUSTIN*
> *G. S.   K. K. K.*

Men might turn aside any questioners in as nonchalant a manner as they could muster. For obvious reasons it was the better part of valor to do it. But in no circumstances did they feel unconcerned. Life was a deadly serious business. There can be no doubt that they felt it so, and acted accordingly.

As the months after election passed, the air became choked with sultry rumors. An ugly story, once launched, would begin to float far and wide throughout the countryside; nor did it ever evaporate, seemingly, but clung near the ground, while new tales pushed their way in beside it to cleave there and multiply. Obviously, the times being what they were, the tales required no substantiation to be believed. Anything seemed possible to men's minds.

It is not for me to say what actually happened in middle Georgia in succeeding months—middle Georgia, which was but the Southern Black Belt in microcosm. I only know the story as participants who were fearful antagonists afterward told it. I know what they said happened to them, and, from first-hand accounts heard in my childhood, what one side felt and did about it.

One thing Southern white men were very bitter about was the "agitation of Negroes" by white and black "demagogues." Negroes were told, they said, that so surely as those "rebels," those "secessionists," won an election, so surely would black men be virtually re-enslaved. They were told, said these Southerners, that the Southern white man hated them; that he would allow their children no education; that he would cheat and exploit them, as already, it was claimed, he was cheating many, keeping their share of the crop, for instance, on pretense of its being owed him for "furnish," then grinding them down into debt, and, by clever means, holding them to work for him year after year to pay it. Negroes were told, it was claimed, that their former masters would not let them buy land unless they took steps to force the issue; that they would not let the black man vote, except as there were U. S. Army troops about to make them. The worst thing that Negroes were told, men felt, because of its implications, was that Southern whites would not treat them as equals, although, so said the "demagogues," "all men are created equal."

In this last suggestion, indeed, was seen the root evil of the agitators' "unprincipled demagoguery." Many Southern white men felt that it was for this that Loyal Leagues existed. Why else, they asked, did Negroes crowd to the meetings as to a revival? What but this could be the essence of their secret oaths and ritual? What other than wild exhortation—"You're as good as any white man!"—need go on behind such closely guarded doors? From mouth to mouth flashed stories of Yankees who ate at Negroes' tables, attended their social entertainments, danced at their balls, called them "Mister." On Greensboro's own streets occurred one such instance (nor did it long go ignored) of a young Northern white man named Gladden, come lately to the county to teach in a colored school. One rainy day, to the town's horrified amazement, he was seen to walk down the main street holding his umbrella over a Negro woman!

Yet far worse to Southern white men than what was being said to "stir up the Negroes" was what was rumored to be going on—a thousand dark rumors of dark deeds. Could not men recount a hundred tales with slight variations of Negroes "becoming very insolent," of "uppitiness," "sassiness," molestation of whites, all intolerable beyond words to former owners of slaves? Was it not said that ladies on the streets were being subjected to gross insults from former slaves? That drunken Negroes were burning down plantation homes? That "overseers . . . had been driven from plantations, and the negroes asserted their right to hold the property for their own benefit?" Had not black men been known to attack a country store to strip it of its goods? And armed recruits, former slaves, been said to roam the countryside demanding of white men to get their vehicles off the road to make room for these uniformed freedmen? Had not secret meetings of Loyal League branches been agitated by carpetbaggers, who baldly exhorted the Negroes—the rumor said so—to go forth to burn and destroy, saying: "Matches are worth only five cents a box; here is a remedy for your grievances"? Were not white women in lonely places "raped by lascivious black males" ("Rapes were being committed"; "ladies were ravished by some of these negroes")?

In what sense true or false? This is beside the point, when it came to the effect upon Southern whites who looked on such tales from the former slaveholder's viewpoint and could and did believe many of them.

In my childhood, Father only told us of Negroes' "insolence" and "uppitiness." True, when he talked, it was as though his words were wrung from him, for he obviously hated the memories. Yet it seems that he felt he must tell the story, lest we have no concrete images such as haunted him. "Lest we forget," he would say to us. "On the streets of Union Point, a darkey," so he put it, "pushed me off the sidewalk and spit on me. . . . And we were helpless: the military . . ." He also said: "My mother, walking down the street, was jostled by a negress, who then sassed her, nor would the woman give an inch of sidewalk to let my mother pass." Certain worse things he never spoke of, at least to us girls, things not suitable to girls' ears, according to Southern standards, things only to be hinted at. We should fear them, of course, but must only guess at their meaning. Of course we could guess; we even knew quite plainly from headlines of lynchings in our newspapers, or when books like *The Clansman* and *The Leopard's Spots* came spilling from the presses in the early 1900's. We would read these avidly and in due time come to the cliff scene, for instance—the chase, the hinted-at rape of a white girl. "The leopard cannot change his spots. . . ." Thus was cast the moral.

We were told how our world during reconstruction was ruled by "scalawags"—those native white men who by every loyal Southerner were scorned as base renegades; and also ruled by "carpetbaggers"—unprincipled without exception; Northerners; interlopers; men who were "nigger-lovers" or pretended to be; rank outsiders who had come in, so it was said, to feast like harpies upon a prostrate country; to agitate and use for personal aggrandizement the hapless black man; to dare to rule in place of the South's own foremost leaders. And to be ruled by Negroes! Ruled by black men! To have those born in the womb of slavery, those children of dark ignorance and lowest race, as they were spoken of, put in office over white men! The slave ruling over the master! They who but yesterday were masters and rulers could only look on this as something intolerable beyond words. Nor could they ever shake off the feelings which had once overwhelmed them. Thirty years after reconstruction, I, a child, must still feel it. Seeing the faces of older men suffuse with emotion when some untoward thing stirred their hardly buried memories, I, too, would feel namelessly oppressed.

This much is certain. To my people, as to me in my childhood, who was reared in their history of those fateful months, no "two sides" to what happened was conceivable. To them there was but one side, made up of true Southerners engaged, they verily believed, in a struggle for existence, for this is what "white supremacy" was to them.

6.

WE WERE never told just how the summons first went forth, except that ways were found to have it reach those who could meet the tests for candidates. "Are you now, or have you ever been, a member of the Radical Republican party, or either of the organizations known as the 'Loyal League' and the 'Grand Army of the Republic'?" "Are you opposed to negro equality, both social and political?" "Are you in favor of a white man's government in this country?" "Are you in favor of the re-enfranchisement and emancipation of the white men of the South, and the restitution of the Southern people to all their rights, alike proprietary, civil, and political?" These were some of them. Nor was it difficult, apparently, to find a host of Southern men of all ages who could and did answer these queries fervently.

Anonymity, we learned, was the first and foremost weapon. The times demanded this, men said. One of the "prescripts" provided (this I did not hear from Father): ". . . I will never reveal to any one not a member . . . any initiation, signs, grips, pass words, mysteries, or purposes of * * * " (the three stars representing the name). It also said: ". . . or that I am a member of the same, or that I know of any one who is a member. . . ." It provided as well: ". . . Origins, designs, mysteries and ritual of this * * * shall never be written. . . ."

It seems that this anonymity was carried very far indeed. With what meticulous care, for instance, a notable man such as General John B. Gordon took pains to guard it! General Gordon allegedly was Grand Dragon of the Invisible Empire in Georgia—he was generally so regarded, even in my childhood. In 1871 he was called to testify before the Committee of Congress investigating "outrages." He said: "I do not know anything about any Ku Klux organization, as the papers talk of it. . . . I have never heard of anything of that sort except in the papers and by general report." He then went on: ". . . In 1868—I think it was—I was approached and asked to attach myself to a secret organization in Georgia . . . by some of the very best citizens of the State—some of the most peaceable, law-abiding men, men of large property, who had large interests in the State. . . . The organization was simply this— nothing more and nothing less: it was an organization, a brother- hood of the property-holders, the peaceable, law-abiding citizens of the State, for self-defense. The instinct of self-protection prompted the organization; the sense of insecurity and danger, particularly in those neighborhoods where the Negro population largely predominated. . . ." He said further: "I am not going to state what my position was in that particular organization, I will say that I certainly would have known if there had been any . . . effort or purpose [for political control] which there was not."

A Congressman asked General Gordon if he did not know what the organization was called. "No, sir," he answered, "though I ought to know. The truth is that I never was at one of the gatherings in my life, if they had any gatherings. . . ." He was asked if there was a chief of the whole order in the state. "Well, sir, such a thing was talked about; I do not know that the organization was ever per- fected. Such a thing was talked about for the purpose of keeping down any general movement on the part of the negroes; but I do not think it was found necessary. . . ." He could not name other men who might testify, he said. "My opinion is that nobody knows anything more about it than I do. . . ." Nor could he say where the organization originated. "I have no idea in the world—not the remotest." The purport of the oath, or "pledge," as he called it? "I have no recollection of it at all, except that it was to the effect that we would unite as a band of brothers to protect each other from violence and aggression on the part of the negro." Or signs of recognition? "I think they did [have them] at first; but I think that passed away in a very short time. . . ." Their meetings? "I do not think they have had any. . . . We did not have any organ- ization like the Loyal League, meeting and counseling together . . . but one purpose to serve . . . to protect the safety of our people . . . The apprehended occasion never arose; the danger passed away; the alarm and apprehension were gradually dis- pelled. As with most of the evils of this life, we found that we had anticipated a great deal more than ever occurred."

So it went with less important men who were questioned. Said the Mayor of Savannah: "I have never heard of any such organization. . . . I do not think it could possibly have existed without my knowledge of this fact." And a newspaper editor of Athens: "I have no idea that there ever has been any organization in the State of Georgia, known as Ku Klux, or any other sort of secret organization, except the Loyal Leagues, since the surrender." He said also, in reply to a question: "I never saw any man on the face of the habitable globe who admitted or said that he belonged. . . ." A middle Georgia farmer, who was a Union man, said that during the two years since 1868, there had been perhaps a hundred men sent for from different parts of his county—men suspected of being active in the Ku Klux. "They have been sent for by the grand jury and asked if they knew anything of the organization, and they said they did not." And he added, suspiciously: "Some of the members of the grand jury, perhaps, were members of it."

Who can say with certainty, therefore, what went on in middle Georgia at the time this Invisible Empire was sending out its unknown men to perform its unnamed missions? Certainly, so far as we as children ever heard it, the missions were never described by ex-Klansmen, except occasionally little visits to unimportant, unnamed individuals. Father, who had been but a rank-and-file young member, told us certain things about those days, but not these matters of importance, if indeed he knew them. Nor did other men do so who sometimes would join him in tales of old times.

The most we heard were accounts of this nature. As in the case of many other sons of planters, the summons had come to Father, and he had answered it promptly. By day he might try to keep his mind on law under Alexander Stephens's tutelage. When night came—those nights when a call came to him—he would mount his horse and ride toward a deep forest or some remote abandoned building, on the way donning his mask and covering his horse so that he might arrive white-robed and white-hooded. When the silent company had assembled, the ghostly horsemen would start forth on their midnight mission.

It was almost an invariable rule, so Father told us, unless some

Uprooted

unusual crisis demanded differently, for companies of men bent on a mission to carry it out in a county not their own, while Klansmen of the county they visited saw to it that each and everyone had a conspicuous alibi. Apparently this was quite general practice. It was repeatedly spoken of. Robinson, Oglethorpe's "scalawag" official, said: "They were tried in the committing court and discharged. . . . They would say they were not there. . . . They had witnesses to prove an alibi. . . ." A Negro, referring to his own beating, said: "Nobody has been punished for it . . . it is the hardest thing in the world [to prove anything]. A man gets forty or fifty men to swear that he was at some other place that night."

Our story continued: They would ride up to a remote cabin in their horrendous white robes, looking like enormous hobgoblins in the dim shadows made by clouds flitting over a waning moon. They would call a man out of his cabin—a Negro who had voted Republican and talked boastfully about it, they said; or one who had been "insufferably impudent" to a white man; or for whatever reason the visit was being paid. They would call loudly to him to come forth from where he might be hiding with his wife and children behind his cabin door. If necessary some of the robed men would dismount and bring him out. Then, so Father said, they would begin to talk among themselves so that the man could hear them. One figure would speak of how he had died at Gettysburg or some other battle and how thirsty he got in hell. Then he would order the quivering man to bring water, buckets of water. One of the robed horsemen would take the bucket of water and drink and drink; then he would ask for another and drink it. Gallon after gallon the trembling man would bring; gallon after gallon to all appearances would go down the gullet of the great white figure, though in truth it but trickled out along the shadowy ground through a convenient little hose which the rider had brought along. This particular story delighted us as children; we thought it funny to an extreme; our shrill young laughter would ring out whenever it was told. "And did it scare them?" we might ask. They seemed to think it did. Before they left, the leader would tell the Negro what was expected of him in "good behavior," Father told us. Maybe thereafter he would give them "no more trouble." He and his family might suddenly move away. Or, as Father would say,

91

the man might return to his former "humility." Perhaps this tells very little. In any event, it is about all we heard from ex-Klansmen.

At the time, it would appear, people were particularly exercised —people up North, I mean, and the "Radical" leaders in the South— by the accounts by men who held public office of visits paid to them. This was natural, no doubt. It would seem very striking if a judge or legislator or some other official person said he had received threatening notes, or was beaten, or had decided to leave town because he was told to. Of course, being non-Southern, how could they understand that these men were simply "scalawags" or "carpetbaggers" or even some of them Negroes?

On the Invisible Empire's part, it was insisted that the organization was completely non-political—"It had no more politics in it than the organization of the Masons," General Gordon put it. Moreover, it was said that if any of the men were visited, as they alleged, that aside from there being no such thing as a Ku Klux Klan, it was certain no one in their particular county had done it, and moreover they had heard that one man who was beaten, for instance, had been "caught stealing," another had an "adulterous relationship in his home," another had been "impudent to a white man," and so on.

As for the stories these more prominent individuals told, they were all quite similar. The "scalawag" Robinson, of Oglethorpe County—he who was elected County Ordinary by Republican votes in 1868—said he received many "warnings," and two or three times left the county for several days because he "feared" attack. Notices were culled from middle Georgia newspapers like this one; which listed names of specific men, saying: "The Ku Klux Klan has arrived, and *woe to the degenerate.*" Also an editorial gave notice to "radicals" and "scalawags" of some terrible doom impending, adding: "Let traitors beware!"

Several Negro legislators in the middle Georgia country had accounts to give of visitations. The Greene County Negro legislator Abram Colby said that one night ten or fifteen men in white robes rode up to his house, broke his door down, took him out of bed, "and took me to the woods and whipped me three hours or more and left me in the woods for dead." He said they beat him "with sticks and with straps that had buckles on the ends of them." He told much more of his beating, but this was the gist of it. They told him, he said, that "I had influence with the negroes in other counties, and had carried the negroes against them." They said: "Do you think you will ever vote another damned radical ticket?" This was the way he remembered it two or three years afterward. Lieutenant Hoyt of the United States Army chanced to be at Greensboro on another case and was called in, he said, on the Colby beating. He told of going out to Colby's house with a squad of men. ". . . He was in a very bad condition." Hoyt said he questioned townsmen in an effort to get to the bottom of the affair. "They . . . said they did not believe that this party [that visited Colby] was from that vicinity, that they thought it must be from down in the country. . . ."

Monday Floyd, who was in the legislature from a group of counties that included Greene, insisted that he was advised by white men that he would do well to leave the county. He also produced a note that he said came to him in the mails and which read:

Hell Town, Ga., At Night.
Monday Floyd: You are requested to resign Your place in the Legislature and retire to private life. We think it the best thing You can do under the present state of affairs. And we hope will comply without further trouble and save us from being provoked to put a dire threat into execution. And we take this opportunity to inform Mr. Dukes that he had better do likewise and warn You to acquaint that Mr. Dukes with the fact that Your own skirts may be clear, for we swear by the powers of both Light and Darkness that no other Negro shall ever enter the Legislative Halls of the South. Sir, a word to the wise is sufficient. Heed, we beseech you, friendly advice, and take warning.

Haste, O Mondy, to be wise,
Stay not for the morrow's sun.
K.K.K.

Also, a Negro legislator named Alfred Richardson, over the line from Greene, in Clarke County, declared he had suffered two attacks after his election. Richardson had been a slave until the surrender, and then became a house carpenter and store owner. Before his first attack, he said, he had been warned by a "wealthy white man," apparently in a friendly spirit. The white man told him, as

Richardson related it, "There are some men about here that have something against you; and they intend to kill you or break you up. They say you are making too much money; that they do not allow any nigger to rise that way; that you can control all the colored votes; and they intend to break you up, and then they can rule the balance of the niggers when they get you off." Others gave him similar warnings. Then one night the hooded figures came. "They were a parcel of disguised men"—some twenty or so, but they "had him in too hot a place to count them." Richardson said he had "sort of expected them," so had made preparations. It seems he fought back. He was wounded, and so was one of his visitors. However, he left his farm after that, moving into Athens.

Then there was Romulus Moore of another county in the area, who had held office first as registrar, then as delegate to the Reconstruction constitutional convention, then as legislator. He had been a free Negro since 1858, having bought himself at the division of his master's estate. Since then, besides being pastor of a church, he had plied his old trade of blacksmith. He had gone home for the week-end from Atlanta when his visitors came. "I was in my house sitting back against my fire-place, reading my Bible. They came to the door, with a kind of war-whoop, expecting that I would run; I did not, and they came into the door. I knew pretty well who they were, and I said, 'Come in, gentlemen.' A whole parcel came in and commenced cursing and abusing me." He said they "abused him" for his "political principles" and for "misleading the colored people, as they said." They accused him of "raising disturbance." He said: "Gentlemen, what fuss do you have reference to?" They replied: "There is a great fuss in the settlement. . . . From your political course heretofore." They gave him to understand, he said, that he "should not control his people politically." They finally said they did not come to hurt him. "They talked a great deal, and said, 'We didn't come to hurt you tonight; we haven't got on our grave clothes.'" But soon after that, so he told the story, Moore's wife, a teacher in a Negro school she had started, also received some "warnings." So he told her they had better pick up and move to Atlanta for the time being, and that was what they did.

It would be hard to judge from the stories, which were more

important in Invisible Empire eyes, the little or the big people. Naturally, there being only a few important persons, there were few stories about them, and there being thousands of little people, a great many stories were told of them. Indeed, any tales we heard as children were about these unimportant people, who were being obstreperous about working as farm hands, and voting, and trying to build schools, and, so it was said, being "impudent" and "saucy" on such matters.

In any event, the Invisible Empire must have thought it worth while to send its missions out to folk such as a certain aged colored man of Clarke County, who said he was called on one night by hooded figures. They whipped him because, he said, they told him, he had stolen a beef; and told him also that "if he ever voted any other ticket besides the democratic . . . they would kill him." Or a Negro named Poldo in this same county, who while working on a road got into a quarrel with a white man named Middlebrooks. Poldo, the account went, "stood up as if he were willing to jump in and fight the white man if he hit him. . . . No more was said that day." But at night Poldo had a visitation, he claimed, of fifteen or twenty "disguised men," who broke in his door, caught him and beat him, and told him it was because he had most impudently "sauced Middlebrooks." Likewise, a Negro man named Dannon. He was a blacksmith. His story went that he had been doing work in his shop for a white man named Kemp, who for over a year had not paid him. Dannon complained to another white man who had rented him the shop, and was advised simply to lay aside Kemp's work until Kemp paid him. However, Kemp would not hear of this. He put his buggy on Dannon's anvil, saying: "Don't you move this off till you take it off to work on it." This was Dannon's story. But Dannon said his landlord told him: "Set the buggy aside, and go on with your work." Kemp was furious. A few nights later, it was said, a score of "disguised men" came to Dannon's door with the usual sequel. Stories were told of Negro women being beaten. As one Negro legislator described it, "A white lady has a colored lady for cook or waiting in the house. . . . They have a quarrel, and sometimes probably the colored woman gives the lady a little jaw. In a night or two a crowd will come in disguise to take her out and whip her."

95

To all appearances, schools and school-teachers—for Negroes, that is—were much objected to by Invisible Empire men. To be sure, the white school-teacher Gladden had upset Greensboro's citizenry by walking down the main street holding his umbrella over a Negro woman; people would think this looked like just plain "social equality"; he was also an interloper, being a Northerner and a white man teaching Negro children. In any case, his story went that he was called upon around the hour of midnight and given a walk in the company of white-robed figures, who escorted him all over town, he said, ending up at a fish pond, where he was informed that "if they found him there in the morning they would do something to him." Even before this the colored school where he taught had "lost" several teachers it was said. An old man named Shropshire from a county near Greene had a school story to tell. Shropshire was a farmer, born in Oglethorpe, who had begun to vote Republican though he called himself a "Jackson Democrat." The white-robed visitors said he was "an old Radical." This farmer said he gave the Negroes on his place permission to build a schoolhouse. But the midnight callers arrived and told them they would have to stop doing it. They did stop, but Shropshire told them to go ahead and use a cabin on his land. This cabin, so he said, was burned to the ground under mysterious circumstances. But the old farmer, being a stubborn man and thinking to do on his own land as he pleased, proceeded to put up a building himself where a Negro school could be held. He implied that this one was allowed to stand.

At a time when white men were very much needing laborers, it was said, "some [went] to the houses where colored men were living off to themselves, and told them if they did not leave there and go to some white man's yard and live, they would come in on them some night. . . ." "I heard of one case," said a Negro man, "in Jackson County. . . . One or two families left their houses and went to some white man's yard to live. They complain they do not know what to do; that they are afraid on account of the Ku Klux. Then the citizens tell them, 'Come to my house and stay, and I'll be bound they won't pester you.'" Some laborers it might affect this way, but others, Negro leaders alleged, were so disturbed that they were leaving the country districts and crowding into the towns. One man said that several Negro families had bought land around his place and settled there, but "since this thing has been going on," they had been selling their lots for little or nothing and moving away. "They go away to some large towns where they lay around and get whatever they can." "There are lots of men down there," he said, "whose crops are running away with grass, and they cannot get hands on account of this thing; the men are running away so and leaving the county. A heap of farmers there can't get labor enough to make their crops." They were going to the towns, he said, feeling that there they were protected. Some planters go to town and try to get hands, said this man. The colored man will ask what part of the country he lives in and say: "We can't go down there, the Ku Klux is down there. If it wasn't for the Ku Klux we would go down and work for you." Another man declared: "Here, in this place [Atlanta], I suppose there are three or four thousand colored people who would today be out on farms if they could be allowed to stay there; while here they hardly make their bread." They are afraid of being "run off by disguised parties." Romulus Moore, the legislator, said he argued this problem with a white planter of his home town. "Captain," he said to this gentleman, " . . . this Ku-Kluxing arrangement you have got up . . . will injure you financially; you will drive all the labor out of the country."

Those who looked on the Invisible Empire with agitation and dread spoke of it this way: "If they don't whip, they ride anyhow, and scare people; they ride up and down at nights. Sometimes they ride through a whole settlement and never touch anybody. Sometimes they go by colored people's doors and shoot some five or six balls through the door and ride on without stopping." This was called being "Ku-Kluxed." "It frightens them," they would add.

How long could this go on?

Certainly such a strange state of affairs must have had the whole countryside in fierce turmoil. Just one such incident in a community would surely be enough to stir it up for weeks: everyone taking sides, and each side according to its view blaming or praising; the press chiming in, sometimes trying to calm people, but sometimes just the opposite; the authorities arresting people and perhaps turning them loose again, because they said there was no evidence; that part of the community which knew the attackers, or could guess, feeling tense and right and defending what was done; and those who had been attacked, or thought they might be, feeling frightened and angry and some longing to make reprisals. If one such incident would arouse a storm of tension and fright and belligerence, what must it have been in Georgia between 'sixty-eight and 'seventy, when the Invisible Empire was sending out its hooded horsemen maybe several times a week; when the sides were becoming ever more sharply drawn as between Negro and white; when the Federal authorities were coming in to investigate?

Apparently, it must go on until the mass of Negroes "came to their senses," and their leaders, "black, white and yellow," had been ousted; until all and sundry—"scalawags," "carpetbaggers," and Negroes—learned the lesson this organization said it went out to teach. Thus "crimes" were punished; "bad men" were treated according to their deserts; "restoration of order" was envisaged, and "putting the darkey in his place." It would go on thus—so said the aim—until "white supremacy" was re-established.

Thus it did go on. Then one day it ceased. Suddenly, so men said, there were no more rides. Suddenly, it seems, the nights were quiet again, except for the normal hoofbeats of horsemen taking their normal course around the countryside.

It is true, one must add, that a "bogus" Ku Klux Klan is supposed to have made occasional visits for a few years afterward. But it was frowned upon. Father told us of it. So do written accounts. It was made up of "bad elements," so people said. It "disgraced" the old order and was contrary to the strict injunction of the old order's leaders, who declared it never should be revived. The old order was made up of the "best people." True, the notion seems to have been allowed to get around at the time that midnight visits under the "real" Klan were but the work of irresponsible "rowdies," "hoodlums," wild young men of no social standing or stability, the work of the "poorer classes." This rumor was allowed, it seems, to throw dust into the eyes of prying authorities. Georgians then knew of the "original" Invisible Empire, as a certain John Calvin Reed put it many years afterward (he said he was Grand Giant in Oglethorpe County and that the son-in-law of no less a man than Robert Toombs was chief in middle Georgia): "It mustered, not assassins, thugs and cut-throats, as has been often alleged, but the choicest Southern manhood." General Gordon himself described the unnamed organization as a "brotherhood of property-holders. . . ." So we as children emphatically understood it.

But the "real" Klan was dissolved, and very suddenly.

It was no accident, apparently, that its dissolution came—so it is believed—after the elections of 1870.

In those elections Georgia Democrats were restored again to power. They won two-thirds of the legislative seats and five out of seven representatives to the Congress. In the localities they quickly re-established themselves. At the next gubernatorial election in 1872, they won the governorship away from the incumbent Republican. Then, indeed, was completed the "Restoration," as Southern men came to call it. Others, who felt very fervently, said "the Redemption."

7.

THE SOUTH might be "restored," but not the old life for Father. Even into the late 1870's, shortly after his marriage, he might again think it would return. So much so that he would write to his young wife, "I think the chances are slim for Register"—this was Register in Bankruptcy for the Northern District of Georgia. "I wrote Gen. Gordon but don't know how he will succeed. I think I had as well make arrangements to go to plowing next year." He might for a while think the law would be sufficient for his needs, only to find the seventies and eighties no time to make a financial success of law. True, he would hold onto his license in this profession of his forebears—to the end of his life he remained "attorney and counsellor at law." But meantime after he was Register, he took another salaried position. This was in the eighties when agricultural hopes in middle Georgia were very bad indeed. The expanding railroads beckoned, so Father took a post with a Georgia railroad. This, as it turned out, marked the final uprooting. At the outset it meant he must move his family. He must leave the town where Grandfather had settled, there in Greene County adjoining Oglethorpe. First came a middle Georgia town farther away; after that, other Georgia towns; and finally, a move away from the state altogether to South Carolina.

Within the first three years of my life we lived in three different towns in Georgia—Macon, where I was born, and two others. Within ten years we had lived in two states, three different locali· ties, and no less than eight different homes. A Southern Methodist pastor's migrations dictated by the rules of his church were hardly comparable. The humor was not a little wry when a country place where we remained all of two years was dubbed by the older children "Nomad's Rest." Being very young I thought they were saying "No Man's," which all but confirmed my worst fears.

Singularly enough, once we had transferred from Georgia to South Carolina, Father's office remained in the one city, Columbia, and in the same building on the same floor, while in that time his family's place of residence changed eight times.

It was far from unknown in the annals of seaboard "old" families for members to migrate elsewhere. There was the William Lumpkin, a William not in our direct line, who left middle Georgia behind in the year 1837, having succumbed to the fever drifting eastward from the fabulously rich cotton lands in Mississippi and the Delta, sold what he could not carry, and made the long overland trek with family and possessions from the wastefully depleted soil of old Georgia to the virgin new acres in the west. "We shall have upward of 60 negroes [said he in a letter to his son William, who had gone before], 32 horses & mules, about 50 head of cattle, beside the white family, consisting of your Mother and myself, 4 daughters, 4 grandchildren, Mr. Mayer & I, & perhaps 2 young white men. I have a coach & 4 white horses, two large waggons 5 mules in each, a 2 horse waggon & a Deabon waggon, & my Sulkey—Mr. Mayer has 2 large Waggons a Coachee and cart & 14 head of horses & mules—So you may see we shall have a very large cavalcade, & a very expensive one—Through Divine Mercy & goodness we are generally in good health thanks be to God. We expect to start in 4 or 5 days [the letter was dated 13th November] so you may justly imagine it will be 15th Decm. or after according to the weather before we arrive with you if our good Lord blesses

& prospers us. . . . " Even if such a pioneer country had offered set patterns of social exclusion against newcomers which they had to overcome, and it would do it only slightly, in any event, this William bore with him sufficiently convincing evidence of his good estate.

Circumstances made all the difference. The shifts and changes of disinherited former slaveholders in the decades after the Civil War were something born of that unique period. With not a single Negro, not a horse or mule, or carriage, or head of cattle, not the smallest suggestion of a "cavalcade," did the William Lumpkins of Oglethorpe County, Georgia, in hot, grimy day coaches of the Southern Railroad, cross over into South Carolina as the old century turned. The Lumpkin drop-leaf dining table from Father's old home, the Du Pre piano, the Morris sideboard, a little "what-not" on which we kept a few pieces of imported old blue china, a lowboy or two; some precious daguerreotypes of the Lumpkins and Pittards, and the Morrises, Patillos and Du Pres; two fragile gold lockets loved by us all for the soft gray locks in them of our grandparents' hair; and the great family Bible on whose pages, stained and faded with age, was entered the solemn record of births and deaths. These few things, lost to all eyes but ours among our nondescript necessary furnishings, alone of our material possessions could have told the world of our "old days."

The Lumpkins came to the Palmetto State as strangers. To be a Georgian in South Carolina was not to feel immediately at home. We were torn loose not alone from our past and from all its material symbols of superiority and comfort; we were set down among the clans of Carolina for whom name was paramount, and to whom our Georgia name in South Carolina genealogy was unknown.

Not by words so much did Carolinians convey their attitude toward outlanders. In their manner it was plainly evident if they were unfamiliar with one's name. Where to others they could quickly strike up a connection, "Oh, you are related to the Gibbes," or to the Stoneys or Gaillairds or DesPortes, with us it would be a raised eyebrow, an inflected tone, "That is not a South Carolina name?" By the time I was a grown woman, in remote Carolina towns I would be asked, "You are the daughter of Colonel Lumpkin?" But that was after many years.

In Georgia, too, one's name had mattered. With my first awakening understanding "Lumpkin" was a title of merit. Joseph Henry, Wilson, Samuel, were some of the Lumpkin names we rolled around our tongues. Back in Georgia the name never had to be spelled, and no one ever put an "s" on it. They merely asked, "To which branch do you belong?" One had taken "Lumpkin" for granted, and here in South Carolina it was not known.

It is easy to imagine the exchange about us when we first settled in the state. "Do you know the Lumpkins who have just moved into the Smith house? They are from a Georgia family." "Are you going to call? Are they nice people?" "It's a Georgia family, of course, but I hear they have background. They lost everything in the War." "Jenny said she met them, and they seemed to her a little cool, and proud as Lucifer." "Well, and why should they be cool?" "Are they related to South Carolina families?" "Not that I've heard of."

In every Southern town, none more so than in South Carolina, it had long ago been established who were the good families. When newcomers arrived it was a subtle process by which they learned to recognize and to be recognized. The absence of material signs of superior social station made for confusion.

Nothing was easier if the strangers were related to already established families. From then on it was "Cousin" this and "Cousin" that without any more ado. If the new family hailed from a distance and, as in our case, even a different state, the problem was complicated. Undoubtedly it helped that we were Episcopalians and immediately established our connection with socially elite Trinity Church.

How the process took place in our instance, how slowly or rapidly our Georgia family "background" was recognized, who can now say, so inconspicuously do such changes come about? When other families came in after us I sensed that an informal investigation ensued, engaged in by the ladies of the neighborhood. In keeping with courteous custom, they must duly call on the newcomer. Not to do so was an affront meted out only to those definitely known to be *de trop*, either because of their lack of background or that they were Yankees. It was really not hard to ascertain something of the strangers' forbears and standing in the place from whence they had come. "From Oglethorpe County. . . . Really. . . . I've never been there, you know, but we South Carolinians do cling to our native state. Had Mr. Lumpkin's family *always* lived there? Since before the Revolutionary War? Virginia? . . . Oh yes, so many old families came from Virginia originally. Though not South Carolinians, you know. Now, *my* people came directly . . . Huguenot descent . . . Charleston . . . low country plantation . . . Columbia after the War. . . . Well, Georgia suffered as we all did . . . Sherman. . . . You *like* South Carolina? Your husband's business, I know. . . . Not like the old days. . . ." No offensive questioning, inasmuch as all were ladies. Having a common language, as they would if the new family were people with "background," the interchange could be smooth as melting butter.

No other state save Virginia perhaps would have made acclimitization so difficult for a newcomer. It was no fault of theirs if by reason of counting cousinships to a distant degree everyone seemed interrelated excepting one's own family. Back in Georgia we too could have said "Aunt Sally," and "Cousin Sam," and "Cousin Jenny." In South Carolina away off in another part of the state lived a Cousin Tony whom we saw rarely, and after some years we discovered residing near us a five-times-removed Cousin Jane.

Growing out of babyhood one learned how from "good family" was derived something called "family pride," which would let a person "hold up his head" however little he had of material possessions, because, his family being what it was, no man was "better" than he.

If it were possible, the move from our native Georgia exaggerated for me the sense of "old family," "good family," "family standing." Inevitably so. South Carolinians had pride of family position? Well, so did we. The delicate contours of my mother's face, the fine texture of her smooth skin, the slender beauty of her expressive hands, meant in my childhood mind a secure sense of "background."

No one ever sat us down saying, "We will teach you about family." The meaning of "family" was warp and woof of our heritage of ideas, and with it, of appropriate actions. One knew without being told that social position depended upon "family"; that "family" strictly determined what children we could play with and those we must avoid, though, the times being what they were, it often took careful guidance to help us make our selection. Under the hurly-burly of democratic public school attendance we might sometimes have to submit to gentle pressure to pry us loose from embarrassing engagements we had made on our own account, and from which others might flow. Even our near neighbors might occasionally be socially unacceptable, as an Irish family with a large and to me intensely interesting flock of children, who, though the father was a streetcar conductor, owned their home. Unfailing courtesy was laid upon us as an obligation, but not intimate social exchange in such circumstances, not borrowing butter or a cup of sugar, or sending over a sample of fresh homemade rolls. Not even calling and being called upon. And for us children, not playing in their back yard, as we did in our other neighbors'. It made especially fascinating the stolen moments with them, delightful forbidden fruit which we chewed on with relish while it lasted.

Among our acquaintances, "family" was the frame of reference for almost any conversation.

Many a home rejoiced whose school children happened to draw a teacher from good family. "My child is in Minna Blank's room. Isn't it lovely? She's of old Charleston stock, you know. Think of his being under so refined an influence in public school. What a pity she has to work!"

When Cole Blease of "demagogic" fame was making his perennial race for governor—and several times winning—the situation was loudly bemoaned, especially among the ladies, largely in terms of background. Why had men of good family stepped out of politics? Why did they let such a man run the state? How could such a governor carry out his necessary social duties? Who would now lead the grand march at the Assembly Ball?

Obviously the trait of "good family" could not be acquired. A girl who married a boy of lower social stratum, or vice versa, had a severe handicap to overcome. It is true lines were already becoming blurred, but among the older generation standards did not change. With great relief a mother would find her child to have chosen a mate of genuine "old stock," however poor he might be. Even if a boy had chosen the occupation of mechanic, as one boy of our acquaintance who was grandson of a well-known planter and political figure had had the temerity to do and of all things joined the labor union of his trade, it was forgiven him when he married a girl of equally good name. It must be said that his family and friends were not satisfied until the lad had given up the trade on which he plainly doted and taken on respectable ownership of a farm.

In any event, possessions were no longer the determinants they once were. When we settled in South Carolina it would be hard to imagine the varied assortment of conditions among families, from well-to-do to virtual poverty—if their true stringencies were known—who yet had the common denominator of aristocratic name.

It was no time at all before we learned in which homes dwelt "old families" regardless of what the outward appearance might be. A new and unusual Spanish style stucco house on our street, with porte-cochere and fine carriage-house in the rear, of all things belonged to a Yankee. One of the few ostentatious places near us, with great white pillars, stained glass decorative windows, formal hedges and flower borders, a conspicuously well-kept lawn, occupying the prize corner of a prize street, was put there by a local manufacturer of very ordinary background in our eyes, whose prosperity was strictly post bellum. A few men, offshoots of the old regime, had built modern dwellings. As I look back I can count them on the fingers of one hand. More often than not along our street, names as revered as any the state boasted could be found tacked on the door jambs of ordinary, undistinguished frame dwellings.

A few families had managed to retain their old family places, very often under hard conditions. A maiden lady of ancient Carolina lineage turned hers into a select day school for children. On a corner across the Green was a sweet old place, conspicuously in poor repair because the sons of the household, later to be prosperous enough, were still young boys. We lived for a few passing months in a furnished dwelling, every room mellow with antebellum dignity; the sons, later men of prominence in their own right, were then struggling through college on the rent. I was too small a child to recognize fine antiques around me. What I drank in was a sense of age and exceeding stability.

In a land where a separate servant class existed and help came exceedingly cheap, it might be supposed the old families, so recently slaveowners, would at all costs provide themselves with domestics in plenty. And so they did when it could be managed. A few were able to have two or three Negro servants, aside from their gardening and laundry work. It was not so for the general run. Most of us were glad to have a Negro cook, paid something around two and a half dollars weekly, with a new face in the kitchen every few months. Now and then a time would even come when we might do our own cooking for short periods, so closely was figuring done.

Hardly any of our mothers but undertook practically all the family sewing, unless there was a wedding to come. Had circumstances allowed, we would have hired a dressmaker to come in regularly. As it was, the sewing machine would hum under our mothers' busy fingers a good many hours in the week. Not only dresses and undergarments were made for Mother and the girls, but even our woolen clothing. For men and boys nothing was bought save suits and starched collars, and in our family my father's special stiff-fronted shirts. Many hours of my early years were spent playing around Mother's sewing machine on the floor where she might keep an eye on me, and as a very special treat, let me oil the machine or rearrange the tangle in its drawers. From those years it remained an effort for me to throw away basting threads, so habitual had it become for us to pull and wind them carefully on empty spools.

Of course we made every effort to keep up appearances. Each of our mothers had her silk dress that rustled, bonnet or hat touched with velvet ribbon, dainty black shoes, and black kid gloves. Even if our Sunday-best garments had seen long service, softly glowing light sifting down through stained glass windows shed a charitable glow over them. The unknowing could hardly have guessed we did not come out of our lost mansions when Sunday came, and one old family after another would tread with infinite pride and dignity old Trinity's deep-carpeted aisle. As prime a necessity as bread was payment on the family pew at Trinity.

Withal it remained true, regardless of present circumstances, that "old-family" still meant the good things of this world—land, houses, servants, everything on a luxurious scale. The difference was that one could only enjoy these by turning one's gaze backward. Only by a tenuous claim upon the past could old families establish their station in this all-important way. "We lost everything when the slaves were freed"; "Mother couldn't keep up the old place when war came and took the men away"; "Sherman burnt down our place and took every last thing we had."

One move, never consummated, might have altered many things for our family. Who can surmise the "may have beens"? This time our goods and chattels were packed and lodged in freight cars under a thrilling sense of acute anticipation. Our voices sang through hurried labor and bustle of making the rented house disgorge everything. Weary though we were after days of packing, we could be gay as we drove away from the deserted dwelling, smiling happily at the vacant windows left staring in the sun.

Father being a railroad man, we traveled on passes. Our passes to the new abode were in his pocket. This we knew because we had begged to handle them. At our night's temporary lodging place before the early morning train we set out our overflowing luggage to rearrange its motley contents of leftovers, so that it could be more easily closed in the morning.

Then Father came to us. Even I, a child, could read something of what was in his face. By some means that I was too young to know, he had learned that the title to the place was dubious or had been challenged. He had bought it in good faith, made his down payment—I could only sense the burden this involved. It had been ours to own. An old plantation—oh, elusive goal—in good Carolina farming country. Was our restless march now nearing its end? None of us had seen the plantation save Father, nor ever did. Now it was gone. For three days we lodged sadly with distant cousins, the only relatives we had in that part of South Carolina, until Father and Mother found and rented another dwelling.

Just another house, we found it, blood brother to all the previous frame houses we had known. Situated on a "good" street, in a "good" neighborhood, with small yard, sparse lawn, few flowers and shrubs, as many rooms as could be secured for the rental, size being primary for a family of nine, no particular color,—be it gray-green or green-gray or yellow-brown—the floor plan varying hardly at all from every other. It was only another house, as I thought of it, from which sooner or later we would inevitably move on.

BOOK THREE

A Child Inherits a Lost Cause

1.

Men like my father spoke of the Lost Cause. It was little more than a manner of speaking. Even of the war they would say, "We were never conquered . . ." and of reconstruction, "I'm an unreconstructed rebel!" They would sing in gayer moods:

> *I've not been reconstructed,*
> *Nor tuck the oath of allegiance,*
> *I'm the same old red hot rebel,*
> *And that's good enough for me!*

Seriously, they would say: "We need not and will not lose those things that made the South glorious." If new features must be permitted the Southern edifice, so be it. At least the fundamentals should be kept intact. It became the preoccupation of their kind to preserve the old foundations at all costs.

In my father's case, as far back as 1874 he had launched upon his career in behalf of Confederate veterans. In that year there met in Union Point, Georgia, then his home, the first regimental reunion of Confederates—this was the claim—ever to be held in the South. This was a gathering of his own, the Third Georgia Regiment. Thenceforth, Father was ever at the beck and call of his comrades' interests.

These were the years when in towns and cities throughout Georgia, South Carolina, and all Southern states, men raised a slender shaft, topped by a tall soldier figure—the Confederate soldier. With solemn ceremony, a "rebel yell" from assembled veterans, a band playing *Dixie*, and oratory of a bygone day, these sacred monuments were unveiled. My father soon became a favor-

111

ite orator on such occasions: he could be counted on to drop everything for them; also, he spoke such things as his audience wanted to hear, and in the way they wanted—feelingly, eloquently. I should hesitate to guess how many of these shafts in the small towns of South Carolina had the veil lifted from them by his devoted hand.

Besides this there were the Confederate reunions, Southwide, statewide, and even on a smaller scale. Father was an inveterate reunion-goer and planner. So were literally hundreds of his kind, men who were also of the Old South's disinherited, who had lost so much and regained so little, materially speaking. It may well be that these men were a mainspring of this "Lost Cause movement," kept it pulsing, held it to fever pitch while they could, firing it with its peculiar fervor. Where but in the past lay their real glory? Who more than they would have reason to keep lifted up the time of their greatness?

Theirs was certainly a tireless effort in behalf of the Lost Cause, and a labor of love if ever there was one. These men expected to get nothing from it save people's warm approbation, perhaps, and the personal satisfaction that comes with performance of a welcome duty; and of course—indeed above everything—their sense that by this means they were serving the paramount aim of preserving the South's old foundations. Father would say: "The heritage we bear is the noblest on earth; it is for us to say whether . . . we will make the home of the South what the home of the South once was—the center of a nation's life; it is for us to keep bright the deeds of the past, and we will do it." For him it was sufficient reward that people could say, as they did on one occasion of my older sister (nor did anyone mind the fulsome language still so dear to the heart of the South at the turn of the century): "Daughter of an eloquent father, reared in a home where the Confederacy is revered as a cause, holy and imperishable. . . ."

We had lived in South Carolina less than five years when I was dipped deep in the fiery experience of Southern patriotism. This was the Confederate reunion of 1903, held in our home town of Columbia.

It was but one in a long line of reunions. In South Carolina they had a way of placing the first in the year 1876—"the grandest reunion ever held in any State, one of the most sublime spectacles ever witnessed," "thrilling the hearts" of the people of Columbia. They called it the first, but "there were no invitations, no elaborate programme, no committees of reception, no assignment of quarters, no reduced rates of transportation, no bands of music, no streamers flying." Of it they said: "The State was prostrate. The people had with marvelous patience restrained themselves from tearing at the throat of the Radical party. Hampton had been elected governor, and yet the tyrannical party would not yield." (Wade Hampton and his "red shirts" had just overthrown reconstruction.) At that moment, the story goes—"It was the supreme moment of the crisis"—there appeared, coming into Columbia from every direction, by all the highways, "men in apparel which had become the most glorious badge of service since the history of the world—those faded jackets of gray." They came, it is said, ten thousand of them, converging on Columbia, making their way straight to the headquarters of the Democratic party. They were resolved, they said, "to make this State one vast cemetery of free men rather than the home of slaves." Their voices shouted hoarsely, "Hampton!" "Forth came the great captain who stilled the tumult with a wave of his hand." He said: "My countrymen, all is well. Go home and be of good cheer. I have been elected governor of South Carolina, and by the eternal God, I will be governor or there shall be none." Men said, "There will never be another such reunion."

It was not a reunion of course in the later sense. Since 'seventy-six the South had seen an exceedingly complex organization of Confederate sentiment. The United Confederate Veterans covered all the Southern states. Each state had its division of the parent organization, and each division its multitude of "camps" honeycombing the counties, each bearing the name of some hero, living or dead. Not only the veterans, but their wives and widows, sons and daughters, children and grandchildren, were organized. My father was an active veteran; my mother and older sister, "Daughters of the Confederacy"; my brothers, as each grew old enough, "Sons of Confederate Veterans"; we who were the youngest, "Children of the Confederacy." Thousands of families showed such a devotion. While yet the old men lived, on whom centered all the fanfare, it was a lusty movement and fervently zealous. I chanced to know it at the peak of its influence.

113

The Making of a Southerner

I remember nothing of the Lost Cause movement before the Confederate reunion of 1903. I may have been drinking it in since the time of my babyhood, but all before that is indistinct, cloudy. In 1903 I was verily baptized in its sentiments. Sooner or later in those three event-packed days we must surely have run the whole marvelous gamut of exuberant emotions. Not the least of the thrill was the Lumpkin part in it—the sense of our complete belonging to this community cavalcade which paraded before us in so many wonderful guises. I was too young myself to have any direct share in it; school children did, but I was just this side of being an old-enough school child. It meant no deprivation, however, for I felt part of it. So absorbed in its planning and execution was our family that we all felt a part, even I, the youngest. I was permitted to see it all, everything, excepting only the balls and receptions to which children did not go but of which they could hear the glowing accounts.

In the air we felt a sense of urgency, as though the chance might never come again to honor the old men. The oratory stressed it: "Ranks of the men who fought beneath the Stars and Bars—the beautiful Southern Cross—are thinner. . . ." "Pathos . . . there cannot be many more reunions for these oaks of the Confederacy. . . ." "Not far from taps . . . for many the ties that bind will soon be severed . . . the high tribute is but their honor due." Hardly a year before, Wade Hampton, Carolina's foremost citizen, had passed away. We must indeed hasten. "Gone is the peerless chieftain, the bravest of them all, the lordly Hampton, that darling *beau sabreur* of whom Father Ryan, the priest-poet of the dead republic, sang. To his stainless memory the reunion is dedicated . . . for him who sleeps under the great oak in Trinity churchyard." I do not remember seeing him ride at the head of the columns, although I may have. Vaguely I can recall the great funeral, the vast throng; and clearly the many times in ensuing years when our family would troop in reverent pilgrimage to his always flower-strewn grave after Sunday services at Trinity.

The grand reunion was held in the month of May. It was the ideal time for it. Earlier would not do, lest we have April showers; later would not have been good, after the summer's heat had set in, and a torrid, sultry spell might mow the old men down like grain

114

under the sickle. If luck held, May was the perfect time, for re-
freshing breezes could almost certainly be counted on; trees and
shrubs were at their deepest green, the great elms and oaks casting
cool shade and not yet filtered over with dust as they would be a
little later, when horse-drawn vehicles, rolling along broad un-
paved avenues, stirred up the hot dry sediment, sifting it onto
everything. And when would flowers ever be so bountiful or varied
again as in May, letting us literally strew them on the path of the
old men and smother our carriages and floats with them in the
parade?

Bustle and business of preparation. What child would not love
it, when everywhere was unbounded enthusiasm and her own
family in the thick of everything? Twenty thousand veterans and
visitors coming—almost more people than in the city itself. Committee meetings every day at the Chamber of Commerce. Indeed,
the Chamber was in the heart of it. Its president was a Confederate
veteran-businessman; its secretary, son of a veteran. Why would
not its every facility be poured into this reunion? Good business,
to be sure. But much more than this, it was good Southern patriotism. A true Southern businessman's heart was in it.

Besides businessmen, all the leading people, and some not so
leading, were drawn into the effort. No, not drawn; they had
poured, all anxious to have a part on this paramount occasion—
institutions, organizations, whole families, including parents, young
people, and children. Entertainment, housing, parades, decora-
tions, meetings—these were men's tasks. Feeding the veterans, in
particular manning two free lunch rooms down town, was the
ladies'. Social events fell to the young people, the Sons of Veterans—
Maxcy Gragg Camp—and the young ladies; they must plan for
balls and receptions, and for the good times of over two hundred
sponsors and maids-of-honor, "bevy of the State's most beautiful
young ladies." Local bands must serve. Local militia—"wearing
uniforms as near like the Confederate butternut as U. S. Arsenals
afford"; students of South Carolina College and the two "female"
colleges; school children, two hundred of them, to strew flowers,
sing in a chorus, execute intricate marches which took hours and
days for training; the Cotillon Club, select dancing society; the
town's "riding set" for the parade; the Metropolitan Club; the local

lodge of Elks; merchants and manufacturers and other businessmen to give their time and money and elaborately decorate their
establishments. Everyone must decorate. Stores had stocked their
shelves. Everyone must go home loaded down with red and white
bunting and Confederate flags.

The day dawned. Tuesday, May 13. A brilliant day. On Monday
had come a heavy, prolonged shower, casting us into gloom. But
we were quickly comforted. It but laid the dust and sent cool
breezes blowing. The paper sang: "Under a sky that was an in-
verted bowl of sapphire . . . in an air that kissed and caressed
them as pleasantly as any zephyr that ever swept across the South-
land, the remnants of the thin gray line mustered into Columbia. . . ."

The moment was here. The pageant unfolded. All the way to
Main Street, every home festooned in bunting and flags, and Main
Street itself, from end to end, red and white bunting, incandescent
lights of white and red. By night these lights, in a child's eyes,
looked like one's dream of fairyland. Confederate flags. They were
everywhere, by the thousands, of every size. People thronging
Main Street carried flags. A few might also have South Carolina's
banner—a palmetto tree and crescent against a field of blue—but
all would have a Confederate flag. Dominating Main Street, at its
head, was the State Capitol building, domed and dignified, granite
steps mounting to its entrance. From window to window was
draped bunting, and spread across its face, a huge Confederate
banner. Across from it, both Opera House and City Hall were
festooned and flag-draped.

Under the shadow of the State House dome on the Capitol
grounds was a huge "bivouac tent"—a circus tent—ninety feet in
diameter, they said. Six hundred veterans would be sheltered
there, overflow from people's homes. Everyone talked of it; pa-
trolled day and night by militia units; army cots provided from the
Armory; only half a block from Convention Hall; information
bureau but a stone's throw; General Hampton's grave a hundred
yards away. Mr. Gantt, Secretary of State, not being satisfied, had
the Negro convicts install a lavatory. General Frost, Adjutant General, pitched some smaller tents like a company street to bring
back "old times." They called it Camp Wade Hampton. Hardly a

yard, inside and outside the bivouac, but was hung in bunting. On its highest pole floated a grand banner—"of course the emblem of the Lost Cause."

All Tuesday veterans and visitors poured in. Every hour broad Main Street grew more crowded. Committees of men on duty at Union Station from daybreak until midnight. Father's stint was four hours in the afternoon, several men under him, all wearing their conspicuous badges (how proud I was): "Ask Me. Entertainment Committee." Helping the hundreds of old men; assigning them quarters; handing them badges: "Veteran," open sesame to everything, free of charge, nothing excluded, the city theirs. Band music all afternoon on the capitol grounds—martial airs—old Southern songs—and *Dixie!* Ever so often, *Dixie!*

How quaint it seems, but not so then—the veterans' free trolley ride. All over the city on the rumbling, bumping trolleys, for two hours, "to their hearts' content," no nickels called for, special trolleys provided. This to keep them occupied until affairs began.

Parades. Two of them. Best of all the "veterans' parade." The old men marching. Not too long a march; just from post office to State House, half a mile. They were getting so old, more should not be expected. How thronged were the sidewalks—thousands of people—and the windows of buildings—people leaning out to cheer and wave Confederate flags. Men doffing their hats so long as the old men were passing, women fluttering their handkerchiefs. School children ahead of them, spreading the streets with a carpet of flowers, lavishly, excitedly. There in a conspicuous carriage, the surviving signers of the Ordinance of Secession! Bands playing march tunes until it seemed one's spine could not stand any more tingles. But then—the Stars and Bars, dipping and floating and— *Dixie!* From end to end along the route, shouting and cheering, always wild shouting and cheering, at the Stars and Bars and *Dixie.* For me too there was the thrill of looking proudly for Father marching with "the Georgians." These were a special contingent, come from Augusta on their own train and given "the place of honor" in the parade, right behind General Carwile, the Commander. "The band of survivors—come from Augusta in their gray jeans . . . with their old muskets . . . to give an exhibition of Hardee's tactics." Everyone was chuckling over the special permis-

117

sion the Georgians asked, to bring the old firearms across the border, telling the Governor, "If fired the old muskets were more dangerous to the shooter than the men aimed at." Wonderful old muskets! Father, particular host to the Georgians—"Col. W. W. Lumpkin, always solicitous for the Georgians, will have charge of their headquarters, and will superintend their arrangements. . . ." And march with them on parade. Also I was looking for my sister. At the end of the long line rode the sponsors and maids-of-honor in carriages. Here also rode the reunion orators.

Hardly less wonderful, on another day, was the "floral parade." "Most beautiful spectacle of the reunion. . . ." One somber note was permitted. Behind the marshals where on other years had ridden a military figure, now there walked an aged Negro, John Johnson, General Hampton's old coachman, ". . . now led by the bridle an unsaddled horse . . . charger of the dead hero." Sponsors and maids-of-honor on splendid floats elaborately decorated as bowers by institutions and businesses. Mounted escort, "ladies and gentlemen of the city's riding set." Carriages of everyone who owned a carriage, swathed in flowers, graced by their owners and by "beautiful young ladies." Even three motor cars, one a "large French one" smothered in white and pink roses. ". . . A series of spectacles . . . parade of flowers with its living buds. . . ."

The meetings. The speeches. Even a child liked to listen, punctuated as they were every few moments with excited handclapping, cheers, stamping of feet, music. And such great men. All were veterans or sons of men in gray: the Chamber of Commerce head; white-haired clergymen pronouncing invocations; Governor Heyward, a veteran; Judge Andrew Crawford, veteran and "silver tongued orator." Most revered of all, Bishop Capers, "warrior-Bishop," by then a pre-eminent religious leader, who at twenty-eight had become a Confederate general, in all eyes saintly, epitome of the South's best. Who there would not feel his Lost Cause blessed when so noble a man could tell them, "We all hold it to be one of the noblest chapters in our history . . ."?

All but one who spoke were veterans or their sons. The one was a daughter. It was the opening night. She was to welcome them—"a daughter of a Confederate." A child would never forget this particular moment. Bands playing a medley of old war tunes. Crowds pushing, for there was not room for all; orchestra and dress circle crammed with old veterans; aisles and entrances packed long before time for opening. The stage—huge to a child's eyes—massed with human figures: great chorus of trained voices waiting their signal; sponsors and maids-of-honor seated tier on tier and trailing from their shoulders broad sashes of office embossed in gold letters. Old soldiers who had been bidden to the stage—generals, colonels, majors, captains, every rank, in spick-and-span gray uniforms. Somewhere among them the slight figure of a young woman.

Roll of drums; blare of trumpets; then the first high, clear notes of *Dixie!* All the gathering surging, scrambling to their feet—clapping, stamping, cheering, singing. In time it ended. It must end from sheer exhaustion. Then Bugler Lightfoot coming forward to sound the sharp notes of the "assembly," and with its dying away, the chorus beginning, and every voice swelling and rolling it forth, the Long-Meter Doxology—"Praise God from whom all blessings flow. . . ."

There were speeches, but they were as nothing to me that opening night. The newspaper said: "The veterans were waiting." So was I waiting. "Their enthusiasm . . . seemed to have been kept in check until Miss Elizabeth Lumpkin, who addressed them last year, was presented. . . ."

> *There is nothing stronger or more splendid on this wide earth than to have borne the sorrow you have borne, than to have endured the pain that you have endured. . . . You young men in whose veins beat the blood of heroes, uncover your heads, for the land in which you live is holy, hallowed by the blood of your fathers, purified by the tears of your mothers. . . . If I could write . . . I would tell how the private fought. . . . He came back and fought poverty, ruin, sometimes degradation for his dear ones at the hands of brutal men. . . . Men of the South, the day when the rebel yell could conquer a host is past . . . the day when you fought . . . is past. . . . Think you the day for all action is past as well?*

It was a long speech, but how could I find it so? "Eloquent . . . finished." So said the accounts. It was true, I knew. "Frequently . . . made to pause because of the cheering. . . ." "Time and again interrupted by thunderous applause. . . ." I joined in, beating my hands together and jumping to my feet like the others to stamp them on the floor.

Even the least of our participation was of moment to me. So for Father's every smallest duty; and Mother's assisting at the veterans' free lunch rooms; and my school-age sister's share in the children's chorus; and seeing them march or ride in the parades. It was so when a thirteen-year-old brother spoke before the old men—"In recognition of his gift of oratory and of devotion to the dead Confederacy . . . General Carwile, amid much enthusiasm, pinned the badge of 'honorary member, U.C.V.' upon the child's patriotic breast." It was so, also for the last night of the reunion.

Speeches must be listened to again. Finally, they were ended, and the closing moments came. Lights were extinguished. We waited while the curtain descended and rose again. Gleaming through the darkness was a bright camp fire with a kettle hanging from a tripod. Around the fire one could see men in bedraggled uniforms. One soldier lounged up to the fire—"Quaint reminder of long ago as he stood in the half light, pipe in mouth, pants tucked into his socks, coatless and collarless." He began to tell a tale of war. More men slipped out and settled down by the fire. ". . . A hushed house as the tale proceeded . . . lights gradually brightened . . . the speaker was recognized . . . Col. W. W. Lumpkin, a soldier of the Confederacy again." After that: bright lights, stacked guns seen in the foreground, tents near by, then stories from other veterans, dear to a child's heart, and to adults' too, apparently. A song begun, joined in by the audience, "We are tenting tonight on the old camp ground," rolling up to the very eaves of the Opera House. Then hilarity, the old soldiers frolicking, young soldiers again, gusts of laughter from the audience urging them on. Quiet again, as a soldier thrummed a banjo and began again to sing, and we to sing with him, one after another, the old Southern ballads, plaintive, nostalgic. On the notes of these the reunion of 1903 "passed away into the land of memories."

2.

CONFEDERATE REUNIONS after all came infrequently. At least it was so for us children. We must wait until it was the turn of our town again to welcome the old men. Moreover, reunions could not do everything. They could be counted upon to arouse our Southern patriotism to a fervid pitch and spur us on to fresh endeavors. When all was said and done, however, something continuing and substantial should be going on if we children were indeed to fulfill the part our people had set their hearts upon.

My father put it this way. He would say of his own children with tender solemnity, "Their mother teaches them their prayers. I teach them to love the Lost Cause." And surely his chosen family function in his eyes ranked but a little lower than the angels. He would say: "Men of the South, let your children hear the old stories of the South; let them hear them by the fireside, in the schoolroom, everywhere, and they will preserve inviolate the sacred honor of the South."

Many other men like Father—men of his station and kind, men who like him still lived in the days of their lost plantations—also said such words, said them continually. For my home, I know it did not rest at words. I know that Father not alone preached these things. In very fact he lived them, at the same time impregnating our lives with some of his sense of strong mission.

Nor could it be without weight that ours was a family in most ways of the old school: Father, head and dominant figure, leader, exemplar, final authority, beyond which was no higher court in family matters; one who, even outside our circle, plainly possessed prestige and recognition for the role he played despite his obvious lack of worldly goods; one through whom we could look back to plantation days, and, who knows, maybe look forward to them. A unique man, in our eyes, perhaps in others', even in some sense unique in appearance: Prince Albert coat, stiff-fronted shirt with studs, wing collar, black tie; a clean shaven man, his thick gray hair worn *en pompadour,* sometimes close-cropped, occasionally long and swept back. It was his wont to call himself the "ugliest man in South Carolina"; he could afford to say it; his audience could afford to laugh; he was standing before them. I might feel a bit dubious, being young, wondering if someone might not believe he meant it, despite the evidence of their eyes. I should have understood. I knew even then that his name as a teller of tales was second only to his name as devotee of the Lost Cause; and how profligate he was with his stories, how inexhaustible his store, how invariable his technique—a ludicrously solemn face, never relaxed even to the end, while his audience, be it around our family table or before a large gathering, was convulsed with laughter. In his manners also Father was ever a goal and example. Where other men were courteous, he made an art of courtesy. Who could show so much deference to a lady, and more than any other, to his wife? Who could bow from the hips with more formality and grace than Father? Who could be more strict in the deference children must show to older people? In how many homes, even in that day, did children immediately rise when their parents entered; and Father with us, when our mother came into the room, even if only to join us with her sewing? These were symbols reminiscent in a hundred other ways of a bygone day. Why would they not reinforce my father's authority—make his person in our eyes the epitome of what he stood for?

To be sure, much was handed on to us incidentally. Family customs seemingly remote from the Lost Cause somehow acquired its flavor. Christmas for us was full of pomp and ceremony, gaiety and gifts; overflowing stockings hanging from the mantel; full, rich carol singing. But also, Christmas was reminiscent of the old days; shouts of "Christmas gif' "; Father's childhood rituals—how well we knew from whence they came; and at the day's end the gathering before the blazing logs, and Father's voice in stories of his boyhood Christmases, until we verily felt ourselves living again on the old place.

Or let there come our annual family fishing trips. Leisure was best for hearing the old tales. Here was a leisure Father rarely could give us. The stories would begin even as he was seated on the kitchen porch, sorting tackle, attaching new hooks and lines and corks to the long reed poles we used, a pole for each of us; they went on to the incomparable sound and smell of frying chicken which my mother's expert hand prepared for our lunch baskets. The next day the tales would be picked up again. We might rise at four to get an early start; we might return long after dark had settled in; no time was too early and none too late. Our hired surrey, or perhaps a plain wagon, might be crowded; the dirt highway bumpy; the distance to mill pond or river take us several hours to traverse. It was no matter, but rather an infinitely pleasant thing to listen to the slow thud-thud of leisurely horses' hoofs and my father's voice telling of the old days.

Of course we heard stories from others, too. There were my mother's friends, some older than she, who had been in their late teens in the sixties. How many times I would sit at their feet and ask for the old tales of the plantation but more especially of the war. With all their dignity and white hair, how gay they sounded, or, if need be, how their eyes would fill with fire. It seems there were many young Yankee officers who would have shown them attentions. But *they* let the invader come to call, however handsome and debonair? *They* fail to give him a "piece of their mind" for his uncalled-for presumption? Besides these were stories unnumbered of silver saved, cotton bales hidden, horses driven to the swamps, and almost always interwoven with the help of faithful slaves. The books I read were in the same nostalgic vein. I luxuriated in the school of Thomas Nelson Page and even in the poorly-printed little volumes of Confederate memoirs then coming off many local presses, so appealing in their covers of patriotic gray. Such titles as *Surrey of Eagle's Nest, Black Rock, Diddy, Dumps and Tot,* cling to my memory.

All this was well enough, but it was not my father's way to leave our lessons to chance. Nor yet indeed my mother's, for she too had her part to play, secondary and supplementary though it might be as befitted the Southern lady and helpmeet. Both Father and Mother guided the books we read, but the daily 'task was my mother's. Then it was we knew the firmness in her gentle hand. Try what devices I would, I could find no relaxation in her strict regime which allotted one hour an afternoon for reading aloud under her tutelage. Sometimes it might be Dickens or Thackeray

or Stevenson. But also and often it was Robert E. Lee and "Stone-
wall" Jackson. Even the incomparable Lee's biography could seem
dull and hampering when it kept a child of nine or ten from play.
Father was ever in search of books to nurture us. One new set, I can
recall, had, to be sure, lives of Lee and Jackson, but to our dismay
also brought a life of Grant. We children were especially indignant
at this affront to our loyalties; I thought it not at all unmannerly
when my sister, but a little older, snatched the Grant book away
to hurl it into the woodshed as ignominious trash. Actually, my
mother quietly rescued it. Books were precious to her in any case.
And Father and Mother, I believe, shared in the generous feeling
of many Southerners towards Grant, speaking warmly of his sol-
dierly treatment of Lee at Appomattox. Similarly, they spoke
tolerantly of Lincoln, saying, "If he had lived, the South never
would have been made to suffer reconstruction."

My father devised one special means for teaching us. The de-
sign for it may have harked back to his own young manhood. He
had been schooled in something very similar under his law teacher
and mentor. Alexander Stephens. Occasionally Mr. Stephens would
have his pupils put aside their law books, to stand before him to
be trained in the art of argument and oratory as it was practiced
in the Old South. Father had heard Mr. Stephens more than once
in the statesman's prime days, he often told us, thrilled to the
strangely piercing voice, the burning eyes, the torrent of eloquent
words. With peculiar zest he would remember his training under
the aged man, who handed his pupils topics of their fiercely controversial day, which they must argue before him or present in ora-
tions, with himself interrupting to criticize mercilessly.

Our "Saturday Night Debating Club" was also a training ground,
although to us it seemed much more an absorbing family game. It
was serious business, but never solemnly serious, nor would any of
us have been left out of it for anything. Even I was allowed a small
part in keeping with my tender years. On most weekdays Father
must be away from home attending to the task of making a living.
Each Saturday night he would announce the topic for the next
meeting, but being away, he left much of our advice in preparation
to Mother. She was entirely qualified to give it, although of course
when Father was there we naturally turned to him. Indeed, Mother

turned us, saying, "Ask your father. He knows about that better than I do." Occasionally the subject for debate would be an old-fashioned query—"Is the pen mightier than the sword?" Usually, and these were our favorites, we argued topics of Southern problems and Southern history. I say "we." The most I ever contributed were a few lines which Mother had taught me. After that I was audience.

We would hurry through Saturday-night supper and dishes. A table would be placed in the parlor, Father seating himself behind it, presiding. On either side were chairs for the debaters. Mother and I comprised the audience, although at the proper time she would retire with Father to assist in judging. All being assembled, Father would rap firmly for order, formally announce the subject, introduce the first speaker on the affirmative, and the game was on.

And what a game! What eloquence from the speakers! What enthusiasm from the "audience"! What strict impartiality from the chairman! And how the plaster walls of our parlor rang with tales of the South's sufferings, exhortations to uphold her honor, recitals of her humanitarian slave regime, denunciation of those who dared to doubt the black man's inferiority, and, ever and always, persuasive logic for her position of "States Rights," and how we must at all times stand solidly together if we would preserve all that the South "stood for."

The judges' decision by no means concluded the evening. Then came a truly serious time. Then Father would assume the role of teacher, addressing himself to each child in turn, pointing up delivery, commenting on gestures; always praising where he felt praise was due; always, whatever he had to say, giving it a kindly turn, so that no one felt deflated; and with it all, taking pains to analyze each child's argument, to show its weak points, and wherein it could have been made stronger.

As we grew old enough we expected to be called upon to play some active part. At eight or nine I could join the "Children of the Confederacy." Under a proud parental eye, I could on my own initiative devise a scheme whereby a short-lived neighborhood club of ours held a "benefit" for the newly-built Old Soldiers' Home, purchasing a rocking chair with the proceeds, and in Father's company going to make a personal presentation.

My special assignment in the old men's behalf was a Confederate veterans' camp in a village several miles distant from our home. ("Camp" was the name given to local organizations of old soldiers.) Father would take me there to recite for them at their regular meetings—a patriotic poem, or a little speech he had written for me.

Nothing, it seems, had prepared me, who was but a child, for the humdrum, everyday labor that went into preserving a Lost Cause. Hence my veterans' camp was frankly disappointing. After the first time I went as a duty, but it held no lure for me. Here were no bands, no thrilling songs, no crowds, no excitement of any kind. Here was a slow, dull ride on a trolley car for Father and me; then a long walk across a river bridge; then a sleepy village. The meeting room was above a store on a drab little main street. Gathered there would be fifteen or twenty aged men, droning away at their business and making decorous use of numerous spittoons strategically placed among them. To be sure, when I said my little poem they were gently appreciative. They clapped their hands, and afterward a few of them would say nice things to Father in their slow-spoken way.

They liked my coming. This was plain, for they prepared me a gift and set a day for me to come to receive their offering. Father responded for me. Never had I seen him more gracious, easy, even eloquent in a quiet way as he thanked the old men and spoke for them the old story of the "Lost Cause." When they turned the gift so that I too could see it, I was filled with dismay. It seems they had secured a photograph of me from Father, and here was an enlargement, a huge thing, even tinted, and set in a broad, ornate gilt frame. They had contributed their nickels and dimes to make me the gift.

We did not hang the portrait once we were home again—so much for my heartfelt relief, for I had truly feared that our unbounded loyalty might carry us to this extreme. But no mirth was permitted, no slightest suggestion of disrespect. Father sternly suppressed incipient signs of it in the children, gravely announcing that the picture was too large to hang in our present home.

For many years Confederate reunions had been sounding the slogan, "Educate the children!" This had come to pass in the schoolrooms of my childhood. They had said: "Confederate soldiers, you have made history! See that it is written! Put into our schools history books true to the South!" They would urge: "The South and the cause of the Confederacy have nothing to fear from the truth, but we do not want our children educated out of a book which tries to throw disgrace on their fathers!" They would exhort: "You cannot depend on the alien historian to do you justice. You cannot depend on Yankee school books to tell of the heroism of Lee. You cannot depend on teachers who have not been inspired with the fervor of your active participation in the grand events of the war to properly teach your children what they should know." "Insist," they would cry, "that the truth should be taught your children in their schools. Insist that in . . . your colleges true Confederate history should be daily impressed upon the upgrowing generation—your sons and your daughters."

They told what had been done, how for two decades after the war, histories were written "by those ignorant of the true conditions." Southern people "resented the histories," yet were "powerless to correct the evil." But then Southern writers appeared—true men—who began to tell the "true history of the war." Confederate veterans' camps throughout the South were but waiting for the signal. Without delay, so it was said, they "used their influence with school boards" all over the South. At long last, Lost Cause leaders could say in 1905, "The most pernicious histories have been banished from the school rooms."

3.

THERE WAS the glamorous, distant past of our heritage. Besides this, there was the living, pulsing present. Hence, it was by no means our business merely to preserve memories. We must keep inviolate a way of life. Let some changes come if they must; our fathers had seen them come to pass: they might grieve, yet could be reconciled. It was inconceivable, however, that any change could be allowed that altered the very present fact of the relation of superior white to inferior Negro. This we came to understand remained for us as it had been for our fathers, the very cornerstone of the South.

It too was sanctified by the Lost Cause. Indeed, more than any other fact of our present, it told us our cause had not been lost, not in its entirety. It had been threatened by our Southern disaster (we would never concede the word "defeat"). No lesson of our history was taught us earlier, and none with greater urgency than the either-or terms in which this was couched: "Either white supremacy or black domination." We learned how Restoration—or the Redemption, as men still said in their more eloquent moments— had meant this as much as anything to our heritage. "The resounding defeat of the forces of darkness. The firm re-establishment of our sacred Southern principles." To be sure, we learned all this long after we had begun to behave according to the practical dictates of the "sacred principle" of white supremacy.

In the case of my particular generation, it seems that we first learned both behavior and belief at a time when those around us were peculiarly disturbed. I was born in 'ninety-seven. This was nearly in the midst of the main Populist years which spanned the 1890's. It is safe to say that no years since reconstruction's overthrow had been filled with so much belligerence and anxiety to Southerners of my people's kind. Even after the crisis passed there remained a tumultuous residue.

In Georgia, when I was born, Tom Watson was still surging along his unorthodox road, leading dissident farmers and workingmen into a separate People's Party. More than this, he had swelled his ranks by calling hitherto disfranchised Negroes—disfranchised not legally but in effect—to join his movement. They too, he told them, were being "fleeced" by greedy corporations; they too were being put upon, all the more so by the forces that kept them from making common cause with their poor white brothers. Nor did it reassure anyone who bitterly opposed Watson's course that he said plainly he had no use for "social equality." He frankly advocated "political equality." That sufficed for the predictions of disaster.

Conservative men would not, if they could prevent it, let overtake them this threat to the white South's solid front. It seems they saw white solidarity as their source of strength; they did not intend to let it be sapped away. All conservatives apparently felt this way, whether politically kin to the postwar New Departure men or Old South men like father. But some of them—not men of father's kind—took a peculiar course of action. (It used to seem peculiar to me when I heard of it in childhood; it was one piece of our history I felt slight shame about, although I would tell myself of the leaders' noble motives.) Some conservatives said, it seems, "If need be, we will fight fire with fire." This could mean, as in Georgia, planters and turpentine men taking their Negro hands to the polls and voting them in gangs. It could mean in some towns holding all-night revelries on election eve, serving barbecue, and beer and whiskey "by the barrel." Then marching the "voters" to the polls to the beat of drums—and the tramp of guards, lest some slip off to seek the fleshpots of the opposing side. For, it is said, the "regulars," the conservative men, were not alone in sinning; but they were "more resourceful," hence enjoyed "more success."

It was something that they were not voting Negroes "on principle." This may have comforted those who saw danger ahead. They did not offer "political equality." They opposed political equality as all men knew. This was frankly an expedient. They knew the People's Party had a large popular following, white and Negro. They countered with their own "popular following," by whatever means they could collect it. They were wise in the ways by which obscure voters could be found who responded to certain practical inducements. That is how the story went, and that they dealt out these several inducements with a generous hand.

At the same time, they seemed not unwilling to let the battle turn on the "race issue." The story goes that violence, bitterness, invective, hatred, became the almost daily portion of those Populist years. Here were white Southerners pitted not against outsiders, but battling among themselves.

The struggle did not relax until the late 1890's when People's Party strength had definitively waned. Then conservative men decided they should call a halt. On every side, white leaders began to speak and write of how wrong it had ever been to have brought the Negro back to the ballot box. He was virtually "eliminated from politics," they said, until this fight began. Now he must be "eliminated" once for all. He was, of course, but not without more struggle and especially not without a storm of speeches and writings and slogans rending the South. The battle had gone on in other Southern states. Everywhere they recited the woes that would befall us: at the worst, Negro domination, at the least, venal politics, if the Negro were not "eliminated." Precisely this was taking place in Georgia in my early childhood. In South Carolina this stage had been gone through shortly before I was born.

One is not guessing in telling of the tenseness of our home in the time of these election battles; how thick the air with talk of "black domination" and "white supremacy"; how sharp the criticism, to put it mildly, of the men responsible for such "unprincipled" actions; how "race" was the undercurrent and, sooner or later, the dominant note so much of the time. Of my parents' children I was the youngest. Our family circle had been in existence more than two decades when I was born. The older children were old enough in plenty to be listeners and even participants in all this exciting talk. We can be certain that from the time I could sit in my high chair at table or play about the parlor floor while others conversed, my ears were saturated with words and phrases at all times intimately familiar to Southern ears and in those years of harsh excitement carrying a special urgency: "white supremacy," "Negro domination," "intermarriage," "social equality," "impudence," "inferiority," "uppitiness," "good darkey," "bad darkey," "keep them in their place." As time passed, I myself would learn to speak these words perhaps with special emphasis, given the times and the tones of others' voices saying them, even before I had the understanding to grasp all they stood for.

Of course I did come to comprehend. When I did, it was a sharp awakening. This was mere chance. Unless we may say it was hardly chance. since my father, although only a boy under slavery, yet had been reared to be a master; which in turn made me but one generation removed from the slave plantation; yet being removed —forty years had interevened—while Father had known Negro slavery at first hand, I knew only a child's dream replica of that alluring. bygone day.

Early in the century our family had gone to live on the outskirts of a small Carolina town some twenty-five miles from Columbia, a place to which we moved presumably for the summer but where we remained for more than a year. When I saw the place from a passing train almost a score of years after, it was sadly disillusioning. Perhaps it had been allowed to run down. Even so, there was no dislodging the pleasant memory I had cherished or the sense in which it realized ever so faintly an unfulfilled family dream.

I loved the house. It was a large brick place, square, and it may have been colonial in style, with wide, airy hallways down the center, and large square rooms. A long ell at back provided more, even larger rooms; the figure "forty feet long" remains in my mind. It was our custom to refer to the upstairs ell as the "ballroom," which it may or may not have been at some time; at any rate on rainy days it was a perfect playroom. The separate kitchen, even though we used in its place the more convenient room partitioned off in the house, gave us a warm sense of plantation authenticity.

Extensive grounds spread around the dwelling, shaded by fine old trees. We found a fenced-in vegetable garden, too huge for our family needs, which we planted half in cotton. Our generous pasture lay beyond, down the pinewoods slope and spreading away to how many acres I could not guess, so wide seemed its pleasant spaces to city children. Here was all the room our hearts could ask, for mountain climbing up and down the deep red gullies; or playing Indian in the woods; or hunting the nests of our recalcitrant far-flying guinea hens; or hurtling down the slope, thickly carpeted in pine needles, on sleds made at home of barrel staves.

Our place was located in an old part of town antedating the railroad but now bounded on one side by the tracks running parallel to our sidewalk. A few other houses stood on either side of us, wooden frame structures, less pretentious than ours. In one of them lived the sheriff of the county.

I have no recollection of the man. Possibly I rarely saw him. Certainly at my age I grasped little of what a sheriff was, except vaguely to connect him with the jail. In any small town a child would see the jail with its barred windows and usually the face of a Negro looking out. I knew the sheriff lived down the street in a house that we children held in some awe.

One summer morning I had gone aimlessly out into the yard before breakfast. In the kitchen breakfast-preparation had been stirring as I passed. Of a sudden in the house there was bedlam—

sounds to make my heart pound and my hair prickle at the roots. Calls and screams were interspersed with blow upon blow. Soon enough I knew someone was getting a fearful beating, and I knew full well it was not one of us: when we children were punished, it might be corporal, but it was an occasion of some dignity for all parties concerned. Carefully keeping my distance, I edged over so that I could gaze in through the kitchen window. I could see enough. Our little black cook, a woman small in stature though full grown, was receiving a severe thrashing. I could see her writhing under the blows of a descending stick wielded by the white master of the house. I could see her face distorted with fear and agony and his with stern rage. I could see her twisting and turning as she tried to free herself from his firm grasp. I could hear her screams, as I was certain they could be heard for blocks, "Mister Sheriff! Mister Sheriff! He's killing me! Help!" Having seen and heard, I chose the better part of stuffing my fists in my ears and creeping away on trembling legs.

The thrashing of the cook was not talked about, not around me at least. Nothing was said in the family, although a strained atmosphere was present all day—a tension one came to expect whenever slight incidents of race-conflict occurred. The neighbors said nothing. Although I waited with considerable trepidation—how unnecessarily I could not know—nothing was heard from the sheriff. To my hesitant question, "What had the cook done?" I was told simply that she had been very "impudent" to her mistress; she had "answered her back."

It was not the custom for Southern white gentlemen to thrash their cooks, not by the early 1900's. But it was not heinous. We did not think so. It had once been right not so many years before. Apparently it still could be. Given sufficient provocation, it might be argued: and what recourse did a white man have? All would have assumed, and no doubt did on this occasion, that the provocation on the Negro cook's part had been very great. Few Negro sins were more reprehensible in our Southern eyes than "impudence." Small child though I was, I had learned this fact. I knew "impudence" was intolerable. In this sense I had no qualms about what I had witnessed. But in another sense I did have, and this disturbed me. Naturally I had no explanation for these mixed feelings. I could merely try to forget the thing—a child wishing to feel at one with her surroundings.

We may assume this about it. It disturbed me because I saw it. If it had been remote, if I had merely heard it as a story as one did hear of similar acts toward Negroes in my childhood, if it had thus been completely removed from all sight and sound, surely I could have felt quite pleasantly *en rapport*.

In any event, this much I know. The inevitable had happened, and what is bound to come to a Southern child chanced to come to me this way. Thereafter, I was fully aware of myself as a white, and of Negroes as Negroes. Thenceforth, I began to be self-conscious about the many signs and symbols of my race position that had been battering against my consciousness since virtual infancy.

I found them countless in number. As soon as I could read, I would carefully spell out the notices in public places. I wished to be certain we were where we ought to be. Our station waiting rooms—"For White." Our railroad coaches—"For White." There was no true occasion for a child's anxiety lest we make a mistake. It was all so plainly marked. (Said the law, it seems, ". . . in letters at least two inches high.") Trains were plain sailing. One knew the "For Colored" coach would be up next the engine, and usually but half a car, with baggage the other half. Theaters were no problem. Negroes rarely went, and in any case "their place" was only a nook railed off far up in the "buzzard's roost." Street cars were more troublesome. Here too were the signs—"White" at the forward end, "Colored" at the rear. But no distinct dividing line, no wall or rail between. How many seats we occupied depended upon our needs. Sometimes conductors must come and shift things around in the twilight zone between. If whites were standing and Negroes not, it may be the latter were told to give up their seats. Conductors were the authority. They might handle the delicate rearrangement quietly by just a tap on the shoulder and a thumb pointing back—this to a Negro; but they might be surly or even belligerent, speak in a loud rough voice so all could hear—"Move back." A little white girl would rather stand, however much she knew it was her right to be seated in place of Negroes, than have this loud-voiced notoriety; and also, I think—it is ever so faint a memory—anything rather than have a fleeting glimpse of the still, dark faces in the rear of the car, which seemed to stare so expressionlessly into space.

We knew the streets were the white man's wherever he chose to walk; that a Negro who moved out into the gutter to let us pass was in our eyes a "good darkey." I could have been hardly more than eight when a little Negro girl of our age, passing a friend and me, showed a disposition to take her half of the sidewalk. We did not give ground—we were whites! Her arm brushed against my companion's. She turned on the Negro child furiously. "Move over there, you dirty black nigger!" I know why this recollection stayed with me while others did not. It outraged us so because this particular colored child did not shrink or run, but flared back at us with a stinging retort, remaining dead in her tracks, defying us, and we had no choice left us but to move on.

Less-than-proper humility from Negroes especially troubled our white consciousness. It was a danger signal and would never occur, we said, were it not for wrong policies. Nine times out of ten we linked it with education. Education was wrong. It made Negroes ambitious, impudent, wishing to "rise out of their place," we said. It was bound to result in intolerable situations.

I knew this was so. I myself had met it face to face. For example, when on Sunday mornings we would run into the line of college youths from Allen University, the Negro institution in our town. We were going to church. So were they. As was the custom for college boys and girls in my childhood, they walked to church in a line. We must cross the street they traversed on their way to church. We did not always meet them, but often we did, and there was always the possibility. What should we do? How comport ourselves? We had no precedent, save that of claiming our right to walk anywhere and Negroes to step aside. But a whole line step aside for a family group, white though it was, or hold up its march, or break its ranks? Then should we walk through it, or should we wait? We might perhaps have said politely, "Excuse me, please. May I pass?" (Of course, if they had been white students going to church. . . .) It would be awkward merely to push through or try to. Suppose they did not make room. Being educated they might be "uppity"; it would be humiliating to let an incident occur; and there was the decorum due a Sunday morning. Must we then do that most galling thing, stand waiting in our places while "darkies" passed? It did not soothe us, but just the contrary, that they were nicely dressed, for it might mean, so we said, that they thought themselves as "good" as whites; or that they were "educated," they and their professors who accompanied them; much more than clothes, this could spell aspirations not encompassed in our beliefs about their "rightful place."

Often we spoke of the sin it would be to eat with a Negro. Next to "intermarriage" this was a most appalling thought. It was an unthinkable act of "social equality." To say the words, "eat with a Negro," stirred us disagreeably. In a sense, of course, it was no problem. How could it arise in our protected lives, and surrounded as we were by our racial barriers? It did, vicariously. We suspected Northerners of doing it upon occasion, and shuddered at the thought. We were sure Yankee teachers in Southern Negro institutions were guilty of the sin. That Republicans flaunted it was glaringly confirmed when one day our newspapers were filled with shocked accounts of President Theodore Roosevelt's entertainment of Dr. Booker T. Washington at luncheon in the White House. It was too much—this unpardonable "insult to the South" from the very seat of our national government, this fomenting in high places of "social equality." We were all aroused, on the streets, in our homes, at recess at school. We children talked of it excitedly, echoing the harshly indignant words and tones.

We often spoke of the peculiar inborn traits of this so peculiar race. For instance, the Negro's "thieving propensities." White men stole too, but not "as a race." We verily believed that a Negro could not help but steal. So we acted accordingly. We must lock up our valuables. We children should never leave the key in the food pantry door, but turn it and put it back in its hiding place. Let something be missing; we suspected the cook, unless it was found; maybe even then, for she could have "got scared" and returned it. It was not serious with us; just a disability of the race, we said, that only we Southerners understood and took charitably. Of course in capacity they were different. This was the essence of our sense of difference—we superior, they inferior. But not merely that in their mental development none could ever go beyond say a child of ten or twelve (unless "they had white blood in them, of course"); they were qualitatively different, somehow, though we as children could not have explained wherein. We just used phrases such as "innately irresponsible," "love of finery," "not to be trusted," "slovenly," and a dozen more. To be sure, we would apply to special individuals contradictory attributes. But this made no difficulty about generalization. The innate traits, we said, applied to the race. To any doubting Thomases from the outside we had our irrefutable answer: "After all, we Southerners alone know the Negro."

At the club-forming age we children had a Ku Klux Klan. It was natural to do it, offspring of our warm Southern patriotism. We were happy in it for the aid and blessing it won from our adults. Our costumes, while made from worn-out sheets, were yet cut to pattern with help at home; they had fitted hoods, also, with tall peaks, and emblazoned across the front of the robes were red cheesecloth crosses. Constitution, by-laws, and ritual were something out of the ordinary. They were written, not on paper, but transcribed, as we supposed the original had been, on a long cloth scroll, at the top of which was a bright red cross. Our elders helped us write the ritual and rules and, true or not, we firmly believed that our laws and oaths were in some sense an echo from the bygone order.

It was certainly a game and fascinating as such. But it was much more besides. Its ritual, rolling off our tongues with much happy gusto, was frequently interlarded with warm exhortations to white supremacy. We held our meetings in the greatest secrecy—so we pretended—in a friend's basement near our home (our counterpart of a deep, silent forest around the hour of midnight on a moonless night). A chief topic of business when ceremonies had ended was the planning of pretended punitive expeditions against mythical recalcitrant Negroes. And while in one sense it never was real, in another it went far beyond pretense. We vented our feelings. We felt glow in us an indignant antagonism. These were real. We felt patriotic; so was this real—this warm, pulsing feeling of Southern loyalty. We told of our Cause and our Southern ideals which we were preserving. It was truly a serious game, and in a sense we were serious children bent on our ideals. We liked our clubs to have this idealistic side. Witness the fact that the club to follow our

Ku Klux Klan was a "Knights of the Round Table," although it was short-lived; it broke up over sharp competition for the post of Sir Galahad.

Times would come when even we children must uphold our beliefs in a serious public way. We rejoiced to do it. It made us feel very worth while. So with me once in the sixth grade in school. Our room was divided—"Busy Bees" on one side, "Wise Owls" on the other. We were to have a debate. It was an exceedingly strange query for a Southern schoolroom: "Are Negroes Equal to White People?" It never would have been proposed if we had not had in the room a little blond Northern boy. He being a Yankee, he could with impunity be asked to serve as the straw man for the rest of us to knock down. Patently, his own side of the room could not support him, so it was all of us against one. It was a strange debate. There were just the two of us—the little Yankee boy and I who were actual participants. My debate I can see now, carefully written down in my own handwriting from the copy we had worked on with so much earnestness in my family circle. His came first— one can guess our scorn at the arguments that flowed from his Yankee home. Then I argued mine. Of course I told of our history and how the South had been saved by the courage of our fathers— we always told this. Probably I told of the Invisible Empire—we often did. Obviously, I recited all the arguments we had for Negro inferiority, and that this was why he must never be allowed to "rise out of his place." My peroration comes back to me in so many words, and how I advanced it with resounding fervor amidst a burst of applause from all the children in the room but my opponent: ". . . and the Bible says that they shall be hewers of wood and drawers of water forever!"

4.

WE DID NOT believe the South to be safe in a final sense. We had restored our white supremacy after reconstruction. We had weathered the storms of the nineties and put the Negro voter "back in his place." We had done this throughout the South by the time of my childhood. Some of this we children understood, some not. In any case our fathers did.

But all was not well. This we most certainly understood. For one thing, a demand was rising from numerous quarters, some of them Southern, to give the Negro more education, to improve Negro schools. This boded very ill as some Southerners saw it. We were of this number. It seemed hardly rational to our minds to suppose that an educated Negro could be "kept in his place," the place we considered his race designed for. Yet it must be so for the South to be safe.

In our family we saw one main safeguard against undue encroachments on our white preserves. In the long run, political control by "safe men" spelled the power to keep our Southern situation well in hand. The uncertain quantity here was "safe men." We of the Old-South way of thinking were by no means sanguine of the turn political affairs had been taking since the surrender in 'sixty-five.

An outsider following the course of those events might have been puzzled to understand what troubled us. To all appearances —save perhaps for the use of Negro votes in the 'nineties—the new politicians in Southern legislatures and those who went to the Congress had accomplished as much as judicial obstacles permitted. Whenever the courts let down the bars a little by new interpretations, our political leaders grasped at the opportunity and made the most of it.

It had taken several decades to discover all the needed devices. It had taken astute legal minds to find a phrase such as "equal and separate" for getting our segregation laws by. Perhaps they did not find it sooner because of the term "equal"; they could bring themselves to use it only after the unequal arrangements on trains and street cars, in schools, in public places, on chain gangs, and in prisons, had been firmly established in common practice. Once that was done they could know with complaisance what a gargantuan task it would be if any ever took a mind to try to unscramble the established complex arrangements of inequality.

In any event, they had learned that "equal" could be virtually ignored and, by so much, that "separate" was the key to this part of our problem. To keep the races separate, the inferior from the superior, was the first prime requisite for keeping the Negro "in his place." They went about doing this to the last jot and tittle. Even convicted white criminals on chain gangs must not be chained to their convicted Negro fellows—this would be to insult their whitehood. We can see how very stern was the temper of our late-nineteenth-century Southern legislators.

To prevent any possible modification of this separateness and to assure the white South against sporadic attempts by Negroes to "rise out of their place," legal disfranchisement was from the first sought after. Any white could see that the inferior race should be allowed no political voice. Our people believed it when they first attempted to rule on the matter after the surrender. They believed it with a fierce, tumultuous emotion after the dark days of reconstruction. Men went on believing it and trying to put their beliefs into practice. For a time constitutional obstacles were too much for them. The loopholes they thought they had found were several times plugged up.

Plainly, the new political leaders of the seventies and eighties made the attempt. They were legally frustrated. But in most places they did accomplish *ipso facto* disfranchisement. This was done by the force of custom or, to put it another way, by the force of white influence in the localities. For the most part Negroes ceased to attempt to go to the polls in the seventies and eighties. This may have lulled white senses into a false security. They were rudely enough awakened by the events of the nineties. Thereafter, it became a first concern of white Southern leaders to leave no step untaken until this problem had been settled.

They were able to settle it. Perhaps their sense of urgent necessity stirred Southern men to new inventiveness. Perhaps also more mellow-minded men had meanwhile taken the places of those who in post-Civil War years had taken a stricter view of the nation's fundamental law. Be that as it may, devices were found. They accomplished their purpose with almost startling success.

There was no trifling now with one cure-all for this most threatening ill. The laws provided were like a series of sieves through which men could be successively sifted. If one failed to catch all the Negro voters and hold them away from the polls, there was another that would hold back more, and still another and another until hardly a trickle could get through.

Many men were too poor to pay a voter's poll tax. Most Negroes were. Three dollars to a sharecropper or unskilled laborer was not a sum to be cast on the waters in place of bread. But suppose some tried to pay it who could afford the sum? By this time very few Republican voters were left in the South. This was so once the Negro vote was eliminated. The time when men were elected to office was in the Democratic primary. Democratic Parties ruled: no Negro may vote. This was a major practical eliminator. (It is true that South Carolina said a Negro could vote if he could find ten Democrats to sign a paper saying he had voted for Wade Hampton in 'seventy-six.) But some Negroes might be just perverse enough to wish to vote anyhow. Provision was made for property tests, and education tests. The latter were the heart of the disfranchisement provisions. In this final sifting it was left to the local registrar to decide when a man was sufficiently "educated." If a white farmer stepped forward, he could be nearly illiterate, even entirely so, and still pass. The registrar would know a good question to ask white Farmer Smith. If it were a Negro, then it was up to the registrar: the man could be asked to explain some obscure point of law, or even to recite an obscure quotation. Few would have the sardonic wit of a Negro college professor in recent times, who, in response to the demand to recite the Preamble of the State Constitution, began sonorously, "Fourscore and seven years ago our fathers brought forth on this continent a new nation, conceived in liberty, and dedicated to the proposition that all men are created equal. Now we are engaged. . . ." Nor did he stop until he came to the end, ". . . and that government of the people, by the people, for the people, shall not perish from the earth." At which the registrar exclaimed with unconcealed astonishment, "By G—, he did it!" If a Negro answered one question, another could be asked. In any event, it was for the registrar to decide what was satisfactory. Those who framed this measure could know that their solution was as simple as that.

At the time these laws were passed, some white men had feared that they were being aimed at too. Old Populists predicted that their kind would suffer—poor white men, they said, would be "eliminated" also, especially by the poll tax. But Southern leaders vowed that this was not their intention—naturally they were anxious to get the laws through and not antagonize this potential white electorate. They put the assurance into their slogans. It was so in Georgia. Around 1906 a man named Hoke Smith was running for governor. By this time Tom Watson had come to rue the day when he called Negro farmers to swell his coalition. He had now decided to swing his still-large following behind the candidacy of the man, Hoke Smith. This was Smith's slogan, blazoned over the State: "Elimination of the Negro from Politics . . . by Legal and Constitutional Methods . . . Without Disfranchising the White Man."

We did not realize it at the time, but after the disfranchising laws, even the white vote grew smaller and smaller. If a contest were bitter, some candidates' friends seemed able to find ways of helping poor white men pay up delinquent poll taxes. This was occasional. By the time I was eight or nine years of age, men were speaking wonderingly of the way politics were in the doldrums; of how voters failed to come to the polls; and how "ignorant" men showed an unintelligent indifference to the noble calling of citizenship.

Obviously, Old South men could hardly complain about the new leaders' accomplishments for white supremacy. What disturbed their minds was something else about these men, something they apparently feared could lead to other dire consequences.

Back in Georgia Father had seen the post-Civil War shift from plantation-belt leaders to a new type entirely. These were called "New Directionists," or "New Departure" Democrats. (Some had a way of saying "New Bourbons," meaning they were successors of the so-called "Old Bourbons" of ante-bellum times. But of course we would never have described ourselves in such derogatory terms.) In Georgia Father had seen these new business-minded men, whose interests lay, not in the plantation country, but in railroad promotion, manufactures, mines, and banks, come to dominate the political scene. Even in South Carolina, a less industrialized state, the same trend had been seen.

Meantime, he had also seen the 'eighties and 'nineties give rise to yet another type of leader, the new agrarian. In Georgia, Tom Watson had even led such dissidents as these into his separate

141

People's Party. In South Carolina, Ben Tillman, in his ascendancy, had rejected this separate course; in doing so he became the powerful agrarian leader of the state's Democracy. Populist tendencies were worsted, to be sure. The Negro was at last legally disfranchised. The Democratic Party as sole arbiter of political life was firmly established as a solid entity. This should have brought reassurance—perhaps.

The new men in Southern affairs apparently began to feel free again to let their interests clash. It was this open clashing of interests among Southern white leaders that so much troubled men of Father's kind.

They seemed to think it had happened only since the surrender. Perhaps their memories of ante-bellum times had faded; or perhaps, having come of those who wielded the power, they had forgotten the opposition's futile attempts. There had come talk of unity on the heels of the 'nineties. "Solid South" was on the lips of leaders everywhere. But then with hardly any lapse of time, the struggle was renewed. We believed it did not have to be this way. We believed it was not something about the South that bred this struggle, but merely that the wrong kind of men were entering politics. They climbed into office by appeals to "special interests," when they should be putting "the South" above all. This made us distrust them.

Some were business-minded and spoke accordingly; others declared themselves "the farmer's" friend; some pitted "the poor" against "the rich," the "people" against the "corporate interests." It was for these last-named men that we usually reserved the term, "demagogue."

We learned to think of the "demagogues" as base men. We suspected them, I think, of much more interest in corralling votes than in the "sacred Southern principles" about which they shouted. We especially distrusted those who would condemn "Negro domination" in one breath and attack "the old aristocracy" in the next; or hail the "rights of the poor man" while they vowed for strict adherence to "States' Rights."

The new business politicians were a different type. Some came from planter forebears. Even "self-made" men could have good manners and were usually careful to identify themselves with old traditions. All these men, however, pushed their "interests." I think Father would have said they were too preoccupied with "getting ahead." He could admire it—and we learned from him—when such men regarded their factory "hands" as personal charges in whom they took a kindly paternal interest. This was much as masters had done for their slave charges—Father's kind of master—back in the good ante-bellum days. Of course these factory hands were white men. Then at least they should be treated as well as slaves had been. Hence, it troubled him when mills were closed down, even if times were hard, without any provision on the owner's part for the needy. It especially deeply offended him when he saw a good friend and old Confederate comrade, who had long and loyally served such owners as superintendent or in some other salaried position, suddenly turned out on the world because he was "too old" and efficiency required a change. It is certain he did not feel at home with the firm insistence that "business is business" and the notion that a man could not stand on too much ceremony if he would win out under the fierce competition that the new South had brought.

Even the new agrarians were unlike those who in a bygone day had also come out of the plantation country. These new men frankly appealed to farmer-interests. Apparently they felt compelled to make their appeal to small as well as large-scale farmers, since small white farmers were a not inconsiderable proportion of the voting electorate in these Deep South states. Nor did they usually in this new day couch their statesmanship in that over-all term, "the South," on the supposition that what was good for one was good for all, they being the spokesmen.

It would appear that my father had a special picture in his head of what a "Southern statesmen" and "public servant" should be. I am sure he thought that such men as he pictured had actually lived and breathed and spoken and served in his boyhood. I know I thought so. It is to be assumed that he thought the ante-bellum men whom he put in this category were well above "special interests." After all, he had been a long while removed from an intimate pecuniary relation to the plantation. His life had not for years rested directly on its prosperity.

Apparently, Father assumed that men such as his kind pictured should and could, even in our day, serve the South and be our bulwark against all manner of dangerous tendencies. At least he must have hoped so, as we certainly did, when he came forward to make the test after almost a lifetime's absence from political campaigns. In 1908—I was then nearly eleven years of age—he entered the race for United States Senator. Six contenders were already in the field. Seven was a goodly number to be running for office even in a Southern primary.

We saw my father wage his campaign according to his precepts. We saw how meticulous he was in his conduct; how carefully he observed his code of "Southern gentleman"; how often he would say of his fellow candidates, "They are all my friends"—hence he would speak ill of none of them. We saw in what terms he framed the issues—none of this divisiveness for him; so much so the newspapers would say a little plaintively, "He is hard to place." He was for all the South. So said his platform: "For the great farming interest of the State for I was born and raised on a farm . . ."; ". . . for railroad employees, for I have been one . . ."; "for the commercial interest of our land, for when those interests prosper we all prosper . . ."; ". . . for the labor interest and the laboring man. . . ." He made a bow now and then to the issues of the times, distinctively Southern issues: "Remove the tariff"; "Throttle the trusts." However, we could see that the main burden of his words was the burden on his mind—"made his usual patriotic speech." His speeches were this more than anything: the Confederate soldier, noble Southern womanhood, the desolation of the past from which the State had risen by the bravery of Southern men. We could see the papers often speak of his "eloquence" and how he "captured the audience with the spell of his oratory" around the themes we knew so well.

We soon saw something else. Father was not a "leading" contender in the public mind, not if the press was indicative. The leading men were of a different kind. They epitomized what we had learned to think was wrong with our Southern affairs. They represented "interests," avowedly so. We could not mistake it.

We saw a businessman type. Except that he was not a "self-made" man, none could have been more so. Rhett was his name. He was of an old family and planter stock. He was mayor of

Charleston. But first and last he was now a businessman with large interests, as everyone knew, in railroads, banks, cotton mills, fertilizer concerns. He was a highly respected man. The papers were warm in his praise—a very annoying fact to some of the lesser candidates. The press praised him for saying candidly what he was and what he sought: ". . . a plain businessman who would carry business methods into the service of the people . . ."; "The question before the people . . . now is an industrial struggle"; "We want more business capacity and less political oratory in the senate."

We saw two avowed agrarians. They called themselves farmers, and at least were from the farming country. One, named Evans, was an ex-governor. He had come of the older, Tillman school; he spoke of "his advocacy of measures of the 'nineties which some called anarchical and populistic at the time" who now supported them. He had been a long time in politics, hence, said the papers, he had "an organization." The other farmer-candidate was E. D. Smith, he who later came to be known by the familiar "Cotton Ed." In this campaign we heard him ring the changes on his major theme, "cotton," and base his main claim for preferment on what he had done for the "cotton farmer." (It would seem candidates were wary men; they did not use the term "plantation," it appears; even Father spoke of having been born on a "farm.")

The only figure lacking in this contest was a "demagogue"; one who attacked his fellows if they were "rich" men, or "aristocrats," or in the "service of the corporations," though now and then faint echoes of these appeals could be heard.

It little mattered. The case was clear without it. It furnished proof positive of our lugubrious expectations. "The People" were being pitted, one group and section against another. Then how indeed could the South be safe?

We were filled with even deeper foreboding by another feature of this campaign. In it a leading candidate was accused of Southern disloyalty. It need not be true to disturb us greatly. As it turned out the man was entirely vindicated, as even his opponents conceded. But the accusations were so graphic, and the man against whom they were leveled so respected a man, indeed, the businessman, whose forbears had been planters, who himself was a gentleman. Of course into this entered a child's naïveté. Our elders could understand how such things could happen with no reflection upon the accused; they could be wise in the ways of our Southern political battles and the use to which explosive words had very often been put.

To us, it shook our faith in the men who wished to lead us, who heard it claimed that this important man had "helped" get a Negro, Dr. W. D. Crum, appointed to the post of Collector of the Port of Charleston by President Theodore Roosevelt; that a "mysterious letter" existed which "proved" the contention; that he was a "Republican at heart"; that when Secretary of War Taft came to visit Charleston, Mayor Rhett had met him at the railroad station in a "delegation of prominent citizens" among whom was "Collector of the Port Crum"; that in a party which had conducted the Secretary of War to a naval vessel in the harbor had been "Mayor Rhett . . . and Collector Crum. . . ." And that the accusers would say, the man had "bureaus and headquarters comparable only to Republican campaigns . . ."; or as the main accuser put it, "I wish to keep a senatorial toga from this State from being packed in the elephant's trunk!"

Perhaps we should have noticed, and been reassured, that the leading candidates took no stock in this. They refrained from joining the hue and cry. Father said nothing. The very most these men did when the issue grew hottest was reiterate their own Southern loyalty. Candidate Smith would "denounce the fourteenth and fifteenth amendments as the greatest crime of the century." His supporters would take pains to tell what a tower of strength Smith had been in saving his district from a Negro postmaster. Father "recounted the struggle of Reconstruction and affirmed white supremacy . . ." not once but many times. But this was all.

Also, Rhett himself denied the charges time and again, asserting that he was a loyal Democrat and had always been; that he had "fought Crum from the time I first heard of his appointment"; that he had just recently told an Ohio audience, "The South would always maintain white supremacy." In the end, moreover, he punctured the charges thoroughly by reading to the audience in his own home city communications from three of the State's leading Democrats. They had seen the "mysterious letter" on which the charges had been built. They testified that Mr. Rhett had protested vigorously against the appointment of Collector Crum, and that nothing about it hinted that Mr. Rhett was Republican. They even told why he could not make his letter public. "Allusions are in it of a very personal character to individuals (a lady, for instance) which, we think, it would form a breach of propriety on your part to publish." So here was an act of a chivalrous Southern gentleman. We knew his own people gave the man unquestioning support: "Businessmen of Charleston who are not usually demonstrative sprang to their feet and gave themselves up to cheering. . . ."

All should have been well that ended so well—so far as white supremacy was concerned. We could not doubt that all were agreed, every single candidate, and also the press, and presumably the voters, about the paramount importance of white supremacy.

Something still was wrong. Perhaps we felt that here was a demonstration that our way, as we had learned it, did not work. We could not mistake the eloquent fact that Father nearly touched bottom on the list when the votes were counted. Candidate E. D. Smith had won, beginning a term which would last for many long years.

We may also have sensed that more change had come to our Southern world than we had been prepared for, and this despite the labor of Lost Cause men. This much is certain: we were filled with doubts; we were very unsure. We supposed we felt unsure with the type of public men we had and the course they were taking for the safety of the South and her sacred institutions.

BOOK FOUR

Sojourn in the Sand Hills

1.

AFTER LONG YEARS of waiting, our family moved to a farm. None of us called the place Father had selected "plantation." I was almost twelve by then and could understand how its two hundred acres precluded such a term. I did not realize, however, until we had moved there that it was in poor farming country. Some sections of Richland County had fine lands and prosperous places, but we were not moving to one.

Our place was not in the real Sand Hills. I should not have called it by that term. But it came to be the way I thought of it. It did lie very close to this desolate area, so much so that one could almost believe that the winds of heaven had drifted some of the heavy sand across the border line into our woods and fields—and some of the inhabitants, too, I was ready to believe after we lived there awhile. With their pasty faces, scrawny necks, angular ill-nourished frames, straw-like hair, they seemed to me no different from the real "sand-hillers."

Ours was the "big farm" of the countryside, our house by far the largest although it was plain and simple. Ours had the largest barns and outbuildings. Later, another farmhouse came to rival ours, but not in appearance and certainly not in standing. (The man was a poor farmer who became well-to-do by acquiring land from the neighbors who were in debt to him—at least so men said—and hence had gained a reputation for harshness and tight-fisted meanness and little compassion for those who worked in his fields.) Most of the white farmers in our immediate vicinity were owners, but in name only; the heavy mortgages they carried were ever a threat to their tenure. Most had few acres and very poor little dwellings. A few more were renters, and some were croppers who had nothing, not even a mule or plow. Most of the croppers were Negroes. It seems that a great many Negroes lived all around us. One would never have guessed it, so scattered were they off in their tiny shacks on the sandy side roads, except perhaps when they crowded into their little church on Sundays or came down late Saturday afternoons to watch the trains go through.

We had one "neighbor." We had other neighbors, too, if reticent farmers living near us in dwellings of two or three rooms could be counted. Our real neighbor was a family much more nearly like ourselves. They lived in a comfortable small home across from the railroad station, owned a number of books, subscribed to a daily paper, sent their boy and girls to state colleges, and even had in their yard a tennis court of sorts.

In some sense the father of this family was ruler of the country-side, a kind of super-boss over all its life. Negroes and white men both referred to him as "the boss." He had as many means of livelihood as there were functions to perform: ticket agent for the railroad; telegraph agent for that company; postmaster for the government, which meant not alone sorting and distributing mail, but hanging up the sacks on the wooden arm for speeding trains to pick up, and gathering in the sacks from where they had been flung from the moving trains. He was manager of the village's one industry, a sprawling brick yard. It may be he was local agent for fertilizer, grain, and seed companies. I do not know how many sidelines he had. Besides these things he was the local magistrate, in his person the community's "law and order." The one occupation he did not engage in was the staple occupation of the area, farming. In keeping with his position, though he might go without his coat, he always appeared in a collar and tie. All his functions he performed from one small office shack, perhaps ten by twenty feet, which stood across the tracks from his home at the entrance to the brickyard. There we went for our mail, and sent our tele-grams, and bought our tickets to town; there went those seeking justice; there went the laborers in the brickyard—when it was run-ning—to get their wages. I know he prospered, for before we moved away he had bought an automobile, a Reo touring car. It was not a time when many owned touring cars. He was very chary about using it, treating it as some fragile thing, as well he might. But it was joy unbounded when occasionally we were invited to ride to town, speeding along, incredibly, at sometimes twenty miles an hour.

The "boss" and his family were very hospitable people. We exchanged calls frequently. The children became our companions. Perhaps they felt the need of "neighbors" almost as much as we city children did, who formerly had been used to so many.

Meanwhile, we began immediately to farm. Father hired help for plowing. We got a farmer to furnish a second team. It was decided which fields would go into cotton, which into corn and sweet potatoes. Quantities of fertilizer had been ordered and stored in the barns even before we were settled. The soil in our vegetable garden was prepared. We had a cow and pigs and chickens. All seemed settled.

However, only three months after we reached our new home, Father, while away on a trip, was taken ill and a few days later died. For the time being we could but continue on the farm. One could not in a moment make satisfactory disposition of a place just purchased, or its supplies and equipment, or its fields, some of which were already planted. We were city-bred. None of us knew any farming. But we had no real alternative.

Our field work, of course, was done by Negroes. Many Negroes, for miles around, sooner or later worked on our place. We had to have numbers of people at peak farm seasons for chopping or picking cotton. We tried to have help about the house, a woman to do heavy work at least; but none was trained to it, so we changed often, as we did our washerwomen.

When we needed field hands, my brother would hitch up the buggy or put the saddle on Nelly. If he went in the buggy, I would often go with him just for something to do. One cluster of Negro cabins was on the outskirts of the village. Here we usually took our washing to be done. Here we sometimes looked for laborers. Most of the Negro men in the village worked in the brickyard when it was running, though always they were employed irregularly, so that one could occasionally find hands there.

Most of our field hands came from remote cabins over on the back roads so heavy with sand we must walk our horse in driving.

153

Here and there would be a shack set down in a field of plowed land or broom sage. I came to know these cabins well by frequent calls, though it must be said they were so similar in appearance it was difficult to remember which belonged to what family. Just one room, usually, the timbers hardly holding together, the interior easy to see through the sagging front door. One could take one glance inside and see all there was to see—a bed, or maybe two, crowding the small space, a table and chair or so, and the frying pan and kettle on the hearth of a smoky fireplace where cooking was done. In some the walls would be pasted over with newspapers, perhaps merely to make them more snug in winter, perhaps for decoration; who could say? If the man were not at home we would dicker with the woman, for herself and the children to come to "chop" or pick. If no one were home we would bewail our luck and drive on to another cabin.

On such a trip we once discovered Money. Or, more properly speaking, Money found us. For from that time forth he came to our place constantly and with no little adroitness established himself as our little man-of-all-chores. Money was his real name, his mother told us, given him in the high hope it might bring him good luck. And well he needed it. His father was a sharecropper who lived in his employer's cabin, fed his family on "furnish," and supposedly got half of the cotton he raised. I imagine the dimes Money earned from us were most of the cash his family saw for months on end.

Money may have been any age between eight and twelve. He looked the former, being small and wiry of frame, with hardly any flesh on his bones, but he acted the latter. During cotton "chopping" or picking time we rarely saw him; he was helping his father then. At other times he was apt to turn up almost every day, walking the several miles between his home and ours to do our small chores.

It must be said, I welcomed Money. For some strange reason he was full of laughter; he was always responsive and never silent or withdrawing or shy. He told droll stories and went about his work with easy abandon. I would follow him about when he carried the slops to the pigs, or cleaned out the cow stall, or weeded a few rows in the garden, just to hear his voice.

It was altogether different with the other Negroes who came to work for us. If I knew their names I at once forgot them, contenting myself with "Sally" or "Jim," or if they were old, perhaps "Uncle" or "Auntie"—generic terms we were wont to use for Negroes whose names we did not know. They came, young and old; even babies in arms sometimes, brought by mothers who could not leave them alone at home but would lay them down under a tree on the edge of the field to sleep or wail away the day. I could stand at my bedroom window in the early morning and see the field workers go by into our barnyard. If it was cotton chopping time, they would go to get their hoes; if cotton picking, to get their sacks: big sacks for those old enough and small sacks for the little ones. If they were working in the fields near the house, I would climb up on the fence to sit there and watch them, or find shelter from the heat under a nearby shade tree and see them at work.

From whence, who knows, I had thought to see "jolly black laborers" singing in the sun as they trudged along between the cotton rows. I had thought to hear jokes bandied back and forth, and see "white teeth gleaming with happy grins." I had thought they would treat me—well, the way Money treated me—deferentially, of course, as would be right to the white landowner's daughter, but outgoingly, responding with hearty pleasure to my little attempts to be friendly, as I thought. They were polite when I spoke to them, but so reticent, it seemed, so very remote. A "Yes, ma'am," or "No, ma'am," and nothing much besides. Men, women, and children it seemed to me worked for the most part silently. If a youngster lagged in the row or stopped at the end under the shade, there might be a sharp loud rebuke from a parent, "You Car'line, get back ter work befo' I whup you." They would pass remarks among each other, of course. But it seemed to me they talked very little. Even at lunch hour when they took out their cold corn bread and fatback and sat around munching it, I would listen for their laughter, listen for a "gay chatter of voices," and I could seem to hear little of it. They would eat their food and hurry back to their labors. They were paid by the hour for chopping and by the pound for picking. There were but so many hours from sunrise to sunset and so many weeks out of the year when so much work was to be had. The sooner they finished our fields, I learned, the sooner they could move on to another's, and the more coins they could lay by to see them through the unpaid months ahead. They did not so much hurry at their work; rather one felt a monotonous rhythm, which varied hardly at all from morning to evening, except for the children who had to be prodded. Of course some hands were better than others, and white farmers would say that "all Negroes stood watching" lest they not pick clean in the rows and grab too much trash with the lint; or when chopping, leave weeds to throttle the young plants or fail to leave a good stand. Chopping cotton was especially a ticklish job, a task the youngest children were not permitted to do, even if they could have handled the heavy hoes.

One can but guess what I had expected to see as I watched our field hands. But certainly not these somber strangers coming and going, who seemed not to care whether they worked for us or someone else, and who, besides, seemed like people carrying some kind of burden with which they were preoccupied.

It was also disappointing to me to find work on a farm so hard. In some sense I felt this because I was doing hard work myself for the first time. We were trying to farm without Father's knowing hand to guide everything and without the hired help that would have lightened the load. Every meal almost would see anxious consultation. My brother, a few years older than I, must himself do some of the plowing. We could not always hire it even when we wanted to. And well it was that wise old Nelly pulled our plow. How often she must have straightened my brother's row for him, avoided the stones which could have broken the plow tongue, called for a rest by stopping in her tracks when he did not know that the heat was becoming too much for them.

There was much even a girl could do on a place with no regular hired man. Besides housework, I could pump the dasher up and down in our old fashioned crockery churn. I could fetch fresh water from the spring in small quantities. I could feed the chickens and even the hogs, if need be, though carrying the heavy bucket of kitchen "slops" out, with the squealing animals as likely as not spilling them over me, was not a job I relished. I could work a little in the vegetable garden weeding and cultivating. Presumably I could learn to milk, and did try to, since my brother usually did it and did not always wish to be at home for the evening milking.

He would not permit Mother to do this hard work. I certainly found it exhausting, especially since no cow likes a green hand at her udder. Our animal was gentle enough, though I never really trusted her or her way of showing her displeasure at my clumsiness by daintily kicking over the bucket with what little milk I had managed to make her give. A few times I helped at planting, only however when my brother was working alone. It was not seemly for me to work in the field with others. In a plot near our house I followed my brother's plow to put corn in. I crawled along between the rows to help him set out hundreds of sweet potato plants with each one having to be put in by hand and each one watered.

Once I even tried my hand at picking cotton, but this was by my own choice. When autumn came I asked to do it to earn a little pocket money. We had to pay it out anyhow, I argued, and why not to me?—being not a little nettled by the quizzical look in their eyes when they said I might try it. It appeared easy. I had seen children far younger than I picking all day. So one day, when the Negroes were working in a field far removed from our house where they could not see me, I was told I could go to the cotton field near by where Mother could keep an eye on me. I believe I stuck to the task longer than they expected, but only from sheer pride. One hour of that back-breaking weariness would have been enough. As light a bag as I dragged from my shoulder, as little cotton as I put in it before emptying the white fluff onto an out-spread sacking, as frequently as I rested, it seemed to make no difference. It was the bending-and-picking, bending-and-picking.

Besides the farm as such, my life was chiefly filled with school-going, at least for the months when there was any school. A few days after our arrival in the country I had begun school again. Father had led me along a path skirting a plowed field and through a patch of pine woods, perhaps a walk of half a mile, to the clearing where stood the building.

It was a new school, which was surprising. But lately a breath of prosperity had come to the countryside. It seems the brickyard had been running with some steadiness for a while. This meant some cash in people's hands. It may be that the legislature had lately sent out some increase of funds to rural schools. In any event, there it stood, a brand-new building, even painted white, with a bell in its tower, and having two rooms. When I saw the old structure, the improvement was apparent. It had been unpainted, was very small, and had but one room; by then, too, its roof was caving in. The present school was so new the brush had hardly been cleared away from around its door. The boys were still busy about it. We had but one teacher, as it turned out. The second room went unused; apparently the new prosperity could not quite pay for two teachers; nor ever did within my knowledge of the place, which extended over many years after we left it.

It would be an exaggeration to say that I came to know the children in my school. For a while, at least, I only saw them every day, studied at a desk in the same room with them, recited my lessons at the sides of the older ones, ate my lunch at recess while they ate theirs, listened to their conversation, of which I could be only slightly a part, being such a stranger, and even tried to play with them, insofar as they played. There was everything, it seemed, to keep us separate and hardly anything to bridge the gap save our common childhood.

My clothing was different. In the city I had thought my clothes nothing in particular: gingham dresses, neat high shoes and black stockings, a red jacket for cold weather. But here, save for the daughters of our "neighbor" who were in the school, I saw on the girls only faded, worn, unstarched, ill-fitting calicos; and on the boys, patched shrunken overalls. The stockings to cover their legs were all over darns or full of holes; their shoes were heavy brogans, which might or might not fit, and in any case, as soon as the first warm weather came, they would be put aside entirely to be hoarded for winter.

My lunches were different. This I found myself wishing I could hide. It disturbed me to take from my kit at recess good beef or cheese sandwiches, a boiled egg, an apple, and piece of cake, and parade it before their heavy thick flour biscuit or corn bread, with at best a piece of fatback on it.

There was the matter of manners. I too might feel a little diffident among children so new to me, but not this shyness they showed, not this reticence so extreme one felt strained to be around it. They recited their lessons for the teacher, but haltingly, seeming to have it dragged out of them by an effort of self-will. When recess came the younger ones played, if it could be so called, even shouted occasionally, but as I looked on it felt heavy, lethargic after the shrill boisterous noisiness of our city school recess where we dashed around in sheer exuberance. The older girls stood about and talked a little, but only snatches of words, which seemed to get nowhere. Now and then they would giggle a little and let their eyes drift over toward the cluster of older boys. And the boys would glance at the girls from where they lolled apart, making remarks, some apparently meant to be overheard but mostly among themselves.

Even our language tended to separate us. I was a city child and talked like one. I was a "cultured" child; I used more or less correct English. I could not have made over my speech into the image of theirs if I had tried. I think I would gladly have done it, so hard would they stare at me when I talked, as though I were some kind of foreigner, as indeed they regarded me; and worse, as though I were "putting on airs."

That they might think me trying to "put on airs" became a bugbear with me. I knew as long as they thought that they would never really accept me. Their murmuring voices would continue to die away whenever I joined them. They would continue by a sort of passive nonresistance to shut me out. They were children and I was a child. They were my schoolmates. It became important to me not to be excluded. In any event, they drew me in some strange way. I wanted them to like me.

Of course my knowledge was different. Why would it not be? Mediocre though my schooling may have been, it had gone on for nine months a year since I was six years old. I had finished a half year of high school, with algebra, physiology, and Latin begun. But these boys and girls, the ones of my age and older, save for the "boss's" daughters, were years behind. They had gone to school perhaps three or four months a year, with these interrupted when they must stay out to help at home. The year I attended, this school shut down in April or earlier—I seem to remember wild violets were in bloom—to let the children help their parents in the fields. True, once I was settled in, there was less difference, in our lessons, that is. The poor homely little woman who struggled to teach us had a half-year less schooling than I had when I entered—she had never been to high school. How could she carry me on into high school

subjects? Perforce I was leveled down nearer my fellows. Some
thirty children were pupils—not that thirty were ever present, attendance being spotty. Our ages ranged from seven-year-olds to a
few of fifteen. She must take us in turn, in groups of twos or threes,
whatever our "grade" was, while the other children sat at their
desks and studied. At every grade-level she must teach arithmetic,
spelling, writing (in old fashioned copybooks), and reading. For
us who were older there was also history and geography, and instead of the "Blue Back" speller, we studied spelling from the
dictionary, beginning with "A." My group was still in "A" when the
term ended. Our neighbor's daughters alone matched my learning,
by dint of having been tutored at home. But they had lived here
for many years. Theirs was not my problem. They had found a
niche of their own—among the people, yet not of them. They could
do this, being the "boss's" children. They did not seem to mind
parading their knowledge or knowing the answers when the farm
boys and girls missed them. To me it was disturbing. It was as
though I had a pre-arranged advantage in a race which made me
always win. I longed to hide what I knew if thereby I might escape
from always having the better of them. I felt unfair and that they
would think me so.

It must be said that most of these were new sensations for me. If
they were hid away in the mental baggage I had carried to the
country, I did not know it. As a city-bred child little of destitution
had passed before my protected eyes, or at least it had not impressed me. Seeing any poverty, I no doubt accepted our scriptural
lesson to explain it: "The poor ye always have with you." This
would account for the poor whites among us. Negro poverty I
would have taken even more for granted.

In fact until we moved to our farm, I knew little and thought
not at all about the "poorer classes." We had a sufficiency for the
needs of life; we had always lived in the "best residential areas."
Being children, we had seen little enough outside of this.

Once the school term was ended I saw little enough anyhow. All
the young people were busy in the fields. Once the farm season
was really under way, there was more work than could be done
even when young and old worked all day. From then until the last
boll of cotton had been picked in late autumn, all worked. Not

that these children or their white parents hired out for field labor. Except for something like plowing, when a white farmer would come with his team to "help," whites did not work in the fields for other whites. In their eyes, this was "nigger work," to hire out for cotton chopping or picking. A white farmer's children would no more go out as field hands for others than they would work in others' kitchens or do others' washing. Whites—men, women, and children of a family—worked in their own fields, if they owned them, or were renters, or even if they were croppers; in the latter case still feeling they were working on home land.

Thus it was I never say any of my schoolmates coming to work in our fields. The truth was, I rarely ever saw these white children, once school was over. They seemed to melt away into the countryside. I rarely saw into any of their homes, though we often passed their places driving and were told, this was "so-in-so's" cabin. Only sometimes down watching the trains come in, or maybe at the crossroads store, I would catch a glimpse of the children. The one time I would be sure to see them was on Sundays if I went to the little Baptist church on the hill.

2.

In August crops were laid by, and while it was good to have a let-up in heavy field work—good to the men and boys to be able to hang around the crossroads store, chewing and smoking and swapping tales and speculating about the crops, good to have this breathing spell before the hard labor of harvesting—these were not the best that August gave them. August was revival time. Then a preacher would come to stay at least a week, perhaps longer if his "harvest was rich." The people had time to go to church every day in the week, during the day, and even long into the night, if perchance the saving-current were running strong.

Negroes, too, held a revival over at their little church, the one we passed on the main highway coming home. We could hear them any evening we cared to listen from our front porch steps under the brilliance of summer stars. It was cool to sit there and listen. Dark came down, and with it frogs would start their mighty croaking down where the creek ran at the foot of our hill. And then a stillness would fall, as though the old bullfrogs themselves stopped to listen to the colored preacher's deep, booming voice drifting across the silence, calling the hymn's first lines. It was far away, the words blurred to us, but we could hear his tones and could know the song, as wave on wave of rich harmony floated across the valley to us.

At revival time, however, we were not often there to listen. The whites were having their own revival at the little Baptist church on a hill about two miles distant from our home.

Long before my first revival I had come to know the tiny church. We began attending soon after we came to the country. We went except when we could go to town for service, hitching up Old Nelly to drive the twelve miles to our Church of the Good Shepherd, there to bask again in our own familiar ritual, hear the solemn words of the liturgy, join again the confessional—"We have left undone those things we ought to have done, and done those things we ought not to have done, and there is no health in us . . ." receive Communion, and after the service see our friends. But at best this could happen infrequently. It was no small thing to wear out one's only horse not to say our human patience in such a journey. So, most of the time we must be content to perform our religious duty by attending the little country church. Moreover, it was seemly. People would not have understood if we had failed to do so.

In truth I wanted to do it. It seemed hardly at all like church to me, but I was intensely curious to see the people on this one occasion when they joined their voices in song and some of them let themselves pray aloud. It was the one gathering-time of all the people for miles around. Almost everyone came, save a few special sinners, and everyone knew why they did not come. (Even the sinners were apt to come at revival time.) People came in numbers even on those Sundays when we had no preacher, but only a deacon, who read the Bible and prayed and announced the hymns and perhaps murmured a few words of exhortation. In a rural Baptist church, of course, preaching was the main thing, that and the long extemporaneous prayer. Surely it bespoke keen hunger of some kind that they came when there was no sermon.

The deacon was section boss on the railroad, his house, owned by the company, a little way up the tracks from the station. Already he had some ten children and another was coming, although it was hard to believe that the emaciated, bowed-down little woman who was their mother could bear any more. I knew the children because they had been in school with me; indeed, there being four or five who attended, they comprised about a sixth of our school. They were curious replicas of their father, sallow as he was sallow, angular as he was, with lusterless hair and eyes like his. Like him they were painfully diffident. Of all the children I knew in school they seemed to me most retiring, hardest to be friendly with, almost frightened of any approach. When all the family trooped to church on Sunday, with the latest baby in the mother's arms, they would fill almost two benches.

How the father, taciturn, withdrawn man that he was, brought himself to perform the offices of deacon I could but wonder. I felt he did it as a stricken man who must fulfill his bounden duty to God. Certainly he was borne down with that sense of duty and the everlasting hell awaiting any who failed to perform it. He told us so. It was his one theme when he muttered his few little words of preaching. Reading the Bible was a torture to him; he could scarcely read in any case, our neighbor told us. He would hold his eyes pinned close to the verses, mumbling when he came to the strange, hard names and places which lie in wait in Holy Scripture. What could such as he do about "Nebuchadnezzar," "Hezekiah," "Ecclesiastes"? Or even New Testament words like "Pharisees," "hypocrites," and "whithersoever"? It seemed as though they came in every line. I had been reading the Bible aloud to Mother every evening since I was a small child old enough to read; I had been memorizing the New Testament, a few verses at a time, from my early years, until I could recite by heart far along in the book of Matthew. I had never dreamed there could be so many words one could stumble over. His misery pained but fascinated me. Even at the hymns he would hardly open his lips in singing. The songs would wail out from the throats of the people in high-pitched strident singsong, but with him it seemed hardly more than a forming of the words. Only in prayer did a change come over him. I knew, because, although I stood as others did and bowed my head, I furtively watched him. He would close his eyes tightly, drop his chin to his breast, and then the words would come, slow-spoken but now flowing like a stream on and on: "Almighty God . . . poor sorrowful sinners . . . wash us clean in the blood of the Lamb . . . bring wandering souls to repentance . . . we have sinned in thy sight . . . cast us not into hell . . . we have gone astray . . . our Savior died for our sins. . . ." Until the congregation began to shuffle their feet, and snuffle in their noses, and cough; until babies began to whimper, and little children to whisper almost aloud. Suddenly he would seem to come to himself, would hurriedly mutter, "Amen" and announce a hymn.

Once a month we had a regular preacher, a man who served our church and several others in this section. Even so, it was a mighty effort to raise the little share of salary we paid him, perhaps a hundred dollars or so a year. Besides this we must raise the sum to pay the revival preacher, a special man from a distance.

Long before revival week, the people began preparing for it. The church was spruced up, swept cleaner than usual, and benches and pulpit dusted thoroughly. The grove surrounding the structure was raked and made neat. People began to go to Wednesday night prayer meeting, which usually was poorly attended, praying the Lord to let his spirit descend upon the coming meeting. One of the "boss's" daughters played the little organ, the kind one pumps by foot. She gathered in a few young people for choir practice. Seven or eight of us must have been in the choir. I particularly liked to sit there because our chairs were at one side of the pulpit where I could watch intently all the faces. I had heard of revivals all my life, but it was something new to experience one.

People began to speculate about the sinners. Would they come to Christ? From my friends, the "boss's" daughters, I first sensed the existence of these sinners, and more and more came to smell and taste the backwash of talk that went slipping in and out about people; sometimes I caught echoes in sly little words and giggles that occasionally fell on my ears at school. Men drank, and this was wicked. But drunkenness was talked about almost boldly, everyone knowing who were the heavy drinkers and who at each annual revival might come up to the mourner's bench to vow again to forsake their old past. Men played cards and threw dice, and these deeds were wicked; it was a dark sin to do either. But these things too were almost open sins, freely admitted when men and boys came up to be saved. For those "living in sin" it was different, that occasional woman or girl who was free with her virtue or even had children by a man whom she had never married. Their sins were not paraded openly, not from the lips of righteous folk; yet nothing seemed more pervasive of our country than the presence of these sinning ones. I was removed enough from the main stream of gossip around me; yet even I could know of this swampy backwater, to which even the most pious folk were ever turning their fascinated gaze. I could hear the hints, the whispered rumors, see the glances of scorn when a miscreant passed. Not the men involved, but the women, were outcast, and their children with them, if they were wrongly come by. These women were the truly black sinners, for whom hell and eternal damnation were almost certainly the penalty.

This revival year the rumor was going around that a certain young woman who already had three children "in sin" was just about to have another. They were all by the same man, it was murmured, a big, red-faced farmer whom I often saw passing, and who was known for his heavy drinking as well as for his philandering. It came about that bitter dissension arose among the worthy people whether this man should be received again, some even murmuring —certain women nagged at their husbands to talk to the "boss" on the matter, he being magistrate—that the man should be forced to marry the girl and make her a "good woman." I think the men had reason to be a little timorous toward this burly fellow, who was so mighty in his anger when he had drink in him, and had never seemed to welcome advice from any quarter.

There was also the older woman whom all called "Miss Sarah." They seemed not to dare actually to treat her like a sinner, though she had lived with a farmer with no marriage words said over them, keeping his house for him for many a year. They were convinced of her sinning. But Miss Sarah, they said—and I knew it too, for I had seen her numerous times—walked proudly as if she had

165

nothing to be ashamed of, and this nonplussed people. She ought to bow her head in shame and did not. She never went to church during the year, only to revival; yet never, in all the years, they said, had she come to Christ; never had she bowed her knee at the mourner's bench, nor asked forgiveness, nor acted as if she wanted to. She just came and went away again as if she had a right to. So people even spoke to her in passing, indeed, almost timidly, it seemed to me, as though fearing a rebuff from her. When in the prayer meetings before revival a pious member would pray, "Oh God, save those who dwell in stiff-necked pride in their sinning . . ." everyone knew who was meant by it.

With such sinners as these always in the offing, and not a few young people who should be about ready for conversion, the week drew near with rising excitement in the air. Even I, who did not have the feeling of danger and fear, which sent shivers down the spines of these country people, lest some poor souls among us should die unsaved, was caught up a little in the tension as we practiced our hymns: "Why not; why not come to Him now. . . ."

People came on foot, in wagons, in buggies, on mules, any way they could manage. They came in whole families; the babies of course had to come, since there was no one to leave them with. The women and girls would go decorously into the church as soon as they arrived; the men and boys would loiter outside until service began. The boys indeed lagged behind, well after the first hymns, some even waiting until preaching. Then in twos and threes they would slip into the back benches, which by some sort of common consent were always left vacant for them. Save for hardened sinners, it seemed to be expected that the boys would be the last to come to Christ. People looked for this harvest on the final nights of revival.

It must be said it seemed very dour to me. I would feel tingles of excitement, but depression too. There was so much grimness in the preacher's face as he greeted a "sister" or "brother"; so still, so tense a look on the women's thin, lined countenances; so withdrawing a solemnity about the pious men, who were pillars of the church, as they moved about distributing hymn books or straightening benches. Only the girls in their best dresses and hair ribbons showed an air of expectancy in eager looks and shy little motions, and the boys outside, in their persistent talking and feigned indifference to the coming events.

Some revivals, I know, have abandon in them, where singing reaches a pitch of almost wild, solemn fervor, where free mourning and shouting seems to undo pent-up emotions, and hearts burst forth in loud prayer for salvation; and where preachers give a message, not alone in tones of condemnation, deep, harsh warnings, but in fervent exultation, with even a sort of joy in it, of tender, mournful promise of happiness in that beautiful Beulah Land. I witnessed such revivals in after years, but not in this countryside. The preacher, knowing his people, may have felt he could not break through the thick encrusted reticence even with the power of religious emotion. It may even be that he tried. It may be that at the times he shouted loudest and exhorted and wheedled and prayed, he was even then beating his pumping arms and strident voice against this unyielding exterior, thinking perchance he might fan into life an inner flame that would burn right through.

True, when people sang at revival their voices rose to a pitch I had never heard from them hitherto, shrill and rending in sound; when they prayed, those faithful ones whose souls had long ago been saved, it was in such insistency as I had not heard at ordinary times. But whether in song or prayer, I felt a tight constriction in them—tensions, suppressed excitement, even fear, that they could not seem to let out. It almost worried me, I think, lest the crust might suddenly be burst—and what might happen?

Each night would come the invitation, climax of everything. The choir would begin its song, at first softly:

> *Rescue the perishing,*
> *Care for the dying,*
> *Snatch them in pity from sin and the grave.*
> *Plead with the erring ones,*
> *Lift up the fallen. . . .*

The preacher would cry, "Will you come?" And my eyes would turn to watch almost anxiously. Would they come? I never knew whether I wanted them to come or to resist this luring voice pushing against them:

> *Jesus is merciful,*
> *Jesus will save.*

He would repeat it: "Jesus is merciful . . . Will you come?" True, he had to make them. What was a revival unless people were saved? Who would be the first one? Each night there must be a first one. It seemed hard to lead the way. Usually they were young people. Most of the older folk years ago had been converted and stayed converted. A young girl would go up, her face flushed, her eyes shining; the preacher would take her hand and say, "God bless you, daughter," and kneel her down at the front bench. Another would somehow get the courage. It seemed so plainly to take a kind of courage, even though they were all ready for conversion, being of the right age. As the week moved on a boy would finally pick himself up from the back benches and stumble up the aisle, and I, looking back at his fellows, could see their heads duck and bodies fidget: their turn had come and they knew it. Some came, but some were a disappointment, as everyone said after revival. Well, maybe another year. . . .

Through it all stood Miss Sarah. I could see her plainly from my seat in the choir, though her face was in shadow from her gingham sun bonnet. She never joined in the singing, never lifted her voice in "Amen" during preaching as many did, just stood there if there was singing or praying, or sat there during the invitation. And after all was over, she left the church directly and alone, with dignity—it must be said, almost with condescension.

Not so the burly, drinking farmer, he of the brood of unclaimed children. Once again he was true to his past. Once again the devil and hell and the fiery pit became too much for him; again he repented and went up to the mourner's bench. The preacher plainly knew him, knew with whom he was dealing, for he stopped the hymn on that night and knelt down beside the man, praying mightily that Almighty God would redeem him from his darkest sins. I had felt many stirrings of embarrassment for others who had been converted, my schoolmates especially; it seemed so public somehow to my Episcopal soul. But this man decidedly disturbed me. In my thoughts I had warmly taken the side of those who thought the man should be made to marry the girl who had borne him children. And here he was, come forward to be saved again.

When it was over, when the week was spent and all who could be brought to Christ had been, then remained only the baptism.

On Saturday water was hauled in barrels to be poured by sweating men into the tomblike pool hidden beneath the pulpit. To church on Sunday the converts came, the girls in white dresses, if they had them, the boys in old pants and white shirts. The preacher descended into the water, and while we sang, took his quivering converts one after another, to dip them bodily in the rite of immersion, calling down the blessing of God on each one. It was hard for the young boys and girls to keep a proper countenance, even boys and girls so reserved as these. How could they help coming up gasping and spluttering and making an exceedingly strange appearance (in my eyes at least) with their wet clothes clinging to their gangling bodies? If I had been a little stirred in the long tense evenings of wailing hymns, strident preaching, anxious waiting to see who would come, I was not now. It was broad daylight of a hot August noonday; flies were buzzing around my face, yellow jackets zooming, my clothes were sticking to me uncomfortably with the oppressive heat. People were not excited now; they seemed sunk back in the old lethargy. Preaching on that last day seemed almost interminable. Service over, I could scarcely wait to climb into our buggy and urge my brother to let us get home.

However, I had certain pleasant residues from the revival. It enabled me to learn almost every white person in the countryside, by name, I mean. Now I could know to whom I was speaking when I passed folk on the road. I had even glimpsed behind the heavy veil usually across their withdrawn countenances. But more important to me, out of the revival had emerged a little social coterie —young people who had found each other. Those who sang in the choir were the better-off farmers' sons and daughters, those who lived in two-story dwellings; and while the boys worked in the fields by day, they owned neckties to wear with their collars and dressed up in them for revival. More than this, they laughed and talked, were almost easygoing, at least seemed so in contrast to the others. I had not known them before—they lived at some distance. Now we had a little company that promised to come together occasionally.

Late autumn came, bringing school near again. It was decided that our neighbor's two daughters and I should drive some three miles behind an old nag to attend another rural school, one with two teachers, one of whom was able, it was thought, to carry forward our preparation for college. It was a more prosperous school, moreover, as were the farms around it. It held entertainments, "socials," a "commencement." There was a piano, with one teacher able to give music lessons.

As it turned out, our hope for Latin and mathematics at high school level was quickly blasted. The woman claimed to be a high school graduate. She may have been, but she knew no more Latin than we did, and studied it less; finally we stopped studying. Thenceforth, it became a game for us to unmask her ignorance, if we could, to shatter her magnificent aplomb. For while she was a handsome woman, vivacious and ready-tongued, and could make school interesting outside of lessons, with it she was a coarse tyrant, swift to anger and free to punish those who were helpless against her wrath.

It was this I resented: she would not vent her spleen on us; we were "important," I discovered. We were children of the farm country's well-to-do. I knew she tried to curry our favor even as she showed her true colors against the poorer children. I could feel righteous in my scorn for her. It took but a few occasions of her stinging ruler striking the cringing hands of helpless little boys and girls to launch us, who apparently had nothing to fear from her, on a year of joyous insubordination. Let this teacher be guilty of any act of injustice—we being the judges—and our revenge was swift and sure: that day she could "do nothing with us." She said so complainingly, and we knew, and the children knew. Nor were we long content with our own misdeeds and the wide-open eyes of our fellow pupils at our daring; we found ways of leading our fellows astray while enabling them to escape retribution. If at long recess we should lead them all down to a stream so far away none of us could hear the bell and keep them there until she must come and get us, what could she do? Could we not plead plaintive innocence, and if this failed, how could she punish a whole school? In this I discovered, moreover, something very exciting: the children loved it. We were making their eyes sparkle and bringing shrill laughter to their throats. I am sure it slightly intoxicated me, who but a few months ago had been a stranger in the midst of

remote and apparently docile children. True, these children were
not a complete replica of my other school fellows. On the whole
they dressed a little better, brought better lunches; some of their
homes I knew were better, a shade better, for we passed them
driving to and from school. They would play if one of us tried hard
enough to make them; it was like "pulling eyeteeth" at first; they
seemed to know few games; but at least they seemed to want to,
and I, for one, never wearied of making them. On my part, much
had happened. I had lived in the country for nearly a year now—
more than a year by the time our school term was in full swing.
I felt more at home with country children, sensed their ways better, was not so afraid of trying to beat down their reticences. Moreover, it could not have been entirely uncongenial to me, whose
own upbringing had been authoritarian, to enjoy this pleasurable
little conflict with authority.

Meanwhile, and this was what most mattered to me, our introduction to this more prosperous farming country added a few
more young people, farmers' sons and daughters, to the circle that
began with our revival choir. During the chill winter months when
plowing was not heavy and horses and mules were freer for riding
and driving, we had a few socials. My brother and I would hitch up
Old Nelly to drive the several miles to a farmer's home to spend
an evening pulling taffy and playing games.

We insisted upon going. Or rather, I insisted. My brother had
no problem: "A boy can look out for himself." Even in my case,
when Mother hesitated, I think it was only because I was young,
and boys and girls of all ages would be at the parties. This did not
mean we had undergone a change. We were still "people of family."
Nothing had altered that. I had no sense of its being altered, at
least. I think my mother had simply accepted as inevitable that
so long as we lived our life here it must be among the people as
we found them. From the outset she herself had set us an example
of careful courtesy, and laid upon our minds strict injunctions for
our guidance. She explained how kind country people were, how
helpful to each other, how sterling were their qualities of character,
how hard working. We must never hurt their feelings by holding
ourselves "above them" so that they could notice it. That we were
"above them," I must surely have gone on assuming. I was con-

cerned lest they discover it, especially lest they might wish to leave me out. If parties were going on, I wanted to go to parties. I had just entered my teens.

It was our misfortune, perhaps, that we were not content with these simpler socials. We developed more grandiose plans. We would have dances, round dances. We could have them at the Woodmen of the World hall. It was an old abandoned store in our village. The "boss" had started the WOW lodge for the handful of farmers and their older sons who could afford the dues required; he headed the lodge and kept it going. Some of the boys in our crowd were WOW members.

It was daring, because to dance was very sinful in the eyes of church people. Round dancing ranked with cards or drinking. It was not a problem for my brother and me, or for the "boss's" children. We had always danced. For these country boys and girls it meant a step of great moment. It was strange, too, that some knew how to dance.

Our music was a harmonica, skillfully played by a young farmer, who danced as he played, the only inconvenience being to his partner, who must do without his right hand to guide her. Inconvenience was nothing. We liked to dance. At first we liked the feeling of wickedness.

The rumble of the coming storm began after our first dance. From then on through succeeding months it grew louder and louder. When the preacher came for his monthly round, this was what he preached about. When he was not there, the deacon and other influential elders prayed. Our companions became the butt of constant chiding, reproaches, outright demands to cease and desist, for their very souls' sake. Perhaps if we and the "boss's" children had not provided a hard inner core which was immune to these pressures, the group would have flown apart almost at once. But we persisted. The others could not resist.

As time passed, however, the fun began to be squeezed out of the dances. Our companions began to look guilty and feel guiltier. They began to dread what people said to them. The harmonica lost its gay lilt, becoming mechanical and almost tiresome. We began to spend our evenings together as much listening to the latest denunciation against us as in floating around in a waltz.

Sojourn in the Sand Hills

The storm broke with the August revival. Since the year before, I had gone less and less to the little church. We were looked on with suspicious eyes because of our sinful dancing. I was not invited this time to sing in the choir. We were outsiders now and would not be welcome. Some of our friends were asked. It was with some little foreboding that we heard they had accepted. I did go to some of the revival meetings. The very first night, the preacher, aflame at our arrogant wickedness, began his denunciation of our stiff-necked ways, our straying on the downward path, our risking of our precious souls to eternal damnation. Each night it was the same. This was something to test his mettle, and he bent himself to conquer it. Then it began. First one, then the other of our erstwhile companions with the hymn and invitation began to go down that fated aisle, tearful and contrite.

Our friends avoided us thereafter, ducking their heads and speaking shyly, all the old comradery gone. It angered and depressed me. I felt somehow as if a trap had been laid for them, which all unwarily they had walked into.

Actually it mattered very little to me. Thus I consoled myself. We would soon be away from the place. Once our crops were in, we were moving back again to the city, and from thence I would go on my way to college. I was not prepared for college, of course. But I had been tutoring, and, when I reached the little Georgia institution where my sisters had also gone, I could make up more of the schooling I had lost.

Thus my last months in this sandy country ended in a sort of ignominious isolation from the people around us whom once I almost felt I had come to know. We met questioning looks again and diffident greeting as at the beginning. It may be the older, more pious people among them blamed us city folk, certain that it was we who had brought their children into temptation, from which they had hardly rescued them. I could harden my own heart against this, feeling even a little condescending at the moment at such "narrow-mindedness." Certainly I was ready to forget them and this ill-begotten country in the wide and expanding life toward which I could now turn my eyes.

BOOK FIVE
Of a New Heaven

1.

THE TOWN of Gainesville lay fifty miles from Georgia's leading metropolis, Atlanta. It was distant enough to place the town deep in the foothills of this northern corner of the state and well away from any sense of big-city mindedness. My college, Brenau, was located in Gainesville. It was here I went when we left the Sand Hill country after our last crops were in and Christmas had passed. It was here my undergraduate days were spent, spanning the years 1912 to 1915, and also two years more while I served as a tutor. All told, nearly six years of my life were lived in these surroundings. They could be six crucial years in mental development. Yet one would surely have supposed the place and circumstances to be indistinguishable in their Southernness from all I had hitherto known.

That they seemed so to me when I first went there is certainly true. If anything I felt more at home than I would have in most Southern towns. I was in Georgia again, the place that we of my name always had felt was home. Far from needing to spell my name here, there were girls who came from a Lumpkin County and a town of Lumpkin. I could feel a sense of history here—our own family history. Our family had once during my infancy even made its home in this town.

The Gainesville I now saw was probably very little different from that earlier Gainesville. After all little more than a decade had passed. And it would be a full quarter-century more before a president of the United States would stand on the public square of this town to say (why this particular little north Georgia town, I have never known): "Georgia and the lower South may just as well face facts—simple facts. . . ." "These [better] things will not come to us in the South if we oppose progress—if we believe in our hearts that the feudal system is still the best system. When you come down to it, there is little difference between the feudal system and the fascist system. . . ." Of course back in 1912, we could not have heard of fascism, and feudalism was something belonging to the Dark Ages of Europe.

As it was, I felt at home in Gainesville. Nearly all I knew and had formerly experienced, and my people before me, was daily an open book for me to reread here. The townspeople were like my people in speech and manner and thought and action. Their ways had all the warm familiarity of the ways of my upbringing. Their likes and antagonisms were the old likes and antagonisms which were then my own.

I had come here believing I belonged to a people of a special mold. Surely I could continue in this pleasant prepossession. I was accepted as one of them. I shared the sense of being knit to them by harsh conflicts gallantly weathered. I knew in my own experience the traits of geniality and generosity which were handed down and preserved as something precious, even if they could not be observed precisely as they had been under that time of abundance—for those who had abundance—of the ante-bellum plantation. In my head I carried the picture of the Southerner which we cherished, and whose likeness we had been reared to aspire to—of a courteous, kindly people, swift to sympathy, hospitable, gay, affectionate, withal proud, and of noble spirit and high ideals. I knew how warm a South it could be to its own, how outgoing, friendly. To me, the very soft air we breathed gave off an essence, and the welcoming wide-open doors of our homes, the little neighborliness in which we liked to excel—among our own kind, to be sure. I knew the generous width of our streets, at least where my kind of people lived, and the great spreading elms and oaks lining them. I found them here; and the easy, slow-moving give-and-take of our business sections, where time waited on the human amenities. It is true, I also knew here, as I had always known it, our "peculiar institution" which was our heritage from slavery. But had it not also been fashioned by the hands of our fathers, who in passing it on to us told us to maintain it?

Of a New Heaven

When I came to this Southern town and college there was certainly nothing visible to me to hint that contrary streams of influence were moving in the South. Indeed, were they moving? When does a trickle become a stream? When did it in the South? Surely, it was not until long after the time of my second awakening to a consciousness of race.

Of course, even before college we knew some purported critics were among us, some Southerners who advocated measures of which we disapproved. We knew we spoke out against those occasional misguided persons who urged more educated Negro leaders and improved Negro educational facilities. We thought of them as occasional. We did not guess that the number had become fairly large and respectable, even including a few politicians now and then. We knew we decried those who from within criticized lynchings. Not because we approved of mob lynching. No respectable person did, we said. We stood for the majesty of the law and justice to all. But the occurrence of lynchings was entirely understandable, the noble motive of outraged white males attempting to protect "white Southern womanhood." We did not know that some Southerners even then were beginning to doubt the motive as well as the punishment.

The more pronounced trickles of counterinfluence that began to appear just before the first World War were quite unknown to me, at least, and I am sure to my fellows. Here and there Southern men and women were doing things and saying things which we had no notion of. A few were speaking out against "yellow journalism" in treatment of racial issues; a little company of them came together about this time and enlisted the aid of certain Southern journalists. A few clergymen scattered about the South had begun to address themselves to "our problem." I would listen to such a man ten years later in a large Baptist church in Atlanta— Jones I think was his name. He may already have begun to speak during my college years, and I not have known it. Occasional professors, a businessman here and there, a few lawyers, would take their stand for "equal justice," "equal sanitation," and other similar equalities, none of them, of course, infringing on our basic separateness. (Southern men were careful of their language; no doubt, also, careful of their thoughts. It behooved them to be careful, they would feel, in a land that had a bitter epithet, "nigger lover," for those at whom it wished to cast sharp stones.) It would seem that as far back as 1906, when a fearful race riot overran Atlanta, Dr. Booker T. Washington had hastened there from Tuskegee and persuaded certain influential whites and Negroes to sit down and consult in the same room over causes of the plague that had overtaken them. Some came to call this the first instance of "interracial co-operation" as a movement. Of course the term was quite unknown as well as inconceivable to us then. We remained ignorant of it even as first co-operative steps were taken during the first World War. Our student Christian organizations—YWCA and YMCA—were making tentative excursions into this uncharted field. But we had not then heard names such as W. D. Weatherford's—YMCA leaders who were making cautious suggestions for making their group active. We did not know that our women's organization had begun to employ Negroes on its staff to do work among Negroes, in the wake of which had come certain limited "co-operation" between white and Negro staff members. So quietly were these hesitant steps being taken that we who were Southern college students in that day had not heard of them.

More dissent than these meager beginnings would suggest must have actually existed. For when something organized emerged, the number who could be counted was patently far too many to have sprung full-blown from just nothing at all. They had been scattered, it seems, usually unknown to one another, each one thinking his uncomfortable thoughts in isolation.

Here then was a feebly breathing, hardly existing South. It could conceivably reach with its puny influence into our campuses. Yet even if it did, why would it not suffocate and die there before it could for any of us penetrate the thick overlay of the old-ways-are-right in which we Southern students were encased?

As it turned out, it was of some account that we lived in eventful times. Large forces had begun to shake the world, even our remote piece of it closed in snugly there in the foothills of north Georgia. A time came when we could feel the tugs at the fringes of our pleasant horizon.

At the outset, I think, the extent of what we noticed was some sense of unease. It took circumstances touching us directly to drive the issue home. Nor was this in the first place the outbreak of war in 1914. Before 1914 affairs at home, even in the South and presently right in Georgia, had taken a turn for the worse. It was presaged by men's disturbing talk of hard times coming. Too many of our elders had lived through deep depressions not to be cast down in anticipation. We could not mistake the gloom and foreboding in the heavy atmosphere.

But then down in Georgia came true cause for alarm. The same year that war broke out in Europe, the boll weevil, that most insidious cotton enemy, had crossed over the Georgia line from Alabama. The news spread like a brush fire, bringing a sinking of heart to Georgia growers. They knew what the boll weevil would do. There had been many years in which to learn since it first invaded the soil of Texas. They knew a cotton farmer must stand almost helpless beside his fields and watch havoc wrought. The most he could do perhaps was to turn aside and try to secure an extension on his mortgage and maybe more credit to put off the day of ruin. They saw even their prosperous creditors suffer—banks, supply merchants, that entire pyramidal credit structure of the region's cotton economy. Some banks and merchants at the lower levels even went into collapse along with their debtors. Incalculable indirect consequences followed in closed down cotton gins and cotton oil mills and lowered land values. It took time for all this to happen in Georgia, some two years after the first boll weevil appeared. By then the plague had made its way to every cotton-growing crevice of the state and crossed over into South Carolina.

Finally came war on the European continent. Cotton men knew what to expect, and voiced their gloom. (It is true that in August 1914 I was so ignorant of our cotton economy as to feel astonished at men's lugubrious countenances when the news first came. The boll weevil—yes, that destroyed cotton. But that a distant war could upset markets. . . . The little boll weevil and war taught my introductory course in economics.) Cotton prices took a sudden plunge in the face of war's uncertainties, from which they did not immediately recover. The boll weevil went right on with its ravages. Many of our students came from Black Belt counties. Some time in this period we understood that affairs were bad, very bad indeed. Our college administration began to take cotton bales in place of cash tuition. Here were hard-driving blows against the wall of seclusion surrounding our student minds, blows that mounted in kind and force as we drew nearer to the time when we entered the first World War.

2.

MEANWHILE, it seems, I had taken too much for granted. I was by no means entirely at home with my old heritage. Enough had gone on in the time-and-place limits of my short lifetime to disturb this seeming rapport. It could have come to nothing, of course—a passing flurry of doubts, and then forgetfulness. Perhaps it would have come to very little if I had chanced to be a student in less dynamic years.

Something, it seems, was begun out there in the Sand Hills. Something apparently had been taken away, even if at the time I did not acknowledge it. For where was the full glamour now of the "old plantation," when in recent first-hand experience there was only a "farm," and this under circumstances of poor country, hard work, and people who seemed not to enjoy it at all? Why would not the old picture be blurred by the insertion of this new one, in which Negro laborers came and went as strangers, among whom were no counterparts of the slave names so familiar in one's family annals? Negro laborers, moreover, who seemed borne down by extremities of destitution which I had never witnessed even for Negroes.

In the Sand Hills for the first time in my experience I had been set down to live day after day in close companionship with deep poverty suffered by whites, a poverty to which I had not hitherto been imperceptibly hardened. In any event, in that isolated countryside all human beings aroused my interest, whoever they might be. Perhaps, therefore, I saw more than I otherwise would have. Evidently the images of the people were photographed indelibly on my mind and with them their surroundings and hardships, even though I might think I had forgotten them. It was not for nothing apparently that my would-be playmates were patently children of destitution, so that I perforce saw their state very intimately. Seeing it and liking them, my mind was stirred against what I saw—at deep levels perhaps, not consciously—in this "the best country and people."

Also, rather than have no companions, or next to none, accustomed social distinctions were allowed to melt away in that remote country. Indeed, it came to seem rather commendable than otherwise, so that one began to explain it in terms of "democracy." I found I was doing this when I reached college. Of course I had no notion why.

Something else was begun in the Sand Hills. When I entered college it was in the role of skeptic. True, it was a skepticism in keeping with my still quite tender years. And presently I was to recoup the loss, at least in a manner of speaking. But the Sand Hill religion meanwhile had been my undoing.

Perhaps if I had been reared as are the vast bulk of Southern children, in evangelical churches, I should not have felt the shock I did. There would have been a contrast, but not a sharp one. As it was, it was a far call for me from the Antioch Baptist Church of my father's ante-bellum upbringing. On his marriage Father had entered my mother's church. What I knew was sedate Episcopal ways.

To my childhood it was hardly church at all without vestments, an altar surmounted by the cross, our ritual and solemn liturgy, the Book of Common Prayer in my hands, our soaring hymns and anthems, a chancel at which to kneel for Holy Communion, a short dignified sermon (and woe, in my mind, to the clergyman who made it long in a service already lengthy). I was unaccustomed to the word "conversion"; it was something to feel reticent about; I knew only "confirmation," the Bishop's solemn "laying on of hands," at a time when one came of age to say: "I think I would like to be confirmed." Hence, I found strange the simple, unadorned auditorium of most evangelical churches, with rostrum and reading desk the main appurtenances and with the clergymen wearing garments little different from street clothes; also the long sermons and long extemporaneous prayer. My Baptist and Methodist friends in the city on their part had plainly felt the difference.

183

They had often refused to attend church with me, saying, with some asperity, that they never knew when to rise up, kneel, or sit down.

Of course, too, there were our more lenient Episcopal ways (we liked to call them "tolerant"). Nor was I unaware that my evangelical friends looked on them with some dubiety. I could see it was suspect in their eyes that we regarded dancing and card playing as innocent pleasures, so long as proper respect was rendered Sundays and Lent. Not that my city friends usually went so far as to consider these pastimes actually sinful. To indulge might be to play with fire, but they often did indulge. So I could not take this kind of difference between us very seriously.

Our beliefs I think I assumed to be much the same, whether we were Baptist or Episcopalian. In any case as a child I would not be much concerned with dogmas. Our theological tenets had sifted as softly into my consciousness as snow floats down on a still winter night and one wakens to find the ground blanketed. They had come in the form of words, to be sure, but words to stately music, and candlelight, and flowers on the altar, and communal voices repeating familiar phrases of poetic quality.

The Sand Hills put an end to this. Beliefs suddenly loomed before my mind. I saw and heard what purported to be the same religion I believed in, but it seemed very changed. With astonishment I would listen to the deacon's heartrending stutters, as he determinedly read a passage like the "begats" of St. Matthew, from "Abraham begat Isaac . . . " through "Josias begat Jechonias . . . " through "Salathiel begat Zorobabel . . . " right down to the end. When I had set out to memorize the book of Matthew, Mother had let me skip the begats and begin with: "So all the generations from Abraham unto David . . . " But here everything was apparently sacred and momentous. The deacon evidently felt he must read these verses, heavy cross though they were to his limited literacy. No less than words of the prophet Isaiah: "In all their affliction, he was afflicted . . . in his love and in his pity he redeemed them . . . " or the Psalmist's: "The Lord is my Shepherd . . . " these begats were for him the very Word of God. When the preacher came, he used terms with which I was familiar. Our Episcopal creed had them, and our theology. Hear-

184

ing them at revival time somehow made them sound entirely different. Or perhaps it is truer to say I heard them for the first time. They seemed to awaken antagonistic responses in my mind, hearing them as I did against the sound of flat, hopeless voices singing: "Wash me whiter than the snow. . . ."

Even before the Sand Hills something was begun, and right in the bosom of our family. When I arrived at college I took for granted a lively intellectual interest. It had not occurred to me that it was untypical of our South, where girl-rearing was concerned and for girls of my background. In our family we had come by it naturally. My mother in particular had had a hand in it. It was a possession of hers. In the midst of busy years of homemaking and child rearing and her church and Daughters-of-the-Confederacy duties, she still found her moments to read and to have her children fill their minds with books. Her own early learning, moreover, was a proud family possession, more particularly among her daughters. Perhaps we took peculiar pleasure in it, feeling our own prestige advanced, who were but females in a world of male superiority. As a little girl back there in Augusta, Mother had sat at the feet of a tutor, Mr. Neely, an Irish clergyman of the Episcopal Church. Certain it is he had few preconceptions about woman's intellectual inferiority, whose young pupil at eight years was set the task of reading the Greek New Testament and at ten was put to work on Locke's *Human Understanding*. With sparkling eyes Mother would talk to us of Mr. Neely, his charm and grace and seemingly limitless learning, and we, as eagerly, would listen to her stories, learning to say his name, even as she did, with reverence. He made a schoolteacher of her. She had begun to be a teacher in the 1870's, when for a girl of "good family," even "without prospects," to practice a profession was very unusual. She met my father and was married. She never lost her interest, however. Consciously or otherwise, and female child though she was, Mr. Neely had made her feel the worth of her mind. Very likely it was her hand, quite imperceptibly, which guided this one of our family beliefs along lines somewhat different from what others around us held.

The situation was anomalous. In some sense it remained with us the woman's part to sit silent when men were speaking; not to pit our opinions against the more knowing male's; indeed, to look on woman as a figure on a pedestal—Southern woman, that is—to be treated accordingly; even to regard her as a creature of intuition, who was meant to lean her feeble strength on the firm, solid frame of a male protector and guide. In most ways I think we shared with those about us this still prevalent idea of "woman's place."

Yet in our family circle the something different had crept in to counter this. It was a saying with us, carrying all the weight of my father's prestige and my mother's training: "Those who have brains are meant to use them." As a result, no real distinction in this regard was made between boys and girls. Not alone our brothers, but we as girls talked of "what we would do some day." To be sure, "woman's place was in the home," but it was conceivable that girls could entertain these other thoughts. Nor in doing it did one think merely of making a living. This possible something that we might do was intrinsically interesting and desirable, a future which might hold infinite variety.

As it chanced, college fed this incipient intellectual interest. At least, one instructor did. So far as I was concerned, this one man was my education. He was not a brilliant personality, carrying us along by sheer weight of his presence, but a shy, modest person who was not even "inspiring." We found in him, however, a quiet persistence which demanded that we use our minds, go to the sources, have no truck with undocumented hearsay, keep our eyes always on the vast play of forces—"discuss the social, economic and political significance of so-and-so"—and we would try to do it. It seemed to make no difference that he was diffident, retiring, and vastly overworked, with a teaching load covering most of the history courses, plus economics and sociology—once he even taught us logic. He could seemingly forget everything else in the intensity of his intellectual fervor. Hence we forgot to find him unapproachable.

A group of students were drawn to him, although it meant they had to "use their brains." He was by no means an easy taskmaster. He required hard mental labor and showed evident impatience at anything less. True, many took his courses because they must to fulfill requirements. But some of us took them all and asked for more. Of those who comprised this little company, while I can remember no names, I recall plainly certain facts about them, and from them, too, I believe I learned. All were Southern students; none were well-to-do, as seemed the majority in the college; few were girls "of family" as one customarily reckoned them; certainly, few belonged to the campus social elite, for whom college was more a finishing school than a place of learning; all except one or two were student leaders; all were planning to "do something" after college. Whether they all did is lost in oblivion for me—only two of the eight or ten was I ever to encounter in later years. If certain special windows of their minds came afterward to be opened, as happened for me, there was no indication of it when we parted.

As time passed I could sense no limitations in the earnest searching of my teacher's mind, nor would he seek to place them on others'. He was a devout churchman, a Baptist, yet when later on a few of us asked him to teach us from the little books of Harry Emerson Fosdick, who was then the flaming "modernist" in most Southern religious minds, he showed no hesitation. He was Southern in his roots, but in after years, when I went to him with questions growing out of my Southernness, he seemed entirely unperturbed. I found in him no disposition to censure or to say: "It is wrong where you are heading."

3.

THERE CAME the years of 1914 and 1915. Audiences of students in our section of the nation had found themselves listening in rapt attention to a new message. Elsewhere it may have sounded before 1914. Our campus heard it in the spring of that year. It was not of heaven and hell and eternal damnation. It was not a call to repentance such as revivalists might sound. There was no "wrath of Jehovah" here, or "sins of the fathers visited unto the third and fourth generation," no hint of a vengeful Deity. It was not even a call to staid duty, to fulfill one's religious obligations to believe, and pray, and attend church services, and tithe. It came in an infinitely attractive guise. It had drawing power at a time when these same young people were beginning to feel uneasy at a world out of joint, and less secure in their surroundings and less confident in their elders. It told youth that the day of discipleship was not past. On the contrary, it said the essence of their religion, did they but know it, was old words with a new meaning—"Follow the Master," "The Kingdom of Heaven on Earth." It said God above all was a "loving Father," who was first and foremost approachable, and had infinite concern for the sons of men. As for the Son of God, he had once been Man as well; he had even been a carpenter, one who worked with his hands. Hence it was practical even in the twentieth century to call him "Master." He was a divine example, to be sure, but he could be "followed." Some might say base human nature would not change. Not the new message or the new voices. Let this religion spread, they said, and it could be potent to transform the world by changing the men who made it. To some of us at least these were little short of John-on-Patmos voices—"And I saw a new heaven and a new earth: for the first heaven and the first earth were passed away; and there was no more sea."

I was drawn into this company then and there. Nor was I any more loath than my fellows to weigh our forebears in the scales and find them wanting. We were especially prone to, who, as we supposed, had already cut loose from many of our childhood religious moorings. How, we began to wonder, as we became more and more enamored of our role, had men been so blind for all the generations of Christendom as not to see what we now perceived? How had they gone on, century after century, quarreling among themselves over theological minutiae, bothering their minds over issues of dogma, to the disregard of what all along had been the essence of our religion? Why, our minds demanded, was there still so little "brotherhood" in the world, when "brotherhood" was the very meaning of Christianity? Let enough people but be persistent enough, and "consistent" enough—this latter loomed very large in our minds who had begun to "follow the Master"—and why might not the new day mankind hoped for begin to dawn? We now had something to be and do in the admittedly very bad times in which we lived. Indeed, the further we pursued the matter, the more there appeared to be and do.

Of a New Heaven

To be sure, not many continued to pursue it. Just occasional students here and there on various campuses.

For me it went on soaking into my consciousness for a year without any peculiarly eruptive consequences. But then it came. Why would it not take the form it did? I was a white Southerner living in the South. I was a young person, able blandly to assume that the Word could be made flesh and dwell among men. Except, of course, that I had never seen it in the flesh. Until I saw it, it had not remotely occurred to me what this might be thought to mean.

My college course was over, but I remained on my campus as a tutor. I was now nineteen. In late 1915 a few of us from several Southern colleges were called to a "leadership" conference by the YWCA, the bearer on our women's campuses of the new social Christianity. The place was in North Carolina—I think, the city of Charlotte. I know it was a strictly Southern city, very Southern indeed, for presently I became exceedingly conscious of the mighty cloud of hostile witnesses that might be surrounding us. At the conference we studied and planned for a day or two. Then one of our staff leaders placed a proposal before us.

She was a Southern woman. She spoke to us as such. She assured us that she had been reared even as had we. She said that she could understand our first impulsive misgivings. Once she had stood at the crossroads we now confronted. She urged us to consider the matter. Take until morning. We could accept or reject.

The proposal was this: There was a Negro woman leader in the city then: a woman of education, a professional woman, herself belonging to the YWCA staff. It was suggested that she speak to us on Christianity and the race problem.

If our leader, in proposing it, had just called the person "Jane Arthur," our sense of foreboding would not have been so great. Well, surely, let a "Jane" or "Mary" speak to us, if needs must, and that could be the end of it; we could go away and forget a "Mary" or a "Jane." We had known and forgotten tens of thousands of Negro Marys and Janes. But never a "Miss Arthur." How forget a "Miss Arthur"? And must we too say: "Miss"? Would we be introduced and have to shake her hand and say: "Miss Arthur"? Shaking hands was not unheard of. Many times we had seen our people shake the hand of a "darkey" in a genuinely kindly way, asking how he was, and how was his family, and they might remark afterward, and probably would, in a spirit of warm generosity: "Now there is a *good* darkey." How could one be "good" who came to us as *"Miss"* Arthur? The only time we had ever said "Miss" or "Mrs." or "Mr." was in telling a "darkey joke," or in black-faced minstrels—"Now, *Mister* Johnson . . . " and the crowd would roar with mirth. It had always been a source of slight amusement to us, the way Negroes seemed to insist upon addressing one another as "Mr." and "Mrs." Why do such a thing, I used to wonder? To imitate white people, I supposed, in their desire to make themselves as much like us as they could. We would remark, tolerantly: "See how they try to mimic us. Queer, isn't it? But they're just like children trying to pretend they are grown up. . . ." We would smile, and not mind it in the general run of "darkies," the ignorant and humble ones. We had no such kindly sentiment toward the educated; those we knew—we had heard—always addressed one another just as we did each other; those whose dark brows seemed to grow overcast, whose countenances seemed suddenly to become strangely still and remote when a white man would say to one of them whom he met on the sidewalk: "Howdye, Jim," or "Good evening, George"— maybe a doctor, or lawyer or teacher. (Some of these had walked our streets when I was a child; we knew their alleged profession; always one thought: "How impudent . . . how presumptuous. . . !")

But see it another way. In one sense, was it so out-of-the-way for a Negro to stand before us and speak to us? There was nothing to be *scared* of. (We put scorn in the emphasis.) We were used to Negroes, weren't we? Who could be more so? How many times had we smiled at Northerners who looked at one almost with horror, and exclaimed: "How can you Southerners stand to have them fondle your children, handle your food?"—smiled at them, and said: "It only goes to show how much kindlier we Southerners feel toward the Negro than you Yankees, who are always trying to tell us how to treat them. . . . You don't understand. . . . We are their best friends. . . . They are all right in their place." But this was the wrong thought to let slip in. This really opened the door to thoughts we would like to avoid. "What would people say? What if they knew? How explain?" For to concur in what was proposed, by no stretch of our imaginations, would be other than breaking the unwritten and written law of our heritage: "Keep them in their place."

We were like a little company of Eves, who, not from being tempted—surely, we did not long to eat the fruit which up to now had been called forbidden—but by sheer force of unsought circumstance found ourselves called upon to pluck from the Tree of Life the apple that would open our eyes to see what was good and evil. But here confusion reigned. We had been taught it was wrong to eat this apple. Yet as it was put before us we felt guilty not to. Most certainly we were afraid to do it. Did we have the glimmering notion that if we did, something that hitherto had always seemed decorous and decent might, if our eyes were opened to see its naked reality, seem quite otherwise?

Why did we consent? Or perhaps put it another way: by what rationalizing means did we excuse our consent to something from which we saw no self-respecting retreat? The old Southern heritage could not be thrust aside, even momentarily, except by something insistently strong. On one side was the dictum: "In their place." Hitherto we had assumed it to be immutable and unchangeable. It carried the authority of our kind. For me it carried a special weight, which still could be felt even if much of its old glamour had slipped away, of a Lost Cause termed sacred. What could bring a counterweight and authority against this bulk, something equally reinforced by sentiment, something that could even take precedence over our assumed racial verities?

We knew what it was. Perhaps we sensed from the outset, the way the case was put, that no real choice faced us, unless we proposed to turn deserter. Before our leader let us go to think it over, she had put the matter in this wise: It was written, she read (and how many times in succeeding years did we let this story stand us in similar stead), ". . . Jesus . . . said, a certain man was going down from Jerusalem to Jericho . . . fell among robbers, who both stripped him and beat him, and departed, leaving him half dead . . . A certain priest . . . when he saw him . . . passed by on the other side . . . in like manner a Levite . . . But a certain Samaritan . . . journeyed . . . and when he saw him . . . was moved with compassion . . . bound up his wounds . . . set him on his own beast . . . brought him to an inn, and took care of him . . . Which of these three . . . was neighbor to him that fell among the robbers?" [Who was better than another here—driving home the point—the "chosen people," or the Samaritan who was despised? What, in "the Master's" lesson, made one person better than another?] Oh, for the days when nothing more than the Virgin Birth, miracles, the Trinity, pushed against one's mind as tests of credulity! But surely, we could argue, all the religious people at home, all one had ever known, would have felt even as we wanted to. Many, there came the additional passing thought, would very probably even take us sternly by the hand, saying: "We must get you out of here."

But this latter notion was not palatable. It kept coming back and we rejected it. Here we were, almost of age. "We must consider this matter for ourselves," we finally said.

In after years one might idly wonder: suppose Miss Arthur had never stood before our little group? Suppose she had been taken ill, or had broken her leg, or for any reason had been kept away? Suppose our leaders had heeded our obvious distress and decided: "We are going too fast; we must wait awhile; they will be more ready by and by." Or suppose we had said: "We just can't stomach it; maybe we should . . . but we can't live up to this test of our new Christian consistency. . . ." It was idle wondering. No doubt other occasions would have come. Of course, if they had not chanced to. . . . In any event, she did stand before us, and she was introduced as "Miss Arthur." Moreover, we were told, "She will talk to us. . . ."

What she talked about was not of such great consequence: what mattered was that she entered the door and stood before us. We told each other afterwards—could it be we felt a little gratified?—how our pulses had hammered, and how we could feel our hearts pound in our chests. Be that as it may, it was of no small moment to hear her low voice sound in the speech of an educated woman, and to have my mind let the thought flicker in, even if it disappeared again immediately—If I should close my eyes, would I know whether she was white or Negro?

In any event, when it was over, I found the heavens had not fallen, nor the earth parted asunder to swallow us up in this unheard of transgression. Indeed, I found I could breathe freely again, eat heartily, even laugh again. Back in my Georgia foothills I put it out of my mind, or better, pushed it down deep in a welter of other unwanteds. But still I would now and then find something stirring up an indefinable sense of discomfort—and then remember. Moreover, in remembering, there was just a flavor of something besides uneasiness: ever so faint exhilaration, perhaps? One of the Bible stories of my childhood which never had sat well with me, seeming to my untutored mind a punishment out of all proportion to the crime, was that of the man in the book of Samuel who broke the law forbidding any secular hand, unconsecrated and unaccustomed to minutely prescribed rules and regulations, to touch the sacred Tabernacle of Jehovah; touching it, so said the story, he was promptly stricken dead. Well, so was this tabernacle of our sacred racial beliefs untouchable. How well I knew it; how ingrained in me were the beliefs it housed, and the belief that to touch it would bring direst consequences. But I had touched it. I had reached out my hand for an instant and let my finger-tips brush it. I had done it, and nothing, not the slightest thing had happened.

BOOK SIX
And a New Earth

1.

Nearly five years passed. In this time the war roared ever closer to our doors, while we continued to feel it remote until we entered it. We took our side, Southerners that we were, in the peculiar home battle being fought, which put back into office the president who had "kept us out of war." We waged the contest with that special fervor that Southerners show for political battles which promise to be in their favor. Happily, we could forget, if we had ever heard them much below Mason-Dixon's line, the phrases that were to make Wilson's name sound round the world. He was not to most of us the eloquent author of a New Freedom, but our man who had won—Democrat, Southerner.

However, when we then went to war we seemed to take it for granted. It gave us no pause to put our men into uniform, and raise the Stars and Stripes, and sing *America*. Not even when Southern boys boarded transports to go to foreign battlefields. Southerners of my kind were steeped in calls to duty, especially the call to war. We had already fought one war as a united nation. In that other war, too, our boys had gone to foreign shores, at least to Cuba and the Philippines. We told of this. Our Confederate reunions when I was a child had recited the tales very proudly, it seems, to show how soldiers of the "dead republic" had "proved the sincerity of their surrender, their loyalty to the will of God and their faithfulness to their reunited country." They had especially told of Confederate stalwarts being called to duty, such as General Joe Wheeler (my father's old commander), and General Butler, and one of the Lees. To be sure, there would also be gleeful stories, as of General Wheeler on a battlefield of Cuba in that War with

Spain exhorting his men to "Charge, boys! Charge!" and then an excited slip of the tongue, "You've got the damn Yanks running!" Now in this first World War our patriotism flourished mightily. Outside my home city, Columbia, was huge Camp Jackson mushroomed to enormous size in but a few months. Our streets were filled with soldiers, and not just Southerners. Northerners by the thousands, officers and men, overran the town. It was all one to us. Or so it seemed.

In these same short years we saw war come to an end, and felt the jubilation of that passing hour. After that we saw the aftermath, heard the immense confusion of sound, as groups in the nation contended with one another over why we had fought the war. Some of us thought we saw how much stronger were certain groups than others. Then we witnessed the outcome, among other things— but this came later—the economic crisis of postwar times.

These then were the years when a scattered few of us who were just coming into adulthood had begun to wrestle with our Southernness. One has no means of surmising how numerous we young Southerners were. Those who sat beside me in that room to hear Miss Arthur I could count on the fingers of my two hands. There were others in our woman-student-company, and among the men something similar was occurring. It seems that now and then young men were listening to such a man as Dr. George Carver, who as a notable scientist even though a Negro, was known to pry open Southern minds by the sheer fact of his existence. It was so at least if he appeared before us. To our incredulous minds it took seeing to make us believe or even consider the possibility that Negroes might not *all* (we emphasized the *all*) be as inferior as we Southerners supposed; that they could and did achieve—in some instances, we added; that to them also, or to some of them rather, might belong the full title and dignity of human being.

Even to think these thoughts one must be disposed to believe. Many were not. In few Southern places in that day, besides student conferences of certain church bodies and YMCA and YWCA, were such racial discussions as ours taking place. Many of those who heard them would turn away, and none knew better than we, who had chanced not to, our fellows' sense of devastating confusion, their unpleasant, unbidden repulsions.

And a New Earth

Also our number was small because we lived at the time when the first cautious, exploratory steps were being taken, and our adult leaders, who were a stage or two beyond us, hesitated even to beckon to young people whose mentors they were and for whom they felt responsible. Possibly they were made the more cautious because, we being young, they supposed we were not yet broken to the harness of slow gradualism and so might take the bit in our teeth and try to run away. We may even have sounded this way, as we pressed them back to answer our questions. We had been bidden to foster "brotherhood" in race relations. Now we wished to know what it meant. Where did it lead? How far did it go? And sooner or later we would give voice to our timeworn Southern fear of "social equality." It momentarily eased our minds when our leaders would say: "No one wants it," neither Negroes nor whites, that this was not "at issue"; and that the cogent words were "justice," "opportunity." Our questions went on pressing against the barriers in our minds. We went on asking them.

Perhaps our leaders should have been reassured that we, no more than they, showed much disposition to implement our fainthearted skepticism in any bold way. For even as they, we went on living in our surroundings, following all the prescribed racial rules and regulations which were our heritage, and finding what mental comfort we could in the fact that we were not contented.

We learned soon enough how little we would do, once we left the warm company of fellow-dissidents. Most of the time we must be alone with our thoughts, scattered far and wide into our communities. I certainly felt so on my campus during the years I was a tutor. I was not yet ready to trust my budding heresies to any but those who I knew would not be scandalized.

To be sure, the only Negroes I knew were those I had always known, those who served us. With the one exception. I saw Miss Arthur a very few times at our student conferences, where she made fleeting appearance to speak before a selected few. I could even say "Miss" Arthur now without too much self-consciousness. But most of the time the Negroes I saw were our washerwomen, and maids in our halls, and waiters in the dining-room, and gardeners.

Even here one could feel the inner motion of change. Certain old mental habits began to slip away. I could no longer bring myself to use the term "darkey," substituting for it with what ease I could, "colored" or "Nigra." (It took me awhile to say correctly, "Negro.") I became vaguely self-critical about our treatment of servants, not because I felt we were unkind. Rather, I found irksome the indefinable assumption that we whites were to be served, not as a job performed for which we paid certain specific individuals, but as a duty owed to us by Negroes as a race. By such tokens as these I could believe I was not standing still, except that times would come to make me feel unsure again.

The Birth of a Nation came to our campus in this time. Years before I had read the Dixon books. Now they came alive in this famous spectacle. In the South we had heard the motion picture acclaimed, that here at last we had been done justice. We poured out to the picture, everyone, students, townsfolk. The hall was packed. Several showings were held so that all could come. I went —in truth, went more than once.

To be sure in old reunion days one would have expected a flood of feeling. Here the Klan rode, white robed. Here were romance and noble white womanhood. Here was the black figure—and the fear of the white girl—though the scene blanked out just in time. Here were sinister men the South scorned and noble men the South revered. And through it all the Klan rode. All around me people sighed and shivered, and now and then shouted or wept, in their intensity.

Who knows what the picture aimed to say? Maybe nothing— some said so—just a spectacle, with new techniques. Southerners, I believe, had no doubt of what it said or what they read into it of the nobility of our history, the righteousness of our acts, the rightness of our beliefs. As for me, I did not know, not at the time, that is. Except that I felt old sentiments stir, and a haunting nostalgia, which told me that much that I thought had been left behind must still be ahead.

2.

IN THE AUTUMN that war ended I went North to spend two years, having never hitherto set foot beyond the borders of the Carolinas and Georgia. Too much had begun before I went for me to say now what happened on the Northern side. Too little appeared there of what I had expected, not to leave me with a sense of unpleasant deflation. Too much opened up before my mind in these particular years, which was neither Northern nor Southern, not to obscure a little the fact of a Mason-Dixon's line.

To be sure, it was as a self-conscious Southerner that I arrived in New York. Certain old habits of mind reasserted themselves at this excursion into the other camp. One expected to have one's different speech recognized, and to say off-handedly, "Yes, from the South." One waited for the questions that inevitably came and gave many of them the inevitable answers. One spoke as an authority on the South. We were all authorities. Whoever we were and whatever our knowledge, we could speak with confidence of what we "know." Perhaps this as much as anything first made me skeptical.

I was a student again. There now came back to me my former teacher's undergraduate schooling in the marks of scholarship. His standards reasserted themselves. Until now, it came over me, I had never studied the South. I had never "gone to the sources," "checked facts against hearsay," sorted out "unbiased from biased history." Then how could I "know" the South when all I knew was what had been handed on to me as my heritage and what had come in my limited experience? And how could these others "know" the South, who spoke with my same bland assurance? I began to be unsure that mere place of origin qualified one to speak. I began to doubt my own characterizations, and my fellows' as well. I soon became surfeited with the invariable echoes of the same old themes, and not a little impatient with our clearly-evident complacency.

It was not that Northerners induced my reaction. Few complained openly of our provincialism. Perhaps they were polite. Perhaps the cotton wool of Southern satisfaction in which we had wrapped ourselves for the Northern winter ahead, shut out the chilling thoughts they harbored. As I felt it, they welcomed our Southernness—most of them. They took with gentle tolerance our vagaries and the peppery language we used in defending our history. They liked to hear us say the authentic "darkey," and our kindly condescension in describing the Negro. They appeared to take in quite good part our usual assertion that we alone understood Negroes and should be left alone to deal with them. It is true, I myself could not talk this way any more. That time had passed before I ever went to the North. But leaving race aside, much still remained to be said of South versus North and of Southern traditional ways. And I heard the talk of others incessantly.

In point of fact I went North with mixed mind about Northerners. Once I had had but one picture in my head. This had long since been modified. I had known many Northerners in my college days. My college had prided itself on cosmopolitanism. Our students came from states far and wide. Our principal annual celebration was a "States' Day," with songs and speeches and a parade of flower-decked floats all through the town. I had learned to sing, not alone *The Old North State, Alabama, Alabama, The Red Old Hills of Georgia,* but also "I-o-wa . . . that's where the tall corn grows." I could count among my friends some Northerners. All in all, it had come to seem a far friendlier territory stretching away beyond Mason-Dixon's line.

On the other hand, some Northern students had repelled me. It was not the few who lived up to my picture of typical "Yankee"— those who were proud of their history and scornful of ours; who would sometimes call us "rebels," and sing *Marching through Georgia* mockingly, and say Sherman "gave you what you deserved," and who would criticize us for our "treatment of the Negroes." These I never minded, although I answered them in kind. They were but what one expected. But then there were those—a majority, I thought—who were far from showing any felt antagonism. They aped our Southern ways, took over our terminology bodily, saying "darkey," and even "nigger." To my scorn, some said "coon," a term we never used. What especially antagonized me was that they offered us sympathy—so their words said; my thoughts termed it "licking boots." "You Southerners certainly have a terrible problem on your hands with so many 'coons' around." "How awful

it must be to have them as servants . . . so lazy . . . unreliable
. . . slovenly . . . light-fingered." These were like our words, but
hearing them from their lips had an unpleasant sound, as of something respectable suddenly made indecent. I was not then disap-
proving of our ways. I supposed us right. But also I had supposed
that all Northerners were the self-ordained champions of Negro
slave and Negro freedman. I seemed to feel almost a slight sense
of shame for them.

Meanwhile I had met other Northerners, met them in the course
of recent years. I had begun to read Northern journals which dealt
with Southern problems of our day. I had revised my opinion of
the section and of Northern people. Some of course would prove
very benighted. I expected this. But also I expected to find myself
in a place where fresh, free air circulated. I was going as a student
to a very hub of learning. I sought here mental stimulus, something to quicken my thoughts and supply them with rich, nourish-
ing materials. I sought companionship in learning, a sense of others
striving to unravel the mysteries of why men behaved as they did
and perhaps what could make them behave differently. I expected,
well, perhaps an extension of what my former teacher exemplified,
except in magnified terms, since here would be notable scholars,
great minds, liberal learning on every side.

It would be untrue to say I met none of this, but I had to modify
my goals and learn moreover where to turn my search. For the most
part it was away from my university.

As for Columbia, I sat in the classrooms of some of its best-known
men. The dry categories were like dust in my throat. We may say I
was to blame. It was my fault, after all, that I wished my learning
to seem alive and had certain problems to which I thought it
might contribute. It was my fault, too, that I was looking for teachers who envisaged scholarship as something moving and breathing
and not as a corpse on which men of learning performed a continuing autopsy. It was surely my fault that I took away, as something that applied, the very lesson I could best have done without.

This was not Giddings's "consciousness of kind"; nor yet Herbert
Spencer's "law of evolution"—". . . integration of matter . . .
concomitant dissipation of motion . . . indefinite incoherent ho-
mogeneity . . . definite coherent heterogeneity. . . ." I memo-

rized these as was required. But they did not set my brain agog. Sumner's "mores" did. Here was something corresponding to what I knew. Here was a scientific name to describe what my eyes had seen, especially in our racial ways, and the solemn morality we attached to these practices which after all were but the creations of the brains of men. So far so good, but there was more besides. It appeared that scientific minds surmised that the "mores" were so imbedded in men's social habits as to make it nearly impossible to alter them—at best taking generations of time, at worst centuries. This was something else again. This was a blow at one's weakest spot. Everything around me thus far had fostered a disposition against too much change too rapidly. Now I must go away with a heavy sense of the authority of science confirming my own inclinations. No one chanced to tell me, not my professors and not the books, that the great Sumner had himself been a vehement opponent of such attempts at change as trade-unionism, child-labor laws, legislation for the eight-hour day as gross interferences with the natural law of supply and demand. This might surely have lifted my sense of defeatism a little, that the author of the "mores" himself believed enough in their possibility of change to consider it needful to put obstacles in the way.

If I had expected one thing more than another from the North, it was to see and be thrown with Negroes who had achieved. In my ignorance I had assumed that a large Northern city saw much natural give and take, coming and going, "equality of opportunity," and the like. To be sure, I knew our saying that we "treated Negoes better" down South, that Northerners were cold, and that our servant class was always happier when they came home than ever they had been in the mercenary, inhospitable North. But this I had come to take with a grain of salt. In any case, it was not the poorer Negroes I expected to see, but educated men and women. This was my lack. These, I assumed, up North found themselves in a climate of equality. I wished to test this climate for myself.

I found the discrepancies, and they had their pleasing side. I would say complacently: "The pot calling the kettle black." But I was nonplussed. It confused me to hear it said: "Let a Negro try to register at a Northern white hotel . . . or a white person take a Negro to a 'nice' white restaurant . . . or a Negro doctor practice in a white hospital . . . or a Negro craftsman qualify for a skilled job he is trained for . . . or a Negro family live in an all-white neighborhood. . . ." This was not what I had bargained for. Our friendly Northern critics had not prepared me for their ways or their close kinship to ours that they often belabored. I felt I was handed a stone when I had come here for bread. I could see why we Southerners behaved as we did; up to a certain point it was most understandable. We had a history. We had held slaves. We still clung to our mental remnants of slavery. But not up North. We made it an excuse that *we* had so many Negroes. Not up North. It seemed so gratuitous, these Northern patterns of our ways, these Northern reflections of our outlook that I had thought peculiar to us. Now I found something similar to them here. I wished to berate the North, to scold, to say: "You've no right, no excuse, for behaving this way." Until I bethought me, it was hardly my place.

It would be absurd to say that I saw no differences. Of course I did. How could I sit beside Negroes in subways and streetcars, and more especially in my classes in graduate school, and not know the difference? In particular, how could I overhear what some of my fellow-Southerners had to say about the indignity of having to sit by Negroes, and not know that this climate was different from ours? And of course there were no signs here, "For White," "For Colored"—not written out at least. But also at this time I wished to minimize differences, since this made us less guilty and the proud North share our guilt. Much I could not see as yet. Certainly, I had no comprehension of the vast difference between a "peculiar institution" which is of the bone and sinew of a society, and ways, however prevalent, that are yet non-institutionalized.

Before I went away I came nearer this latter knowledge, and once again, by the instrument of Negroes themselves. One of my expectations of the North was partially realized. In a summer seminar at Columbia, to my surprise, were three Negroes, one man and two women. One of the women was Georgia-born, even as I was. The course browsed in the field of race relations.

Soon enough I realized that these Negroes were very different persons altogether from Miss Arthur. Their educational training and professional position exceeded hers. Also they were traveled and had a large grasp of public affairs. But besides this, they were forthright, blunt, it seemed to me, who had been accustomed to have my Southern sensibilities taken some account of. It was not they who were sensitive to being Negroes, of whom I must be considerate, but I who found myself sensitive to being white, and Southern white at that. They continually held our discussion to facts, which they were versed in. Hitherto my Southernness had protected me from the devastating potency of facts. Here I found no escape from them, nor did one side of me wish to escape but drove my mind open to take the consequences.

Most of all, my fellow Georgian was the instrument of this. She spoke of my section, even of my state, which I once thought I knew. Especially she spoke of Negroes there, of whom I had heard all my life, "We Southerners understand." She shattered this pleasant fiction with figures and incidents which told in plain language the realities of segregation. She confronted one with truths as to what Southern Negroes wished for in education, citizenship, job opportunities, equality before the law, and what in fact they had.

Then at the close of the term our professor invited his seminar to tea.

I went to the tea. It was not without full knowledge of what I was doing. This was "eating with Negroes." In the terminology I once had used this was "social equality." In the whole roster of Southern taboos it was nearly the most sacred. It was a grievous Southern sin for which were allowed no mitigating circumstances.

Once it would have seemed a momentous thing, a personal crisis as great as that first one when I decided to sit and listen to a "Miss" Arthur. It was not so now. To be sure, when it was over, one could feel relief to have had the chance to prove that this taboo no longer held dominion over one's mind. It was a welcome thing thus to see some of our most sacred racial "mores" in this perspective, and know that individuals at least could shake off their domination within a relatively short space of time, and then glimpse the possibility for whole groups, if circumstances could be made favorable. None of this however took first place in my mind. And by so much I knew that what moved me here stood in sharp contrast to that earlier time, when our primary concern had been with our personal religious consistency. The emphasis was shifting. The "old heaven" may have passed away, but not the "old earth," nor showed many signs of it. The earth was our concern. I now saw this taboo as nothing personal at all. It had a large social purpose which we white Southerners had summed up as keeping the Negro in his "place." It was for this it had been made a part of our life, and on this account that it was inserted into the minds of each white generation.

3.

NINETEEN-TWENTY brought me home, but not to a South of happy promise. The time had come of which we had been so sternly warned: "We must put them back in their place again."

The toll of the boll weevil, as far back as 1916, had started a slowly swelling labor army moving out of devastated cotton fields. If corn bread and fatback could not be "furnished," then stranded Negro families must be on the move. Then came the war and opened the gates of hitherto closed Northern mills. These were beckoning eagerly to any and all laborers. Negro migrants began to move in a steady stream to Northern industrial cities. They wrote letters home, telling of high wages, schools for their children, streetcars where they could sit anywhere. There could be riots in East St. Louis or even Chicago. Still, they felt safer up North and said so, writing home. Recruiting agents began to drift around in remote Southern communities, making rash promises about the promised land.

The pull was strong, and the numbers were disturbing. Southern men took steps, though they could not feel satisfied. They passed restraining ordinances in their towns, imposed penalties upon migration, set up rules and regulations, placed bans on agents, let rumors and threats circulate as to what would happen to any whö tried to board trains. One heard of violence even during the war.

At the same time, Southern boys who had been drafted were poured by thousands into army camps and overseas. But these were not alone white boys. This was the point of it. To be sure, races were meticulously kept apart: white boys in this part of camp; Negro boys in that part; white boys in these trenches; Negro boys in others, or, if not in trenches, then on trucks or at loading and unloading, tasks which white men were accustomed to have them do. Even so, white men reminded each other, this was disquieting. Negroes were being put into uniforms, precisely as were whites; they too carried guns on their shoulders; they were given the selfsame army pay. This, Southern men had said, was really very dangerous. Besides, stories had begun to come out of France: Negro men . . . French women. This was more dangerous.

One could hear a calmer view. U. B. Phillips, distinguished Southern-born historian, was very reassuring. He wrote cheerfully from a Southern army camp, for his foreword to *Negro Slavery*, of excellent relations. It reminded him of nothing so much, he said, as the old relations of which he told in his book. ". . . The two great elements fundamentally in accord. . . ." Negro soldiers, he believed, showed the same characteristics "which distinguished their forbears"; "Serio-comic obedience . . . same personal attachments to white men . . . love of laughter and rhythm. . . ." Similarly the white officers commanding them—these were Southern men—". . . reflect the planter's admixture of tact with firmness of control. . . ."

Practical, unscholarly white men also spoke confidently. "Oh, we can handle things. We know how to manage them. We are their best friends, after all." But these also said, as did a cruder, more belligerent kind, "We must teach them their place again . . . after the war."

Once the war was over, the time had come. The surplus labor force had been menaced by the drain to the North and the drain into the Army. The formerly "docile" Negro laborers had come home with "new ideas"—so whites believed—about "their place." These laborers had seen more wages than ever before. Their condition had been bettered in a hundred little ways. This was disrupting. This could upset the entire peculiar Southern economy.

One heard many rumors and saw much done. One sensed that a prolonged struggle had begun, with one side hardly conscious of its opportunities, while the other side knew very precisely the stakes.

There were many facets to the movement thus set going, to pull and push or if need be drive the Negro back into "his place." There were respectable men, men of leadership and name and business position, who did their part. To be sure they used respectable means, as we Southerners ordinarily rated them, so that some were hardly recognizable for what they were. Then there were men who were not so respectable in the best circles; or at least whose methods were decried, even if their aims met not a little sympathy.

The Ku Klux Klan was flourishing when I reached home.

It is true, at least so far as I could tell, that the people I knew frowned on this modern Ku Klux Klan. They would say it was never meant to be revived, but was only an instrument for a special time and condition. They would say that the "best people" did not support the new KKK. They decried violence by hooded men. In fact, however, the numbers grew, and so did the influence of this new order.

One heard the words in which the Klan's mission was couched and knew them for the old familiar phrases, even to their habiliments of lush nobility—"the sacred duty of protecting womanhood . . . maintain forever white supremacy . . . bless mankind . . . a pure Americanism." ". . . God's act to make the white race superior. . . . By some scheme of providence . . . Negro created a serf. . . . We harbor no race prejudice . . . Negro never had . . . a better friend than the Ku Klux Klan. . . ." But now something different was added. We soon learned why, watching the new order spread its baleful wings over the North and West. "We exclude Jews. . . . We exclude Catholics. . . . To assure the supremacy of the white race we believe in the exclusion of the yellow race. . . ." In Southern newspapers were lurid, brief, little items of fiery crosses burning, of masked bands of men, of Negroes beaten, of tarrings-and-featherings, of signs, "Nigger, don't let the sun set on you here." And now and then one would hear of whites who were victims. Of course no one proved this was the Klan. The Ku Klux Klan abhorred violence, it said. Other men—maybe "rowdies" as was said in the old days—could have dressed up in white robes and hoods and burned fiery crosses.

Some spoke as though the Klan were but a simple abscess on our otherwise healthy Southern body. It did not strike us this way, who by now were scanning our surroundings for real signs of change. We read symptoms of a deep-seated infection coursing in our

Southern life. We saw it in a letter, directed by a Southern businessman to a leading Southern business journal, bearing the headline: "Anglo-Saxonism of North, South and West Must Combine for the Good of All," which went on to say: ". . . your liberality of space and your clear-cut discussion of States' Rights and the supremacy of the Anglo-Saxon, so dear—one by written law and the other by inheritance—to the people of the South . . . you cannot begin to appreciate the good that you do the South. . . ."

We distinctly saw it in a filibuster waged in the early 1920's against an anti-lynching bill. It had happened before. It would happen again. But I, for one, had not seen it happen since my mind had been aroused to some sense of its significance. Hence, while I knew that we Southerners had a means of wielding power in the arena of national affairs, it was my first conscious lesson in how this was done, and what it portended. We witnessed the methods, heard the candid assumption of our Southern men that their minority had the right, where they saw fit and Southern interests were concerned, to obstruct the direction of the nation's policy. A leading Southerner, Senator Underwood of Alabama, could say bluntly on the Senate floor: "The only way we can fight it [the anti-lynching bill] and let the country understand we will always fight such a measure, is simply to obstruct legislation until we come to an understanding about it." We saw them demonstrate how this could be done: the innumerable roll calls, the day-long speeches, the endless sessions spent correcting the senate journal, and debating omission of the chaplain's prayer. We heard the repeated reminder: "We may not be able to stop all the business you are going to do, Senators, but you cannot prevent us from having a roll call on every affirmative thing that you want to do. . . ."

Others, who were neither Democrats nor Southern, had used the filibuster. They also could be wrong. But we knew our Southern case was different. Our men could say they were but guardians of the sacred principle of States' Rights. They could call themselves worthy protectors of precious individual liberties. They could assert as did Senator Overman on the Senate floor: "The Negroes in the South are happy and contented. . . ." They could clothe their aim in any language they selected. There was no mistaking their true intent. It is certain Southerners knew what it was.

4.

WE HAD Negro colleagues. I was now on the student field staff of the YWCA. Most of our work was done in separation—Negroes among Negroes, whites among whites. Yet we were associates. We saw other advantaged Negroes, those in professions, business, education. The conditions were most peculiar. Our Negro fellows were always subject to our racial ways. We in turn were blessed with our white privileges. This disparity wore on me day by day. Willy-nilly I was pulled about by choices which made no kind of sense to me.

Miss Arthur was on our staff. She traveled as we did to many Southern communities. She had as much allowance for travel as we did; she covered as much mileage or more. But it was not the same. She could not spend the money. Strange, perhaps, that this should strike us as something new, something we had not comprehended before. In our white hands the money was good. It bought us sleepers and chair cars, meals on diners, rooms at first-class city hotels, good food at excellent restaurants. Miss Arthur had allowance for these; it was worthless in her darker hands. It could buy her at most one ticket to so-and-so, riding Jim Crow.

Miss Arthur came to staff meetings. This was all very well when they were held in our field offices. To be sure, it was just a little suspect for a nicely dressed Negro to enter the elevator in a white office building, and enter our suite and take her seat there. Once inside we could try to ignore the sense of a hostile world round about us. We could be almost natural, have some give-and-take, treat her as we treated ourselves, or think we did, for this passing moment. We could even have stenographers who would take letters from this member of our staff, type them, and bring them back to her, all with seemly Southern courtesy. But also we had staff meetings now and then at someone's home.

The chairman of our board had an annual tea to which she invited us. I went to my first one, not even noticing at first that our circle was incomplete. It was a charming country home. We were gay and congenial. We enjoyed delicious food. Then the swinging door opened that led to the kitchen. Miss Arthur was joining us.

Now our hostess was a woman of unmatched principles and unassuming devotion to high ideals. We knew her dilemma. This was the South. We knew she was brave to have a Negro merely sit with us in her drawing room. We asked ourselves, could we have dared to do as much? It seems it did not occur to us until a later time—and then it was not by our initiative—that we could do without these enjoyable little symbols of good fellowship; that we could omit tea, leave out meals, and simply meet, however drab it might seem, if meeting was all we could do together with our Negro colleagues.

A few years later I heard it said: "Her people do not trust Miss Arthur; too much 'Uncle Tom' in her attitude; too humble with whites." At first we whites saw it differently. Who were we not to accept a little humility which came to us in the guise of Christian fortitude? Miss Arthur could carry on her person marks of her rearing in a harsh white world. Why would we not call it Christ-like virtue, if she turned the other cheek to humiliations that our kind heaped on her, and showed kindly goodwill even to her white tormentors, whom she steadfastly looked upon as potential brothers? She made very few demands on our Christian consistency. We admired this. We said she understood our hard, hard situation. We partook of her compassion when she saw us wriggling around to escape, and welcomed the loopholes she generously provided for letting us slip back into comfortable old positions. We particularly took refuge in the sense she gave us that her race might not desire recognition in fullest measure; at least not at once, not until some blessed far distant day.

We had other colleagues. One we saw first at so unlikely a place as our Southern white student conference. We will call her Miss Jones. The conference grounds we used were the YMCA's. The men also had been laboring for co-operation. So they had lately made provision at the conference place to have Negro speakers. They had built a special cottage for their Negro visitors, calling it "Booker T. Washington." Miss Arthur and the new Miss Jones were to be our guests.

So they were, in a manner of speaking. I was sent to conduct them to their first evening meeting. The path up the mountain was fresh and rough. Few feet indeed had hitherto trod it. The cottage itself was somewhat apart, its face modestly turned to front the mountainside. As I knocked at the door I heard dishes rattle. As Miss Arthur opened it I saw that she had put a tray aside. Miss Jones also had disposed of a tray and risen to greet this white stranger, who was close to her in age and education as well as a member of the same profession. Until now I had not wondered how our special guests would eat. It had not occurred to me. My wants were cared for in the usual way. I had just come from the large dining-room where the several hundred members of the conference were fed. Not these, however.

It seems Miss Jones had not known that these would be the conditions of her entertainment. In her way, it appears, she had much to learn. She had attended a Southern Negro college. She had never known any Southern whites. Her only white acquaintances had been faculty members of her own institution. This was her first "interracial" experience, as we white Southerners provided it.

She was different from Miss Arthur. One was certain of this. I could almost hear Miss Arthur's brain ticking off excuses for this thing we had done. If presently in her secret heart she would entreat in her prayers, "Father, forgive them . . . ", she did not make us feel it. Nor did Miss Jones. Miss Jones confronted one with something infinitely more disturbing than a slight sense of deflated pride. Her quiet personal dignity and composed aloofness spoke an unmistakable message. Miss Jones, one knew with utmost sureness, rejected these symbols of inferiority which had been thrust upon her in this Christian conference. She considered them unwarranted, then or at any time, either for her in her person or for her race.

We came to establish a joint student council, representative of the South, and joint local groups, with both races in them. These were long delayed in coming. We could not solve the primary problem of getting together. Where have meetings? How arrange it so that Negro and white could sit together in a common room? How exercise the intricate care over every smallest detail, the hawk-like vigilance lest slips occur? Besides all this, how explain to these young people, few of whom on either side had sat down to talk with the other race, how to behave and what to expect? Above all, how answer the question on our side, from our kind: "How far does it go?" "Is this, or is it not 'social equality'?" We should have known. By this time, surely, we knew our direction and what we sought. It was not so. If we used evasions, we could not help it. We lived evasions. We manufactured rationalizations by the score. We were on our way, it is true. But perhaps we hoped that if we kept our eyes turned from the signposts they would not be there.

Our Negro colleagues also talked to their students before we met. We could not guess the nature of what they said. Was it: "Be charitable if you can; consider their history; at least these whites are trying"? Perhaps it was far from that. Perhaps that was what we hoped they said, and hoped that was all of it. It may be that if we had heard what they said we should have learned faster than we did.

A few white colleges invited us to bring Negro speakers. It was very complicated. By this time we white staff members were wary of our judgment when it came to arrangements under our white conditions. We would back and fill, consult our fellows. We would try to search out some new *modus vivendi* which fitted into our shifting canons of what the Southern traffic would bear, and into our colleagues' canons of how far they could go in flouting principles of common decency.

There was the matter of hospitality. As honored guests we whites would be entertained in the college guest room, have our meals with the students, move without restraint about the campus. Where would our Negro colleague stay, where eat, and what do, during those hours while she waited to speak before the students? In the end there was little we knew to do, but ask them to come and assume the burden of their own arrangements.

Then there came train time. We could be taking the same train, going to the same place on the same mission. We were professional colleagues with much in common. None of this altered by a hair our "normal" surroundings.

One such journey that I made chanced to be with the Georgia woman whom I had known in my Columbia University seminar.

She had spoken for us at a Virginia college. Our next stop was in North Carolina. We entered the railroad station—but by different doors: hers, "For Colored," mine, "For White." Presumably I was used to this. I had done nothing else all my life. But it was not the same. Every feature of these now peculiar-seeming arrangements thrust themselves against me as something shockingly new.

In this particular station a wooden rail separated the two waiting rooms. (In some it was a wall.) There were two ticket windows. She must stand at one, I at the other, with the rail between. Only on the platform was there no physical separation—railroad platforms must have baffled our Southern ingenuity. So we paced the platform side by side. Even this was unacceptable, as both of us knew. Then came the train. One saw the coach up next the engine, half for baggage, half for passengers. One knew the sign to be found there, and the signs in our several comfortable coaches. One knew one sign was meant to stigmatize, the other to assert superiority. But not for frivolous or capricious reasons. Never had I seen so plainly as on this day how deadly serious the white South was in its signs and separations, or understood in clearer focus its single-mindedness of aim.

In my turn I visited Negro institutions, and occasionally Negro student conferences. At times I was the only white Southerner there, though my hosts did not remind me of it, so that I could seem to forget. What I could never put behind me until it had been resolved was the nagging query that dogged my mind. And yet one day it struck me with stunning force that these men and women were plainly unconcerned with the problem I faced. I might be wrestling with inferiority of race, but not these Negroes. To them it was nonexistent, only a fiction, a myth, which white minds had created for reasons of their own. A vicious myth, to be sure: one with a history, which could and did wreak havoc in the life of their people, but a myth pure and simple just the same.

5.

DURING THIS TIME we had not forgotten our Negro "servant class." We were more than conscious of the uncultured mass of Negroes: cooks and field hands, draymen and laborers in fertilizer mills, ditch diggers and construction gangs.

We could not forget these, for one thing, because they were ever before our eyes in the South, whereas our advantaged acquaintances were few in number and rarely seen. But also so much hinged on these, in the direction our thoughts had begun to take. It was all very well to say of people who had education and culture even as we did: are they not in all essentials like ourselves?

Not so for this mass of Negroes. These in fact were "hewers of wood and drawers of water." These were destitute in large numbers, or at least in dire poverty, with only a few living above the poverty line. Many of these could not write their names, and many who could had no more in possessions or achievement because of it. How could we say they were not this way because they were incapable? What then would become of any equality of races, however hypothetical?

We knew the potency of this dilemma. We knew that the Southern view allowed for this exceptionalism. We knew this exceptionalism was the ace-in-the-hole in the general run of Southern arguments. "Of course. *Some* Negroes have ability; *some* can 'take' an education; *some* can achieve. But as a race. . . ."

Conceivably one might have continued to be suspended here. In our case it proved quite impossible. For meanwhile there had begun to pass before us still another South, one we had known but little hitherto and had not at all comprehended.

For my part, it is true, I had in some sense always known that Southern whites were poor in large numbers. I had grown up using the phrase "lower classes" to describe all those who in common parlance "worked for their living." I knew this meant that they worked with their hands, in contrast to us of the "upper classes" who were the "brains" of society.

Once I had even seen the rigors of Southern destitution; it had been before my eyes in some of its crudest forms; I had known white neighbors who suffered it. But this belonged to the long ago, or so it seemed, and whenever I could, I had put aside my memories of the Sand Hill people.

Besides this, living in the Deep South, I knew mill villages, dozens of them—by sight, that is. I had passed their way times without number, heard the hum of spindle and loom in the gaunt brick structures, seen faces at the windows peering at us curiously; walked down the dirt roads between the rows of company houses, and perceiving their undeviating sameness, idly wondered how, if one lived in such a place, he could ever know his home from all the others on the street.

By so much I knew the South. None of it was unfamiliar. From the best to the poorest, none of it was hidden. The meanest Negro cabin held no surprises, neither the most miserable rags of clothing, nor the corn pone and bacon one would see cooking at open fireplaces. One could ride for miles and miles and see such cabins by the score, set down out there in barren fields or with cotton growing right up to their doors. It came as no surprise that whites lived little better; that their cabins were of comparable meanness; that they had emaciated, undernourished frames and sallow faces, and the women had stooped shoulders while still young, and the children spindly legs. I was familiar with this, for it was home, and belonged to our Southern landscape, yet remote from me.

Now this had changed. When I went home in 1920 it had begun to change. I no longer used the term, "lower classes." These were working people. The South was now an economy, although I knew very little of how it operated.

Much of the spare time of a number of us during these early 1920's was given to learning what the South was like. We sought out experts, went to the census, read official reports, followed legislative battles over limiting women's hours and the ages at which children could go to work. We turned over in our minds the phenomenon we saw, of mill owners who used their influence and power to prevent laws prohibiting the labor of children and laws to protect women from working eleven hours a day. We noted and pondered their advertisements which told their Northern fellows:

"Bring your plants here. Our labor is docile, contented, native white, and cheap."

Then we also learned how meager were the protections that we afforded compared with those of other sections. One could see this was "backward," as was so often said. One could not yet see why. A very kaleidoscope of words was passing through our heads, familiar in color but changing in shade, depending on the side from which the terms were viewed. Nor had they formed any particular pattern.

Ever so gradually we began to learn how poor our Southern whites really were, and how many were poor. We began to comprehend how much money came to them from their wages, and what this could and could not buy. It is true figures taught us some of this, but only because they had come alive.

Mill girls and women would gather in our industrial conferences and at YWCA clubs in the cities. We saw them there. Now and then we might occasionally see them in trade unions—but not many were in unions then. They were straight from their spindles, or cigarette factories, from packing candy and crackers, or making paper boxes. We would hear a conference physician, who had given such girls routine check-ups, ask at our staff meetings, "What do I say?" Could she tell them: "Upon going home, be sure to get more fresh air; drink milk in quantities; eat more fruit and vegetables?" Could she say: "Better take 'correctives' for that posture and stop bending over a spinning frame so many hours a day"? Could she urge them: "Don't bear so many babies as your mother did, and lay off work several weeks before and after; be sure to have prenatal care; go to a hospital for delivery, do not rely on a midwife"?

When our turn came as leaders and guides, we might wish to try this advice: "You began work at fourteen, but surely you see it doesn't pay to let your little sister do it, or your own children." "Doesn't pay?" We soon learned to avoid such an inept turn of phrase. To them it most certainly paid, perhaps five, six, or seven dollars a week; which, added to the mother's ten and the father's twelve (this was in the 1920's) could nearly make ends meet for a large family. It could have, they would say, if there were never slack seasons when layoffs came; or if the older children did not get married and stop helping out at home; or if they could buy their supplies in town where they were cheaper, instead of having them charged against their pay at the company store.

One might be tempted to say in some instances: "Now you are obviously a very bright young woman. You should never have stopped school in the sixth grade. Go back to school. Twenty is not too old. Finish high school. Tending a spinning frame, or folding edges on paper boxes, or even wrapping the outer leaf around cigars, skilled though it may seem, is really only a blind alley when it comes to your ability. Other work would surely open up if you but went on with your education. But set down in that mill village —what can you hope?" A time came, however, when one knew why they had stopped, knew what the answers would be if the question were put: "High school was in town; the mill village had none; our clothes were not good enough; Mother was ill, or Father out of work; or even with combined earnings of all, we still couldn't make ends meet; perhaps planning to get married very soon—yes, to a mill boy, and both of us will work." And usually to crown it all: "What else is there to do if not tend a spinning frame, or wrap cigars, or something else much the same?" Some, it is true, felt differently. They were not defeated in the least, but bluntly wished to know the answers to something better than they had. Then we were baffled more than before. Somehow, "Go back to school," or "Get a better job," had a specious ring. Suppose these individuals could? It was not what their questions meant.

It was not alone the poverty of these masses of Southern whites that pushed against our minds. Some workers were less poor than others. A few even were not badly off, as such things go. One knew this. They might own little homes and carry some insurance. Building tradesmen, printers, and a few others, even belonged to trades unions. But even these in certain ways were no different from their fellows. Such a thought was new, at least to me.

I tried work in a shoe factory. Standing at a bench nine hours a day, I pushed tacks into insoles to hold them to the lasts, while skilled piecework men waited at their machines on both sides of me, one feeding me work, the other waiting for it, while my hands fumbled at the unfamiliar task. This went on but a few weeks, and then I returned again to my accustomed work.

It was not so much that my wages were low—most weeks around

seven dollars. Or that I chose to live on them; this was self-imposed. Or that I must walk the streets for many days to find any work, and when I found it, that it must be in small concerns—the "marginal" kind—since big plants in those middle 1920's did not want inexperienced help even for unskilled tasks. It was easy to see why the conditions were "bad" in the plants I saw, whereas some conditions elsewhere would have been "good." But this was not the point.

Nor was it merely that I found how hard it was to get ahead. Of course, I could change my place of work as fellow workers advised. I would play with the notion of learning a skill, perhaps on a power machine. I would ask stitchers how they learned and only hear: "I just got someone to teach me." I would see how some girls apparently tried to learn, as when our shop hired a "skiver" to use the machine that scrapes the edges of the leather to be folded over; and this young skiver ruined a good many shoes by paring off the edges before she was fired; but perhaps after a few such hirings and firings she might have learned the skill.

True, I grew to like the people with whom I worked, and to admire them for their seeming strong sense of responsibility for one another. So that when they saw me struggling with my lack of skill, even those on piece wages sometimes would stop their work and try to teach me quicker and better ways. Or when they saw how little I had earned, palpably disturbed, they were sure to ask where I lived, if I had any relatives to fall back on, and if I had enough to get me by till next payday. And also I heard them do the same for other unskilled girls or for their skilled fellows whom adversity had struck.

It was not poverty alone. Some I knew in this place were not poverty-stricken—not as income figures went. The highly skilled men were not, so long as their jobs continued. Moreover, knowing some statistics of income, I could do mental calculations and figure how different pay levels stood. My mind would work at these as I stood at my bench. Although I saw into numbers of the workers' homes, here where I worked I saw few extremes of poverty. I had something to compare this with. The South had already shown me what was real destitution. It was not here a case of being overcome in my senses by severe human suffering.

What it came down to was something flatly factual. We were

hardly more than instruments, it seemed, moved helplessly by a larger machine that ran all the smaller ones at which we worked, and which was operated by some remote control, a vast over-all mechanism that was not geared to human consequences. People beside me on the job were being laid off; they had families at home, maybe someone ill; nothing was laid by because it had all been spent at the last lay-off; rent was overdue; credit out at the stores. Management would say monotonously: we are sorry; business is poor; come back another time.

All this was normal, the expected state of affairs and state of mind. It would seem that wage earners grew up with this anxiety, assuming it to be as much a part of their lot as was work itself. By so much, those who at a given moment were not in actual poverty, never knew now when they might be; while those who never had lived above the poverty line never had any relief from uncertainty as to how they would make provision for the bare necessities.

Now by this time, I had learned more about the special and peculiar features of our Southern economy, and by what steps we had come to be in the position we were. The story went back to our single-crop condition, our preoccupation with cotton, and the plantation system which had held back our industrial development. It took account of how our capital had been swept away in the Civil War, and how afterward we must pull ourselves out of the devastation and regional poverty of those years. It told of Northern capital stepping in to finance much of our expanding industry, especially the cotton textile industry which had arisen so phenomenally. It told also that as an area we had become beholden to the North, so that the wealth we did produce tended to go there more than it stayed at home, thus leaving us poor as a region, "with mighty little to do with." But naturally it was to our advantage to go on building up industry, for in this lay our hope for prosperity.

The South could confidently look forward to this, one learned, for one special reason. It was not the greater profitability of mills which were set down right next door to the raw materials, although we had this asset. It was the greater profitability of our labor supply. This was our great attraction, our main drawing-card: we had a cheap, docile, abundant, native white labor force. It was widely argued, one knew, in the press, at legislative hearings, on street corners, around family tables, and when businessmen met and agreed on public affairs, that if anything were to happen to make this labor force less cheap and docile, what would become of us, who were just beginning to grow in wealth and general prosperity? It could stop the building up of native capital and stem the flow of outside capital and new plants into our section. The conclusion derived from this went without saying, although it was said frequently. Even if we were not in any case "too poor," as some put it, to spend money on raising wages and reducing hours or on public welfare frills, it would be disastrous economic policy.

But this seemed to say in substance that we would and must remain as we were, "backward." It appeared to say that for the South to be prosperous the majority of its people must remain poverty-stricken.

At this point the mass of Negro people began to move into the picture forming in my head. For if millions of whites must stay poor, as men seemed to say, to bring Southern prosperity, how much more the millions of Negroes?

Admittedly, even Southern poorer whites were on the whole much better off than Negroes. They had some escape from our depressed, one-crop agricultural economy where poverty extended to its widest and lowest reaches. They could press into the higher paid industrial occupations, in some numbers at least, unlike the Negro, to whom much of industry was closed. And of course they suffered no racial disabilities.

Yet even for whites, it now seemed to me, it was "Thus far and no farther." They might tread a curve that went up and down, but for most of them just so far up. It would seem that the mass of whites in a purely economic sense also had their "place," in which they too seemed meant to stay. If such were the case, then surely wage-earning whites and Negroes were, functionally speaking, not so unlike after all. By so much, the proof of group incapacity, because of poverty or the lowly work men did, lost its persuasiveness.

6.

BUT THEN this people once had been in slavery. White Southerners had sometimes used this fact as a sort of last ditch defense on the supposition that a race that at one time had been slaves must surely have deserved it, and never could warrant in full measure the place of equal in our scale of humanity. By this time, for my part, however, I had begun to learn something different about slaves and slavery, some of it no more than glimpsed during the 1920's, but some of it seen even then for its light on our history.

That once so appealing tale of Runaway Dennis on my forbears' plantation back there in Oglethorpe County, Georgia, had come to sink out of view. I now knew another story of "runaway" slaves, that ran in this wise. From just such plantations, even many whose masters were as conscientious and kindly as were my grandparents, slaves had slipped out in the dark of the moon to walk miles through swamps and along unfamiliar dirt roads until they reached someone whom someone else had told them of. They were in turn sent along to another anonymous someone and thence to another, mile after slow mile, maybe a great distance from their starting place deep in Mississippi or Alabama or Georgia, until they reached the wide stretches of the Ohio River. There still another unknown someone was waiting to slip them across; and on the other side would be others who would move them quietly along; until one day they could stop. They were told that here it was safe; they could settle down as free men. They had done this, not by tens or hundreds, but by the many uncounted thousands, so much so that it was considered an extremely serious matter by those who owned slaves. Moreover, they had left not just "bad" masters, or evil slave conditions, but all kinds of masters and plantations, in short, had simply left slavery.

Also, I discovered that back on the plantations where it was contrary to law for masters to let their slaves learn to read and write, slaves would do it nonetheless. Some masters even let them, it seems, because something inside themselves would not refuse this wish when it was expressed, and when a slave man or woman so evidently groped after whatever it is the human mind wants when it seeks to dispel its illiteracy. Other masters did not, but sometimes there were slaves who by hook or crook acquired the knowledge, in secret to be sure, and kept their secret, lest they be considered "dangerous," or reaching after the stars, which in their status of slave was not thought seemly. It occurred to me that even Grandfather's Jerry—this was conceivable—instead of having the phenomenal memory everyone thought he had, may have worked a life-long deception on his master and mistress, loyal though he was to them, knowing as he would that they could not approve of law-breaking. And so he may have gone through his weekly make-believe of learning that Bible chapter by heart at one or two readings from my grandmother. I do not say it was so, but it easily could have been, and it would have been very like what other slaves sometimes did in order to hug at least to themselves this seemingly precious right to read the printed word.

There could be in slavery, I came to know, a young slave boy named Frederick Douglass who would talk with his white boy playmates, saying: "I wish I could be free, as you will be when you get to be men," would talk of it and think of it continually, so he said. And also an unknown slave boy named Jack, who served Fanny Kemble on her husband's Sea Island plantation, whom she had the temerity to ask suddenly one day if he would like to be free. Whereat she saw a gleam of light shoot over his countenance, and then he began to stammer, hesitate, become excessively confused, while she read his face and saw "the fear of offending by uttering that forbidden wish." At length he replied: "Free, missis! What for me wish to be free? Oh, no, missis, me no wish to be free, if massa only let me keep pig!" I did not know it then, but learned later, that in the very Georgia County of Greene where my grandparents went to live during the war—perhaps right outside the windows of their home—the day the news came of surrender, the cry went up, "Free at last!" And that Negroes poured out into the roads, men, women, and children, aged and young, babies in their mothers' arms, hundreds of people singing and crying and shouting: "Free at last!" That they stayed on these roads throughout the night, feeling in the dirt under their bare feet the right to move unimpeded, with nobody to tell them: "Show your passes," no white man to say: "Has your master given you permission?", no patrols to ride among them, saying: "Go back to your plantation."

I also learned that masses of ex-slaves—it is said nearly two hundred thousand—had volunteered to serve in the armies of Abraham Lincoln. I had heard in plenty of faithful slave servants who, like Father's Old Pete, went with his master to war, waited on him, foraged for him to furnish him food, even fought beside him when occasion called for it—if not for the Confederacy, then for that master and other masters—and after the war remained faithful to the accustomed relationship to the end. But not of the men like those under General S. C. Armstrong (he who founded Hampton Institute) of whom he could say, writing to his mother: "They do not fail us—they are noble men . . . make excellent soldiers . . . do duty well . . . wonderfully persevering in learning to read . . . carry their books with them constantly; many a time have I seen a sentinel with a spelling book under his cartridge-box belt. . . . They will fight and have fought well." These were the men indeed who had chosen as their battle song, "Jehovah has triumphed! His people are free!"

I also came to know how the liberators waited long and hesitantly to let the ex-slaves "fight for their freedom." They hesitated, it seems, to put uniforms on these volunteers or let them go into battle. They even hit upon the strange name of "contraband of war" in their anxiety to seem legal in not returning "property," when thousands upon tens of thousands of slaves poured out of their old habitats into Union Army camps and over Union lines, seeking refuge and sustenance, and maybe even something more that was intangible. At best they were very human in their liberating; at worst not quite as humane as might have been expected, even considering man's well known human frailties. In short, while the liberated might start out by making certain broad assumptions about those who rescued them, their liberators, to put it charitably, were often confused, even, it may be, often very reluctant in the role history had laid on them.

By this time I had begun to learn something of how this newly freed people had attempted to use their freedom. There was a different version, I found, of "forty-acres-and-a-mule" from the one for which we felt such amused contempt in childhood. There were those Sea Island ex-slaves, for instance, who by one federal authority were given possession of the lands their former masters had left; and by another had them returned to the old masters again. But meanwhile the ex-slaves had had time to build schools, churches, roads; establish their own civil government, write their own constitution and laws; plant several thousand acres and reap the harvest from them; raise provisions and purchase stock; sell their own Sea Island cotton in the market and get the proceeds from it. Finally when, under the Johnson policy, the Freedmen's Bureau, in the person of General Howard himself, went to dispossess them of what they had thought was theirs, they met in their church, two thousand of them, it is said, listening to their preachers' "broken and tearful words," singing their "most touching and mournful" songs; and withal, sending stern word to their representatives, who sat with General Howard and the planters' delegate, that never would they work for a white man or under overseers; they would buy the land, or rent it, indeed, begged for the opportunity, except the ex-masters would in no wise consent.

Moreover, one could see from even the most garbled sources that there were very numerous signs of a popular sentiment for the franchise, for labor organization, for expansion of schools, as well as for land-holding on the part of the landless: all this in that interval of time when the bonds of old ways had been temporarily loosened by war and the suddenness of emancipation.

There was of course the assumed antagonism between poor white free man and Negro slave in slavery. So much was this true that on it we had built the notion of "inevitable." This was "inevitable" and "innate," we had said, so what could we do?

For one thing, I at last came to understand a fact about the slave period which hitherto had not been clear in my conscious mind. Not only did I now know how many poorer whites there were. I knew how many there had been under slavery and how few whites all told had been owners of slaves. In other words, that it was non-slaveholders who were numerous in the South; that non-slaveholding was the standpoint from which the vast majority of Southern whites had necessarily looked on the world.

Besides this, there were facts about the actual relations of white free men to the system of slavery. For instance, the not unusual practice among owners of hiring out their slaves, sometimes as house servants or hotel employees in cities; sometimes to work in mines or mills or forests; not infrequently as skilled artisans to do the work that normally would have been done by white artisans. But this of course was at a rate of "rent," so to speak, which could not fail to undercut the wages of white urban laborers and artisans or white workers in mills and mines, and thus stood as a direct competitive threat to these whites and their livelihood. So cognizant were white workers of this condition, it seems, that not once but numerous times they took steps to try to protect themselves. It happened in Atlanta, Georgia, a budding manufacturing center with workshops, foundries, and rolling mills. In the fifties white workmen organized and used press and public opinion to aid their cause, petitioning the city council to ban the use of slave mechanics, whose masters, they said, residing elsewhere, were hiring out their skilled slaves to local manufacturers, and underbidding the local citizen-mechanics of the city to their great disadvantage. Or again, in Athens, the city so near my grandfather's plantation, a Mechanics Mutual Aid Association was formed, claiming that contractors had a most "strong antipathy" to the masonry and carpentry trades of their white citizens; that they showed a preference for giving employment to Negro workmen, which had greatly "cheapened" the white man's labor, even sending many of them from the town. They went so far as to suggest to poor white men, reminding them that they were a majority, to send to the legislature men who would make it a penal offense for Negro mechanic labor to be preferred over the white man's.

Knowing this, it seemed more than reasonable to expect that poor white men who owned nothing, or mechanics who owned merely the tools of their trade, or farmers who were pushed back and farther back to the poorest lands and onto the rocky soil of mountain coves, would all of them learn to hate slavery, and human nature being what it is and perhaps with a little guidance from above, would come to blame the Negro who was the slave.

We would go on to say that this antagonism was "inevitable" because it continued after slavery. It could be called so, to be sure, if the conditions for it were perpetuated. I went on to learn that precisely this happened, once emancipation came. The ex-slave was evidently land-hungry; he wanted a little plot to farm. So now he became potential competitor in a direct sense even for the land-owning farmer; he could hire out on the land, or become a share-cropper, and perhaps succeed in even purchasing a piece. Besides this he could and did move from country to town. Here he became more than ever a potential and direct competitor of poor white men. If he had a skill left over from the plantation, he even competed with mechanics' trades. He was a wage earner now. By so much he was like a white man and in some sense "stood in the way." He was paid lower wages for the same kind of work. But was that so much an advantage to white mechanics, although they insisted upon it? Or did it only make the Negro more a competitor, since he could be got cheaper, and hence kept holding down a white mechanic's pay?

But then we had, so-to-say, come to reverse the matter. On the score of assumed "innate" and "inevitable," we had taken for granted in our day the Negro's lower wages, his poorer job opportunities, his poorer schooling facilities. We had certainly taken for granted the prescribed ways of keeping whites and Negroes separate, if not at their work, which could not always be done, then after their work. Thus our cities had made certain that whites stayed in their slums and Negroes in theirs, and it would trouble us when we observed some overlapping in these, brought on by careless circumstance. In the country, of course, each race had its own churches and its own schools, such as they were; this was taken for granted on the same score, even though men and women and children of both races might be sharecroppers or field hands for the same landlord. In industry, if some inclination were shown, as occasionally had happened, and would come to happen more, for whites and Negroes to join in the same union organization, it would seem that the larger white community disapproved. It would point out the line that poorer white men must observe of: "Thus far and no farther."

I came to find that, seen in its setting, "innate" and "inevitable" had lost their old validity. What struck me now was the circumstantial convenience of a belief in inferiority to the existence of a slave institution and the perpetuation of its aftermath.

It was no longer possible to shut out, or circumvent, or admit pleasant pretenses about inferiority. Being white, one might not know all it meant to be thus stamped because of race. How could we know all or even much, who had not grown up on the Negro side? I could learn, and did, day by day, as the 1920's advanced, what it meant from our side. I had learned what it meant to be a party to our Southern ways, in which I had once been a willing partner, to have a hand in imposing their rigors, not alone on persons whom one knew, but now on the unknown millions whose state one had learned to visualize. I could be struck, at the least, with a sense of gross absurdity, at the most, with the full effect and intent of these our racial provisions. Now I knew that I had rejected racial inferiority, and with it, the entire peculiar set of ways which it allegedly justified. To be sure, institutions would not melt away as could old attitudes of mind. But if human hands and brains had made them, they could refashion them again. Who should know this better than we of the South who once had been in bondage to slavery?

Time of Change

Twenty years have passed. The old life goes on. The old ways still mold the lives of Southern children. They are still taught as sacrosanct the old abhorrences. The old signs, "For White," "For Colored," still swing over station doors and in separate coaches and in the minds of not a few respected teachers of youth. It is certain that "white supremacy" remains in good repute, when elected representatives, as did South Carolina's in 1944, can "reaffirm our belief in and our allegiance to established white supremacy . . . solemnly pledge our lives and our sacred honor to maintaining it." It is still respectable for men to say "inferior" race, to call "enlightened" those who deny the wealth of findings confounding such inferiority.

The location of Southern power has not shifted. Here and there individual men have won a place, stepped aside from the ranks of the Solid South on some issues, spoken and acted as from a different setting. Not so the more numerous leaders. Apparently their confidence is still unshaken, as is their feeling of solidarity and their sense that they alone truly speak for the South. If something seems to them to threaten "Southern rights," of course as they render them, be it an anti-lynching bill, or abolition of the poll tax, or "fair employment practices," they assert their right to block it. Coalitions have been forged between such Southern men and certain Republicans in the Congress. Some say this spells a new move of increasing influence. More probably it is just the same old Southern preponderance of power asserting its decisive sway over the nation's policies.

I know the old life continues, but not serenely, not without a struggle to maintain its existence.

The Making of a Southerner

Strong forces have been battering against the South. Such were the crisis of 1929, the upheavals of the thirties, the second World War. Industrialization was speeded; mechanization in agriculture was advanced with its threat of dislocation of large numbers of people; huge sums were poured into the South from federal coffers to give work during unemployment, build new roads and schools, bring countless surface transformations to our backward landscape. Something new happened with the breaching of the low-wage wall at Mason-Dixon's line; and the lifting even so slightly of the pall of insecurity; and the tide of labor unionism in its new industrial form that swept over the South, overriding, it would seem, the old antagonisms.

The Southern people are pressing against the enclosing walls. In these years they have done it at decisive points—new labor organizations, the franchise struggle, changing attitudes.

We have seen a recognition among working men of common interests. Not that it has ended all racial bars in unions, or made all leaders and those led cease to speak with contempt of their Negro fellows. But especially the new industrial unions have begun to move in a different direction. Forbidding racial discrimination even in the South, they have established joint unions in steel mills and mines, on docks and ships, even occasionally in factories. Some had already existed, but not in the numbers of these recent years. Negroes and whites have even shared the offices and the direction of union affairs. Some leading unions have made contracts prohibiting discrimination. Some Southern state organizations of industrial unions have taken their stand against "pitting race against race," and on the side of equal civil, political, and economic rights.

We have seen the rising struggle for enfranchisement, its strong momentum, its inclusiveness. It embraces white laboring men and farmers whose voting power was cut down with old laws; it includes many Southerners who have the franchise but who wish to extend it; it finally came to include the Negro. Then the signs were plain—he who ran could read—that Southern white people in large numbers had come to understand that there were not two roads to this freedom, marked "For Colored," "For White."

We have seen a growing struggle of the mind, itself a force battling against the old imperviousness. Numerous men and women are experiencing it. Compared with the 1920's the number is manyfold. It may even be that in millions doubts have been stirred. Not major doubts, but enough to let many take their stand for enfranchisement, or for the right of Negroes to equal justice, or equal access to jobs, or equal educational opportunities. I know the limits of this change. I know that today we white Southerners go on skirting around the truth about segregation, against which we now shut that fateful door marked: "Thus far and no farther." By so much we cannot confront the full realities of what it does to a people on whom segregation is imposed—and also what it does to us whose hands impose it. Yet it is not a slight thing that we strike some blows against these shackles. I think of two decades ago. How fortunate it seemed if a round dozen of us came together for our interracial conferences. But in 1945 at a statewide student convention one hundred North Carolina white students voted to invite Negro students to meet with them in coming years. Of course men of standing tried to dissuade them. But not the president of the state university. He said this: that he must take his stand with the people of the state upon the principle—this in the South, on a racial issue—"of the freedom of students to speak their honest opinions and vote their convictions according to conscience. . . ."

In the lengthening years I saw this come to pass—the old life continuing, yet a rising tide against it. Indeed, it came to me, this was integral to the South. The incongruities of the old life had produced the struggle against it. It was just a step from such a thought for me to understand that precisely this accounted for what had happened to myself.

Change was in my blood. I could see it now. I was in truth its offspring. Once I had been beholden to the slave plantation. I was its child, although I came years after its passing. Then that time passed. I turned against my old heritage of racial beliefs and racial practices. I could even think, as perhaps I still did at the time of my Southern remaking, that I had banished the dominion of the past. Yet the unchanging clung to me. Certainly I was haunted by the old dogma, that but one way was Southern, and hence there could be but one kind of Southerner. I could still half believe this, even as late as the 1920's, perhaps partially remain under the spell of its old authority. I was long indeed shaking off the feeling—

which is as things are meant to be to keep one from changing—that by so much I had turned my hand against my own people.

But then I learned that this was not so. It could not be. What had altered me was the South's own doing. The beginning of the beginning for my change lay far back in our history.

We had been uprooted. Was there ever so much movement in so brief a span of years? It broke us from our past with great violence. It set slaves free by the millions; it set whites free, the vast majority—they who had never owned slaves and never could be free under slavery; it set forces free, which under our old slave economy could not move the South as afterward it moved; it set minds free, in a partial sense, which perforce believed in human bondage while they remained its beneficiaries.

But then there was my kind, we who had, so to speak, been disinherited. In slavery days we had felt secure as had no other class in our society—in substance, in station, above all in our values. There had been financial failures, to be sure; planters rose and fell. It never shook our foundations. We were under attack; abolitionists belabored my kind of people; this did not shake them. Our fathers knew their way was good. All around them men agreed—men who mattered—that they should keep their way of life. But it was shattered, and the South was started on its new epoch. It was hard to see this new day as desirable. Yet it moved us. It set going in my people, and thence from them to me who was born many years after the first blow struck, repercussions which I surely felt from infancy, and as consciousness came, felt more powerfully. I knew the ebbtide of nostalgic memories of a lost slave plantation; the pain and bitterness of our "civilization" nearly overcome, and then the triumph of its reconquest; the harsh strain of the 1890's, in the midst of which I was born, although I did not know until in after years of the fears it held, nor in my early childhood the fierce realities I shared—in feelings if not in consciousness—as we "put the Negro down" by the final statutes of segregation and disfranchisement. Backward movement. On our part we were desperately pulling our boat against the current. Yet we saw change. It affected us. Small wonder we would speak stern, antiquated words in one breath, and in the next mankind's loftiest phrases. I heard and learned such words, and by so much I was the child of this strange anachronism. Like my people, I learned to try to mix in myself these antagonistic elements. Mainly I saw it being attempted all around me. And there entered into me—I am sure this is so —even at that time, even in my formative years, a sense of uncertainty, a sense that I, with all the people of my kind, looked almost askance at our handiwork, felt almost uncomfortable living in the structure we had built.

This may seem incredible, for we know what happened. We know that every effort was bent at the time of upheaval, and in subsequent years, to put the Negro back "in his place," as nearly similar to the old as circumstances allowed. We know that we came to call it a "redemption." We reaffirmed our old values and said they were ours to stay. Down the post-bellum decades, and into the twentieth century, we hardly ever faltered in our fateful course, or lowered the grim old flag of white supremacy. Yet it was too late. What men could say made good sense in a time of slavery obviously made none now that men were free. A child might not know this, but her senses could absorb it, as I am certain mine did, and were ever being stirred by the feeling of these contradictions.

Our skins were now thinner. I am sure this is so. We were far more sensitive to our inconsistencies than had once been possible. In a sense we were seeing ourselves as we had once been, although this we did not know. In any event, we were disturbed. I know how it disturbed me when the newcomers who had now taken our place in ordering society, spoke of the Negro as we had once done. These people, they said, were their hewers of wood and drawers of water whom the Lord in his wisdom had provided for their productive uses. Perhaps it was not often put in this direct form, but rather usually said with our old nuance: that the Negro, the "inferior," had his "place," hence he must perform his "rightful function." Indeed, we believed that this was so. And yet, it seems doubt crept in. If I had lived in the ante-bellum time it could hardly have done so. Then my kind of Southern people had been the ones to hold men in bondage as their means of wealth. We could not have afforded to be thus plagued with unseemly doubts. But now since the time of our uprooting we had come to be very remote from the direct benefits of our one-time plantations. Now we were driven, not as were the new men, who had become society's beneficiaries. What we had left in us was our sense of position, but more especially, our ideals and our fears. We had our love for the South; and we had our dread of the "inferior" race, the dread that had been allowed to breed at the deep levels bordering consciousness. These, our ideals and fears, did their part in the post-bellum years.

The new men needed our fathers' kind for establishing their hegemony; they needed all the forces they could muster in this time of upheaval if they would direct the South along the lines their interests called for. Small wonder then that they spoke so much of saving "Southern civilization"—and it may be believed that this was the nature of their objective. Be that as it may, this was likewise what our fathers desired: they would pass on to their children's children the kind of South that in their hearts they could approve of. So they lent their ardor, their warm devotion, their unremitting labor, to accomplish the goal of preserving "Southern principles." In such terms we saw fixed on the South the institution of white supremacy.

I say all this made us who were our fathers' children inheritors of a very strange confusion. We could be sternly confident in our sense of uprightness. We could be painfully unsure with the doubts that would assail us.

Why did some of us take one course and some another? Why, in my case, did I not hold to things as they were? Patently, my personal quest was for a kind of certainty, a sense of self-consistency in my discordant world. But could I not find it best in the old sureties for which I had the support of all authority, of family, government, even devout religion? I know it is commonly so. In my case it chanced not to be. We may call it chance. We may speak of the mysterious chemistry of individuality. We may say of the very ideals of my personal childhood rearing that they were potentially explosive taken in their combination—"Do your duty always," "Aid the weak and helpless," "He who has brains must use them." We may point to religion, and the way it was turned around on itself —for me, I mean—so that its high authority was fallen back on to justify the very acts which our Southern teaching had told us were unjustifiable. Under religion's felt demand I could first profane the sacred tabernacle of our racial beliefs and go on profaning it in subsequent years, until I no longer felt the need to lean on any kind of authority, save that of the demands of a common humanity. It was these, and yet much more, that set my course. After all I was a Southerner nurtured in the Lost Cause, who looked upon my people's history and conduct of affairs as scarcely short of exemplary. Yet such was our life, that the dynamics of the South itself in its glaring incongruities began to arouse in me a chronic state of doubt. It is true, this awakened skepticism might have come to very little, even to being stifled by our protecting walls of privilege, had it not been for one thing—the sudden breaking down of my isolation from the realities of Southern life. The Sand Hills intervened, and did so at the very time of my changing teens. Here in actuality was the moment when chance circumstance showed me our native Tree of Life, and had me eat of its revealing fruit. To all effects that act shut me out from my erstwhile Southern Garden of Eden. For, once my eyes had been opened, it would seem, I never again could return to the comfortable ignorance which would have let me assume as an unfortunate inevitability the destitution, the drabness of life, the spiritual and material exploitation, which was the lot of so many. And the South being the South, where could such a beginning of knowledge eventuate except at the barriers which had been so vigilantly erected to segregate Negroes? By so much, it appeared, the disrupting notion had overtaken me that ordinary canons of human rights should apply equally to all conditions of people. For a time I supposed that this idea was alien to the South, still immersed as I was in the assumption that our plantation tradition alone was authentically Southern. It took the years of the twenties to show me how diverse were Southerners, and how different the strains of Southern heritage that had been handed on, for instance, by the white millions whose forbears had never owned slaves, and also by the Negro millions whose people had been held in slavery. It took a fresh reading of our past to find buried there not a little that told of the strivings of these various Southerners after a different South. As it came about, it was this different South that in the end drew me towards my refashioning, even as my Old South receded ever farther into history.

AFTERWORD

AFTERWORD

IT HAS INTERESTED ME to reflect that this book was written in the final years of a passing era. In 1946 as I wrote the closing chapter, racial segregation remained fully legalized in the southern states. By this time it had also existed de facto in northern and western cities, once migration from the South had distributed black people into every section of the United States. White Southerners favoring the end of segregation—and there were a good many—had increased in number; and I believed I saw signs that currents of change had begun to push, weakly no doubt, against old ways of thought and behavior. Yet when I was writing in 1946, I am certain I did not perceive that just ahead there could occur a far-reaching and peaceful event that would alter drastically the potentials for change.

During the weeks prior to May 17, 1954, word was circulating that the Supreme Court could be expected at almost any time to render its final decisions on *Brown* v. *Board of Education of Topeka, Kansas*, and four other school segregation cases. I recall my feeling almost of dread. I feared evasion of the central issue, the constitutionality of racial segregation. Attempts to challenge segregation had failed ever since *Plessy* v. *Ferguson* in 1896 had approved the principle of "separate but equal." Thereby the system of racial segregation as I knew it in my young years was fastened on the South.

But in 1954 the highest court did not evade or equivocate. On the contrary, its decision declaring racial segregation in public schools unconstitutional was specific and unanimous. With untold relief I read in my *New York Times* the clear, unambiguous language of the decision: "We come then to the question presented: Does segregation of children in public schools solely on the basis of race . . . deprive the children of the minority group of equal opportunities? We believe that it does. . . . We conclude that in the field of public education the doctrine of 'separate but equal' has no place. Separate educational facilities are inherently unequal."

As I read the incisive words, I found the thought taking hold in my mind: the old era is now being left behind; abolition of racial segregation has begun.

Of course the old was not "left behind," as I well knew. Even when some outward aspects of racial segregation underwent some changes, there were constant reminders, especially in the resistance of southern white people, of how stubbornly old attitudes and ways were persisting in everyday life. Only in a quite limited sense could I feel that a new era had begun, only because segregation had now been stamped unconstitutional by our highest court.

In the years between that day and now, I have followed and experienced the changes that have come to southern life—and to national life also, but now I am writing of my native South. As I considered how these changes came about, I found some questions surfacing that will be reflected in some of my discussion. They are not new questions, although for me they possess a new imperative.

DESEGREGATION of public schools in the southern states confronted a rocky road. The border states (and the District of Columbia), though they were among the seventeen having school segregation laws, had taken prompt steps to comply with the Supreme Court ruling. Eleven states—the traditional "Old South"—began at once to resist compliance in whatever way they could devise.

The voices and actions showing resistance to the Court's decision did not surprise me. On the contrary, I think I assumed that the laws passed in the various legislatures very likely reflected the prevailing sentiment among a majority of southern white people. I did not doubt that shock and fear was felt by countless individuals. As I told myself, given our history and upbringing, it was not surprising. I also knew that such anxiety can cause the same emotional distress whether it is warranted or not.

Afterword

It was in a sober spirit that I followed events as they transpired day by day. The resistance laws in particular gave me a sense almost of crisis. Take the "pupil assignment" legislation. In essence these laws provided that pupils wishing reassignment to other schools (presumably black pupils) were required to apply individually to the designated authority. Included was a long list of criteria, some of them so vague and undefined that it seemed a simple matter, if a board were so disposed, to refuse transfers to most applicants whose complexions were dark. Most states had laws of this kind. There were other laws, but this type struck most directly at desegregation.

In 1956 the resistance spirit received dramatic encouragement from a prestigious quarter. Ninety-six southern congressmen issued a "manifesto," a "Declaration of Constitutional Principles." It was signed by nineteen senators and seventy-seven representatives. Their stand was made clear in the opening sentence: "The unwarranted decision of the Supreme Court in the school cases is now bearing the fruit always produced when men substitute naked power for established law." They "commended" those states "which have declared the intention to resist forced integration by any lawful means," and condemned "outside agitators" for invading the South to meddle in southern affairs. I had a sudden feeling of wry surprise. Had there flitted through my mind a shadowy memory, welling up from childhood?—always give respectful attention to our southern men in high positions of national responsibility. . . . My next thought blotted out any glimmer of surprise. I knew their words would bring powerful support to the spirit of resistance already at work all through the South.

Already there had been instances of extreme reaction, none more so than in Little Rock. Some will recall it. Governor Faubus and the Arkansas legislators and others opposed a federal district court order to admit nine black children to the Little Rock high school, Faubus using national guard units to prevent the black children's admission; then President Eisenhower ordered in U.S. Army units to enforce the federal court's order. The conflict simmered on for months, while the nine children, under soldiers' protection, attended high school despite harassment and some disorder. Eventually the crisis died away. The nine children continued in school. And we must assume that time brought some healing to individuals; how much we cannot know.

Resistance measures had undoubtedly succeeded in holding back desegregation. A figure published in the early 1960s showed only one-half of one percent of black children in the South attending schools with white children.

Around this time some efforts were launched to blunt the effectiveness of resistance legislation. A number of black parents began suits in federal courts challenging the new laws. Attorneys from the NAACP and other civil rights organizations had come to their aid with expert legal help. In time these suits were partially successful, but court cases proved to be a slow, expensive road to desegregation. Meanwhile, with school desegregation at a virtual standstill, there were signs of a growing impatience among southern black people with the still unfulfilled promise of the Supreme Court decision.

In 1955, when southern white resistance was conspicuously on the rise, the Reverend Martin Luther King, Jr., first came to public notice when he became a leader of a widely publicized bus boycott in Montgomery, Alabama. The boycott began when Mrs. Rosa Parks of the local black community took a front seat on a bus, and when told by the driver to move to the back, she refused and was arrested.

One notable feature of the bus boycott was its successful use of the "nonviolent direct action" principle espoused by Dr. King. In the end the boycott succeeded so well that desegregation of the city bus lines was achieved. To many black people this meant that nonviolent action could and did work. When the bus boycott ended, Dr. King moved to Atlanta, his home city, soon to launch his national career.

We come to events of special interest to me. I refer to the role of the nonviolent protest movement in the 1960s and how it was able to a very large extent to put an end to the more obvious, visible forms of racial segregation. At the same time it helped to end the long-standing disfranchisement of black people in the southern states.

The protest began when Dr. King moved back to Atlanta and organized the Southern Christian Leadership Conference, serving

Afterword

as its president. From then on, until his fateful assassination in 1968, the SCLC was the main vehicle for his widespread activities. From the beginning Dr. King stressed the principle of "nonviolent direct action." Wherever he went he explained it and urged its use, and by the early 1960s it was widely known. Unnumbered individuals in countless communities were drawn into the work.

In 1960 nonviolent "sit-ins" began in Greensboro, North Carolina. Four young freshmen from A & T University, a state-supported institution for Negro men, entered a Woolworth store and took seats at the lunch counter. When they requested service, it was refused. They explained their reason quietly to the clerk and continued to sit. Others from the college heard the word, and they joined the "sit-in"; nonviolent action was made a condition. The students' action continued a good while, there was no violence, and Woolworth's lunch eventually was desegregated.

Sit-ins by black youths soon spread all through the southern states, and with them the nonviolent principle. In some places participants met violence; many were arrested, some were jailed, some were charged with trespass and their cases were brought to trial. Supporting organizations came to their aid with legal help. A few cases were appealed, which meant long months of litigation. Some eighteen months later, at least two hundred eating places in the South had been desegregated by these actions.

A Student Nonviolent Coordinating Committee (SNCC) was formed to organize the multiplying activities. By this time training centers had been set going, where participants could be taught nonviolent techniques.

"Freedom rides" began in 1961 with the aim of desegregating interstate bus travel. Groups of black and white young men made trips together by bus, usually into the deep South cities. They were often harassed in the towns they passed through, even attacked and sometimes injured. They too practiced nonviolence, as did CORE, the organization sponsoring the project. Many hundreds of young men made such trips. The campaign continued for many months. It ended when the Interstate Commerce Commission desegregated all interstate buses. In late 1961 three major railroads serving the southern states had also desegregated their trains and waiting rooms.

Afterword

In the next few years, various "sit-in" actions were used to desegregate public facilities. Nonviolent action successfully opened up parks, playgrounds, lunch counters and restaurants, and motion picture theaters. In some cities, groups of local citizens (not connected with the protest movement), white and black, joined forces to open up to black patrons facilities such as hotels, motels, and restaurants. A notable, long-sought change came in the opening up of public libraries—all branches—so that they were equally available to all races.

Oddly desegregation of schools still lagged, though the efforts in many localities were less halting now. Some progress was being made in the hiring of black teachers and black administrators for desegregated schools. Local governments had begun to employ more black men and women; so had local business firms—banks, stores, offices. Opportunities to make a good life were definitely increasing. As segregation walls all over the region came tumbling down, it became ever clearer that black people were done with enduring their undeserved discriminations.

Of parallel importance to desegregation was a swelling movement for the right to vote. Black people in some of the southern states were largely disfranchised by devices to deprive them of the ballot. Some states still had a poll tax on voting that penalized especially the poor; others a "literacy" test. In some places intimidation was used, and there were other methods. The "grandfather clause," once a favorite, had been declared unconstitutional many years before, as was the "white primary." Vigorous campaigns were launched to help black people register to vote. One often saw pictures in the press of long lines of black people, waiting sometimes for hours for the registrar to get around to them.

Because of these campaigns, and later the federal Voting Rights Act, the number of registered black voters in the South increased immensely. From this change flowed an increased interest in politics among black citizens.

Around this time, demonstrations on a national scale were being planned, chief among them the "March on Washington" in 1963. Delegations from all parts of the nation participated in the "March." An immediate aim was passage of the comprehensive Civil Rights bill, then pending in the Congress. It passed in 1964. President Johnson had actively supported the measure from the outset and used all his influence for it. Some writers have asserted that passage of the Civil Rights Act of 1964 was given the necessary push by the massive "March on Washington" demonstration in 1963. Similarly, the Voting Rights Act of 1965 was greatly aided by the impressive mass march from Selma to Montgomery, Alabama, organized by Dr. King in 1965. These two great acts I think of as landmarks, in particular in the way they spelled out the most flagrant forms of discrimination and the protections against them. They specifically provided that the rights and opportunities covered in these laws must be provided "without discrimination or segregation on the ground of race, color, religion, and national origin." Equal opportunity for employment was stressed in the Civil Rights Act, with discrimination forbidden. I take this to mean that the desegregation achievements of the protest movement now were buttressed and undergirded by these new acts. No doubt in many times and places equal opportunity will have to be enforced. Even so, these two acts represent an unprecedented achievement in their fields.

A QUARTER CENTURY has passed since the Supreme Court in 1954 ruled that racial segregation is unconstitutional. Today the years of my childhood and growing up in the South seem far more distant than they did some thirty-five years ago when I was writing this book. In terms of the changes that have come to black people, and white also, I am in a different world, admittedly a world I had not supposed would come in my lifetime. I am grateful I did not miss witnessing the transformations we are seeing in the South, partial though they are. I mean not only those in the surroundings—the facilities and other visible features that have been desegregated; I mean transformations also in interpersonal race relations. In neither regard are the changes in any wise completed; I realize that much remains to be done.

In the past, I believe, most southern white people were acquainted with only those black people who were employed in their homes. Black people at more prosperous economic levels, from skilled labor to professional and business occupations, were rarely, if ever, in white people's homes, or vice versa, and rarely seen walking on white residential streets; they even tended to avoid, if possible, white-owned "downtown" business streets.

Afterword

There was too much feeling of segregation there, of places forbidden to them. And the barriers of all kinds were very numerous. Now all this is changed in most places. Contacts of white people with black strangers, of an economic level similar to theirs, are much more frequent, more natural. While their contacts are mostly impersonal still, yet because they encounter each other more often—face to face, so to speak—I imagine white people are coming to recognize all types and kinds of black people; they perceive a diversity among them where before they may have tended to see sameness. By so much, black people they do not know are becoming persons to them as they never had been before. If by chance white and black people are thrown together occasionally on boards, or on committees, or common community projects, then the feeling of personal relationship is enhanced. To me, this clearer perception of one another as persons will in time, in itself, tend to the increase of simple friendliness on both sides.

One thing further: I believe that neither the visible nor the interpersonal transformations could have come merely by court decisions or new laws by the Congress, though both were necessary. The provisions in the laws could not come alive until they were used by people back in their communities. It is also interesting to think that the two comprehensive acts enacted by the Congress, the Civil Rights Act of 1964 and the Voting Rights Act of 1965, came after, not before, the nonviolent protest movement of southern black people had already secured many of the rights those laws guaranteed. The laws were necessary to make sure there would be no backsliding in the states and to buttress and undergird these basic rights. I think it was good that the order of development came as it did. Some writers assert that the black protest movement—and up to 1965 much of the protest was in the South—was a chief factor in the passage of these two acts. However that may be, the movement's role was an important one, not only in bringing about the new laws, but also in transformations in inter-race relations. In the latter regard, the protest movement furnished incontrovertible evidence to any and all who had failed to comprehend, that black people were asserting that the time was now for an end to their burden of discrimination and segregation.

250

Afterword

The black protest movement underwent changes around 1965. SNCC, the student nonviolent organization, underwent a change in leadership and began to turn away—some members did—from nonviolent action. Northern and western cities, where a majority of black people in the United States now live, began to see waves of protest. Some of these were marked by violence. The most alarming happening came in Watts, the black section of Los Angeles. I suppose it can be said that at last the eyes of city dwellers in the North and West began to open and see the vast increase in their black populations and the flight of their white tax payers to the suburbs and to feel the impact of the complex problems now confronting them.

Most of the conspicuous changes in the status of black people had occurred in the South through the nonviolent protest movement. These remain far from complete. Dr. King was continuing his widespread activities much as before. He was engaged in them in Memphis on the day he was assassinated in 1968.

Need I say that much remains to be done before black people will have equal rights, equal justice, equal opportunities? Overt and subtle forms of discrimination continue to be their daily experience. What is yet to be done, I am certain, is by far the hardest part. Segregation still remains as entrenched as it ever was—de facto to be sure—in housing for black people. Areas for black people cannot be set aside by law, not since a court decision earlier in the century; but custom does permit this practice, and so do methods of businesses by which ghetto habitations are bought and sold and otherwise change hands. Black ghettoes can be found in all large cities, so far as I can learn, in the South and North and West. Within these ghettoes almost all black people of all income levels are constrained to live. It would be one thing if they were voluntarily in these separate neighborhoods and if it were possible for those black families which were economically able and wished to, to find housing somewhere else in the city or outside it if they preferred. Then those who preferred neighborhoods of their own people could remain there without a sense of being forced to.

Within the confines of ghettoes of big cities are found slum areas. The poverty-stricken make their homes in these slums. Although these are areas of poverty, many dwellers there are people who work hard, make the best homes they are able to, and try constantly to rise out of poverty. But tragically these slums are apt to be inhabited by society's unwanted: many small-time criminals and delinquents, many drug users, many derelicts. Much of the housing in slums is deteriorated; city services are often poor and neglected. Even small cities, and there are many in the South, have their "Negro sections," the places where most black people are expected to live. In short, such sections continue to be segregated.

Of special concern is the much higher rate of unemployment among black people compared with white. When economic recessions bring high rates of unemployment, and even when times are good, we know that black people are much more subject to unemployment than white. This is especially true of young people. Recently I read a figure for Detroit on its youth unemployment during the recession that laid off many automobile workers; some estimates said 60 percent of Detroit's black youth were unemployed. It takes little imagination to picture the vicious circle set going by this kind of alarming situation. It is crying out for informed attention and for basic cures.

When I turn my eyes to all that remains to be done, it lets me sound a note of gloom. But my dominant feeling is one of belief in the future. I remind myself of the effort it took in the 1940s, as I wrote the concluding pages to this book, to express a belief that someday I knew southern segregation and disfranchisement of black people could be ended and be relegated to the past. I had no conception then of how it would happen. Now the recent decades have come to pass, with all they have held of greatly needed changes, and the principal instrument was a movement by black people committed to the use of nonviolent action. It was this alone that enabled the changes to come in a human and peaceful way. This knowledge remains etched in my memory, and I am bound to have a lift of spirit whenever it comes to mind.

KATHARINE DU PRE LUMPKIN
Chapel Hill, North Carolina
1980

NOTE ON SOURCES

NOTE ON SOURCES

For the most part this Note lists only those sources which have been drawn on in a specific way in this book for facts or documents. A few books are included to illustrate attitudes toward controversial issues in the ante-bellum and post-bellum periods.

GENERAL SOURCES

Written materials on family history: written accounts by my father and mother of their childhood years (one account by my father in *Columbia* (S.C.) *State*, December 16, 1906, "An Old Time Georgia Christmas"); an unpublished genealogical record, compiled by B. H. Lumpkin, for documents from public archives, such as wills, deeds, etc.; scattered material from secondary sources dealing with Georgia history and men of affairs; newspaper items, some of which are cited below.

Seventh U. S. Census, 1850, by States and Territories, Arranged by Counties; Eighth U. S. Census, 1860, volumes on Population and Agricultural Statistics: for size of plantations, number of slaves, educational and religious facilities in middle Georgia counties.

Ku Klux Conspiracy: Testimony Taken by a Joint Select Committee of the Congress to Inquire into the Condition of Affairs in the Late Insurrectionary States (13 volumes; Washington : Government Printing Office; 1872). (Designated under page citations below as "Ku Klux Report.") This Congressional committee held hearings in Southern communities, and there appeared before it men representing all points of view, including Southern conservatives, white Republicans resident in the South, both Southern and Northern, and Negro leaders. Among these were numerous men from Oglethorpe, Greene, and other middle Georgia counties. See especially Volume I, *Report,* and the two volumes on Georgia.

255

Note on Sources

On agricultural methods and problems in pre- and post-emancipation years: *Southern Cultivator*, a middle Georgia farm journal, published in Athens, Clarke County. See for the post-emancipation period, Vol. XXVII (1869). In practically every issue were letters from planters and small-scale farmers debating the acute labor problems of the time and relating their experiences. Some of the stories in Book Two are drawn from these letters.

Ante-bellum and post-bellum works: Frederick Law Olmstead: *Journey in the Seaboard Slave States* (New York, 1856), *Journey in the Back Country* (New York, 1860), *Journey through Texas* (New York, 1860); Frances Anne Kemble: *Journal of a Residence on a Georgian Plantation, 1838–1839* (New York, 1863); Hinton R. Helper: *The Impending Crisis of the South* (New York, 1857); William Goodell: *American Slave Code* (2nd edition, New York, 1853), for citations on legal status of slaves, also advertisements from Southern newspapers relating to slavery, from which some quotations are drawn (see especially pages 54, 55, 119, 126); Frances Butler Leigh: *Ten Years on a Georgia Plantation since the War* (London, 1883). Albion W. Tourgée: *A Fool's Errand* (New York, 1879), and *An Appeal to Caesar* (New York, 1884). Examples of more obscure works reflecting attitudes: Albert Barnes: *An Inquiry into the Scriptural Views of Slavery* (Philadelphia, 1846); Rev. E. J. Stearns: *Notes on Uncle Tom's Cabin, Being a Logical Answer* (Philadelphia, 1853); M. T. Wheat: *The Progress and Intelligence of Americans, Collateral Proof of Slavery from the First to the Eleventh Chapters of Genesis* (2nd edition, Louisville, Ky., 1862); William I. Royal: *A Reply to "A Fool's Errand," By One of the Fools* (3rd edition, New York, 1881).

For ante-bellum documentary material: U. B. Phillips: *Life and Labor in the Old South* (Boston: Little, Brown & Company, 1939); *American Negro Slavery* (New York: D. Appleton-Century Company, 1918); John R. Commons and associates: *Documentary History of American Industrial Society*, Volumes I and II, *Plantation and Frontier* (Glendale, Cal.: Arthur H. Clark Company, 1910); W. S. Jenkins: *Pro-Slavery Thought in the Old South* (Chapel Hill: University of North Carolina Press, 1935); P. H. Buck: "The Poor Whites of the Ante-Bellum South," *American Historical Review*, Vol. XXXI, No. 1.

For documentary materials on Reconstruction: W. L. Fleming: *Documentary History of Reconstruction*, 2 vols. (Glendale, Cal.: Arthur H. Clark Company, 1906). Also numerous monographs, including C. M. Thompson: *Reconstruction in Georgia, Economic, Social, Political, 1865–1872* (Columbia University Studies in Economics, History and Public Law, No. 154 New York, 1915); Ethel Maud Christler: *Participation of Negroes in the Government of Georgia, 1867–1870* (A -

Note on Sources

lanta University, 1933, unpublished); A. A. Taylor: "The Negro in South Carolina during the Reconstruction," *Journal of Negro History*, Vol. IX, Nos. 3 and 4 (July and October, 1924); F. B. Simkins and R. H. Woody: *South Carolina during Reconstruction* (Chaptel Hill, 1932); P. S. Peirce: *The Freedman's Bureau* (University of Iowa Studies in Sociology, Economics, Politics and History, Vol. III, No. 1, 1904).

General works: Arthur F. Raper: *Tenants of the Almighty* (New York: Macmillan Company, 1943), a book about Greene County, Georgia, the county to which my grandparents moved during the Civil War. On the political and economic situation in Georgia in the late nineteenth century: E. M. Banks: *Economics of Land Tenure in Georgia* (New York: Columbia University Press, 1905); A. M. Arnett: *The Populist Movement in Georgia* (New York: Columbia University Studies in History, Economics and Public Law, Volume CIV, 1922); C. Van Woodward: *Tom Watson, Agrarian Rebel* (New York, 1938); Paul Lewison: *Race, Class and Party* (New York, 1932). Local histories, in particular *The Story of Washington-Wilkes*, compiled by Workers of the Writers' Program of the Works Progress Administration in the State of Georgia (1941); and *History of Athens and Clarke County, Georgia* (Athens, 1923).

Newspaper sources: On the Confederate Reunion of 1903, the *Columbia* (S.C.) *State*, May 5–15, carried extensive accounts, from which some quotations were drawn. For actions of Confederate Veterans' organizations concerning the schools and education, see *Columbia State*, May 14, 1903, and *Louisville* (Ky.) *Herald*, June 16, 1905. On the South Carolina senatorial campaign of 1908, the *Columbia State*, from late June into the early days of August, carried reports. Quotations used in Book Three, Section 4, are from this source.

PAGE CITATIONS

Page 3.

E. M. Banks: *Economics of Land Tenure in Georgia* (New York, 1905), p. 18, data on Georgia lottery acts.

U. B. Phillips: *Life and Labor in the Old South* (Boston: Little, Brown & Company, 1939), p. 177, for slave prices.

Pages 16f.

F. L. Olmstead: *Journey in the Seaboard Slave States* (New York, 1856), pp. 32f., for account of slave markets from *Chambers Journal*, October 1853.

Pages 18, 20.

William Goodell: *American Slave Code* (New York, 1853), p. 109, on action of Savannah River Baptist Association.

Note on Sources

Page 22.

Phillips: *Life and Labor in the Old South*, p. 180, quotation on pricing of slaves.

Page 24.

Ibid., p. 279, on the planter, Tait.

Pages 25f.

Ibid., pp. 197, 279, on food allowances for slaves.

Page 27.

U. B. Phillips: *American Negro Slavery* (New York: D. Appleton-Century Company, 1918), pp. 262f., quotations from plantation documents.

Rev. Thornton Stringfellow: "Slavery: Its Origin, Nature and History, Considered in the Light of Bible Teachings, Moral Justice and Political Wisdom," 1860 (32 pp.).

Page 30.

Phillips: *Life and Labor in the Old South*, p. 327, quotation from *Farmers' Register*, III, 495.

Page 33.

Olmstead: *Seaboard Slave States*, pp. 118f., for the Bishop Mead sermon to slaves.

Page 40.

Olmstead: *Journey in the Back Country*, pp. 48f., on Christmas customs of some slaveowners.

Pages 43f.

Devereaux's North Carolina *Reports*, Judge Ruffin in *State* vs. *Mann* (from *American Slave Code*, p. 126).

Book Two, Section 2.

Unless otherwise indicated in page citations below, see *Southern Cultivator*, Vol. XXVII (1869), especially pages 57, 90, 180, 250, 372, 374, 302ff., for quotations on the labor problem and immigration. Also, "Ku Klux Report," Vol. I, *Report*, pp. 330, 304, for the story of the painted pegs, and for Southerners' comments on the freedmen.

Book Two, Sections 5 and 6.

See "Ku Klux Report," pp. 303, 305, for general comments quoted; and see in the two volumes on Georgia, testimony of the following: Lieutenant Hoyt, the Mayor of Savannah, Abram Colby, Monday Floyd, Robinson of Ogelthorpe County, Alfred Richardson, the farmer, Shropshire, and others, for accounts given by these individuals.

258

Note on Sources

Page 49.

R. S. Cotterill: *The Old South* (Glendale, Cal.: The Arthur H. Clark Company, 1939), p. 323, for figures on conscription and desertion under the Confederacy.

Pages 55f.

James S. Pike: *The Prostrate State* (reprinted, 1935, by Loring & Mussey, New York), pp. 115ff.

Page 56.

Arthur Raper: *Tenants of the Almighty* (New York: Macmillan Company, 1943), p. 50, on taxable wealth invested in slaves in Greene County.

Page 57.

W. L. Fleming: *Documentary History of Reconstruction* (1906), Vol. I, pp. 72, 92, for quotations from masters on freedom of their slaves, and p. 72, for quotation: "The heart of the South . . ." Reprinted by permission of the publishers, The Arthur H. Clark Company from Fleming's *Documentary History of Reconstruction*, Vols. 1, 2.

Pages 58.

Raper, op. cit., p. 73, on emancipation of slaves in Greene County. See also *Senate Executive Documents*, 39 Cong., 1 Sess., No. 2, 1865, for Carl Schurz report to President Johnson. See also Fleming, op. cit., Vol. I, p. 356, for Sidney Andrews, account of sentiment among freedmen for landownership.

Pages 59–60.

Fleming, op. cit., Vol. I, 151ff., quotation from Thaddeus Stevens's land confiscation bill; pp. 450f., from Cordoza speech; and p. 354, for quotation from Georgia Freedmen's Bureau report. Reprinted by permission of the publishers, The Arthur H. Clark Company from Fleming's *Documentary History of Reconstruction*, Vols. 1, 2.

Page 64.

R. P. Brooks: *The Agrarian Revolution in Georgia, 1865–1912*, Bul. of the Univ. of Wisconsin, No. 639 (1914), p. 12.

Pages 64, 65f.

Fleming, op. cit., Vol. I, p. 129, quotation from General Howell Cobb; also, pp. 294ff., quotations from the Black Code of South Carolina. Reprinted by permission of the publishers, The Arthur H. Clark Company from Fleming's *Documentary History of Reconstruction*, Vols. 1, 2.

Page 66.

W. E. B. Du Bois: *Black Reconstruction* (New York, 1935), pp. 174, 496, on Georgia's Black Code. For quotation from Gov. Joseph Brown, see "Ku Klux Report," Georgia, Pt. 2, p. 816.

Note on Sources

Page 68.

Frances Butler Leigh: *Ten Years on a Georgia Plantation since the War* (London, 1883), p. 26.

Pages 69ff.

See *Southern Cultivator*, Vol. XXVII, 1869, especially pp. 206f., 208, 302, 372, for the Colonel Hazard story, and for the several comments on the labor problem by planters and farmers.

Pages 72–3.

Carl Sandburg: *Abraham Lincoln: The War Years* (New York. Harcourt, Brace & Company, 1939), Vol. III, pp. 260, 621, 634.

Emory Q. Hawkes: *Economic History of the South* (New York: Prentice-Hall, 1934), pp. 427, 428, for Sherman on damage done on his march.

Page 76.

American Historical Association, *Annual Report*, 1911, Vol. II, "Correspondence of Robert Toombs, Alexander H. Stephens and Howell Cobb," p. 655.

Page 77.

Myrta Locket Avary: *Recollections of Alexander H. Stephens* (New York, 1910), p. 173.

Pages 79–80.

Arthur Raper, op. cit., p. 82, quotation from the *Greensboro Herald,* March 26, 1868. "Ku Klux Report," Georgia, Pt. 1, pp. 307, 309, for quotation from General Gordon.

Page 83.

Stanley F. Horn: *Invisible Empire, the Story of the Ku Klux Klan, 1866–1871* (Boston: Houghton Mifflin Company, 1939), p. 169, on General Forrest's visit to Atlanta.

Page 84.

Fleming, op. cit., Vol. II, p. 336, item from Tuscaloosa (Ala.) *Independent Monitor*, April 1868. Reprinted by permission of the publishers, The Arthur H. Clark Company from Fleming's *Documentary History of Construction*, Vols. 1, 2.

Pages 88ff.

Horn, op. cit., Appendix II, p. 406, Prescript of Ku Klux Klan, Article VII, for quotations from questions asked members; and "Ku Klux Report," *Report*, Vol. I, pp. 12f., for other quotations from Prescript of the Ku Klux Klan. "Ku Klux Report," Georgia, Pt. 1, pp. 324ff., for General Gordon's testimony before the Congressional Committee. See Horn, op. cit., p. 170, on General Gordon as Grand Dragon of Georgia.

Note on Sources

Page 98.
Horn, op. cit., p. 188, for quotation from John Calvin Reed.

Page 128.
See Arnett: *The Populist Movement in Georgia,* pp. 153f.; also, C. Van Woodward: *Tom Watson, Agrarian Rebel.*

Page 141.
Woodward, op. cit., pp. 380ff., on Tom Watson and the Hoke Smith campaign.

Page 181.
Rupert B. Vance: *Human Factors in Cotton Culture* (Chapel Hill, 1929), pp. 97ff., on boll weevil.

Page 208.
U. B. Phillips: *American Negro Slavery* (New York: D. Appleton-Century Co., 1918), quotation from Preface.

Page 209.
Nation, September 14, 1921, quotations from pronouncements of the Ku Klux Klan of the 1920's.

Page 210.
Manufacturers Record, Baltimore, Md., July 3, 1924, quotation on "Anglo-Saxonism." Also, *Congressional Record,* Proceedings and Debates of the Third Session, 67th Congress, Vol. LXIII, Pt. 1, November 20 to December 5, 1922, on filibuster in Senate against anti-lynching bill.

Page 224.
Life and Times of Frederick Douglass (Pathway Press ed., 1941), p. 93. Frances Kemble: *Journal of a Residence on a Georgian Plantation,* p. 48, on slave boy named Jack.

Page 225.
Raper, op. cit., pp. 72–4, for the story of Greene County slaves when emancipation came. C. W. Williams, *Negro Troops in the Rebellion, 1861–1865* (New York, 1888), p. 324, on number of Negro troops. Quotation from General Armstrong, from unpublished manuscript material in the possession of Mrs. M. A. Armstrong.

Page 227.
John R. Commons and associates: *Documentary History of American Industrial Society,* The Arthur H. Clark Company, 1910, Vol. II, *Plantation and Frontier, 1649–1863,* by U. B. Phillips, pp. 360, 367, gives pronouncements of organizations of artisans in Athens and Atlanta.

Note on Sources

Page 226.

Fleming, op. cit., Vol. I, p. 357, for story of Sea Island ex-slaves. Reprinted by permission of the publishers, The Arthur H. Clark Company from Fleming's *Documentary History of Reconstruction*, Vols. 1, 2.

Page 233.

From resolution passed by South Carolina House of Representatives on February 28, 1944, quoted in *PM*, March 1, 1944.

Page 235.

See "Monthly Summary of Events and Trends in Race Relations," January 1946, Vol. III, No. 6, pp. 170f., for account of action by North Carolina student convention.